Cinephilia and History, or The Wind in the Trees

Cinephilia and History,

or The Wind in the Trees

Christian Keathley

Indiana University Press
BLOOMINGTON AND INDIANAPOLIS

This book is a publication of

Indiana University Press
601 North Morton Street
Bloomington, IN 47404-3797 USA

http://iupress.indiana.edu

Telephone orders   800-842-6796
Fax orders   812-855-7931
Orders by e-mail   iuporder@indiana.edu

MANUFACTURED IN THE UNITED STATES OF AMERICA

Library of Congress Cataloging-in-Publication Data

Keathley, Christian.
    Cinephilia and history, or, The wind in the trees / Christian Keathley.
        p. cm.
    Includes bibliographical references and index.
    ISBN 0-253-34648-7 (cloth : alk. paper) — ISBN 0-253-21795-4 (pbk. : alk. paper)
    1. Motion pictures. I. Title: Cinephilia and history. II. Title: Wind in the trees. III. Title.
    PN1994.K345 2005
    791.43'09—dc22

                                                                2005023392

1 2 3 4 5   11 10 09 08 07 06

For M. E., with all my love

What's missing from movies nowadays is the beauty of the moving wind in the trees.
—D. W. Griffith, 1944

Is the movement of a tree in the wind history? The shape of a hat? Or of a hut? The gesture of a man when he rises? . . . Cannot such pieces of data be used in written history, used because they have some meaning beyond their mere brute reality?
—Robert Rosenstone, *Visions of the Past*

The cinephile joins together the spirit of the collector and the competence of the connoisseur, but a connoisseur who would only collect within his memory.
—Jean-Louis Leutrat, "Traces That Resemble Us"

CONTENTS

ILLUSTRATIONS

ACKNOWLEDGMENTS

It is difficult for me to locate this project's precise point of origin. It has evolved out of many years of sharing my love for the movies—and my love for ideas about the movies—with many friends and colleagues. I should perhaps begin with those friends with whom I first shared (and still share) the experience of cinephilia: Chris Ekholm, Michael DeCasper, Chris Swartout, and Paul Tatara.

The book itself began as a dissertation at the University of Iowa, where I had the great benefit of studying under the supervision of Dudley Andrew. When I arrived at Iowa in 1995, I brought with me some kind of half-formed theoretical interest in something I didn't yet know to call cinephilia or cine-philiac moments. Dudley guided and supported me as I shaped my project, challenging me in the process to think historically as well as critically about the ideas I was engaged with.

Lauren Rabinovitz and Rick Altman also contributed importantly to my experience at Iowa, as did Corey Creekmur, Nataša Ďurovičová, and Garrett Stewart. In addition, there were my fellow graduate students, who helped to create an environment of friendship and intellectual camaraderie of the richest sort. I want especially to acknowledge here Jay Beck, Scott Benjamin, Gregory Flaxman, Alison LaTendresse, and Prakash Younger. Timothy Barnard is to be included in this group, and he deserves special thanks for the generous sharing of his professional translation skills.

Many conversations—some brief, some sustained—with other friends and colleagues influenced my ideas and my work, and though the list could run for many pages, I want to acknowledge here Daniel Eisenberg, Eric Faden, Michael Jarrett, Noel King, Sean O'Sullivan, and Gilberto Perez. I owe a great debt to David T. Johnson, whose suggestions and criticisms regarding the anecdotes in the final chapter were unfailingly on target.

My colleagues in the Film and Media Culture Program at Middlebury College have been supportive of me since I arrived in 2002. Leger Grindon and Ted Perry both read the manuscript and offered helpful comments and advice; in addition, both have been superb mentors. It was my great good fortune to arrive at Middlebury at the same time as Jason Mittell, who has been as fine a colleague and friend as I could wish to have.

I also want to thank the Middlebury students in my fall 2003 Senior Seminar in Film Theory, where I presented some of the ideas in this book's final chapters. Eliza Mitchell deserves special mention, both for the terrific cinephiliac anecdote she wrote (reprinted in the final chapter) and for the assistance she provided in selecting the book's illustrations.

Michael Lundell, my editor at Indiana University Press, showed interest in this project well before it was finished, and he remained supportive (and patient) while I completed it. Thanks also to Jane Lyle and Karen Kodner, who helped guide the book to completion.

I am most deeply indebted to Robert B. Ray, whose influence hovers over this book in many ways. He introduced me to academic film studies twenty years ago, at the University of Florida, and since then he has been a constant source of encouragement, inspiration, and friendship.

Cinephilia and History, or The Wind in the Trees

Introduction

At the climax of John Ford's *The Searchers*, as the cavalry raids the compound of the Comanche chief Scar, Ethan Edwards (John Wayne) charges his horse through the scurrying Indians to find his niece, Debbie, kidnapped five years earlier. Martin Pawley (Jeffrey Hunter), convinced that Ethan intends not to rescue Debbie, but to kill her, chases after Ethan in an attempt to stop him. "No, Ethan!" he screams. Shirtless and on foot, Martin tries in vain to slow Ethan or pull him out of his saddle. As Ethan turns and gallops away, Martin makes a final, desperate leap up onto the rump of Ethan's horse.

Every time I see this film, this is the moment I wait for. As the dust kicked up by Ethan's horse swirls around him, Martin's leap seems to transform his motion. In contrast to the jerking and pulling of the horse, Martin's body seems to float. While the rest of the action remains at regular speed, Martin's action seems momentarily to slow down. This moment—this action—is, for me, the most beautiful in the entire film.

What can the methods of analysis ordinarily practiced in the discipline of film studies tell us about this moment, or about my response to it? Unfortunately, not much. The extraordinary pleasure I take in this moment would surely be classified as a kind of fetishism—something I would quickly and proudly acknowledge—but then it is likely to be dismissed with a condescending snigger. That reaction is strange, though, when one considers that Film Studies as an academic discipline owes much to cinephilia in all its forms and manifestations. While in recent years a number of journalists and critics have lamented that the end of cinema's first century was marked by a depressing decline in interest in movies, or that the end of the twentieth century was the end of cinema's century, film scholars have remained mute. Why has this been the case? More importantly, what might the discipline of film studies have to gain by serious consideration of the phenomenon of cinephilia?

One of the earliest and most provocative pronouncements about the demise of cinephilia came from Susan Sontag in her 1996 article "The Decay of Cinema." She argued that, while it has recently become commonplace to lament the passing away of some fire in the life of cinema, what has in fact faded out is not the cinema itself, but a certain kind of intense loving relationship with the cinema that goes by the name of "cinephilia."[1] In the 1960s and 70s, the cinema was the most urgent and important art form, interacting in extraordinarily dynamic and diverse ways with its cultural and historical moment. Although interest in the cinema as a serious art form predates these years, phenomena like organized film societies, independent filmmaking, serious film criticism, and academic cinema studies had been limited to large metropolitan areas like New York and San Francisco; also, interest had most often focused on European art cinema and/or avant-garde filmmaking. The 1960s and 70s, however, saw a nationwide diffusion of interest in cinema; furthermore, the interest extended beyond so-called "serious" cinema to an embracing of Hollywood film and its history. In the wake of these developments, colleges all across the country began offering courses and even degrees in cinema studies; more and more film magazines and journals came into print (*Film Comment, Film Heritage,* and others); film critics were hired on as regular staff at newspapers, even in small cities and mid-sized towns; and film schools became the new proving ground for future filmmakers. This enthusiasm for film filtered down into general culture to the point that even "average" moviegoers developed a respect and appreciation for the cinema as the art form for the times, and a large public happily accepted the challenges offered by ambitious, personal, unconventional films.

Sontag's essay stimulated a number of other film critics—David Denby

and Stanley Kauffmann among them—to weigh in on the issue.[2] The statements and tones of their pieces were remarkably similar: mourning the decline
of interest in cinema, decrying the current state of filmmaking, and worrying
over the inability of the cinephile critic to do anything about it. In spite of
some slight differences of opinion, there was general agreement among them
that, in most critical discourse, both journalistic and academic, "Cinephilia
itself has come under attack, as something quaint, outmoded, snobbish"; for
cinephilia maintains that films can be "unique, unrepeatable, magic experiences."[3]

But while this discussion has been quite lively in journalistic quarters,
film scholars have largely refused to weigh in on the issue. This silence is even
more mysterious when one remembers that it was precisely this spirited period
of cinephilia that saw the birth of film studies as an academic discipline. The
American cinephilia Sontag eulogized was, of course, the internationalization
of a cinephilia that had been born overseas. For her, as for most others, the
great moment of cinephilia occurred in France and lasted roughly from the
end of World War II until the late 1960s. Hollywood cinema was its primary
(though not exclusive) object of obsession, and this love found expression
most famously in the pages of *Cahiers du Cinéma*. In Europe, not surprisingly,
scholarly discussions about cinephilia have been quite lively. In March 1995,
Antoine de Baecque and Thierry Frémaux organized a conference, "The Invention of a Culture: A History of Cinephilia," at the Lumière Institute in
Lyon, featuring an impressive roster of international critics and scholars. Co-
incident with this conference, de Baecque and Frémaux published a statement about their project that is also representative of the differences between
U.S. and European considerations of cinephilia.[4] Rather than echoing American critics and simply bemoaning the demise of cinephilia, de Baecque and
Frémaux proposed to treat cinephilia as a historical object of study—to engage
in a measured consideration of exactly what practices and circumstances defined cinephilia, what forces brought it into being, and what effect it had on
film culture and culture in general. If cinephilia gave birth to the first histories
of cinema, they argue, then it now falls to us in the post-cinephilic era to look
back and chart the history of cinephilia itself, to construct, in their words, "a
history of the history of cinema."[5] The possible subjects for research in such
a historical project are diverse and far-reaching, including, among many other
things, "the rituals of cinephilic film-going; the networks of ciné-clubs between 1920 and 1960; film magazines and their influence, editorial policies, distribution; and certain intellectual currents that were particularly receptive to
using cinema to disseminate ideas."[6] Some of this history has, of course, already been written, though much important work remains to be done.

But there is more to this project than cinephilia as a historical object of

study. The goal is also to recover for the present some sense of the excitement, the ebullient cinephilic spirit—or better yet, *cinephiliac* spirit, with that adjectival form's connotation of a "disorder"—that marked so much writing about the movies during these years. "What is needed today," de Baecque and Frémaux argue, "is to reintroduce cinema into historical discipline, to recover the materiality of the source, even the pleasure of the gaze."[7] During the great period of cinephilia, the writing that emerged from journals like *Cahiers* was not just history or criticism, they explain, but "a creative act of substitution no less important than the films themselves."[8] As cinema studies became institutionalized, that cinephilic spirit was willfully set aside, and then ultimately misplaced. Can it be recovered? Their historical project demands it. In this book, I take up de Baecque and Frémaux's call. What I offer here is one installment in the *history of cinephilia,* as well as an attempt to formulate strategies for how one might write a *cinephiliac history,* the ultimate goal being to find a way for the discipline of film studies to speak up about cinephilia, and to speak in the voice of a cinephile.

By way of explaining his own cinematic practice, Jacques Rivette once offered a sketch of the successive stages of the evolution of film language, and his chronology—as well as its ultimate goal—may be helpful in explaining more about the specific nature of my own project.

So one might, very schematically, distinguish four moments: the invention of montage (Griffith, Eisenstein); its deviation (Pudovkin-Hollywood: elaboration of the techniques of propaganda cinema); the rejection of propaganda (a rejection loosely or closely allied to long takes, direct sound, amateur or auxiliary actors, non-linear narrative, heterogeneity of genres, elements or techniques, etc.); and finally, . . . the attempt to "salvage," to reinject into contemporary methods the spirit and the theory of the first period, though without rejecting the contribution made by the third, but rather trying to cultivate one through the other.[9]

Film studies, too, has seen a series of stages, and these have been charted by Dudley Andrew.[10] The first stage, the pre-academic period of film studies, saw two important moments. In the 1920s, European intellectuals and avant-gardists, seeing the cinema as the most modern of art forms, embraced its enormous creative potential; ciné-clubs thrived, film journals were started, and the first film theories were written. This first wave of cinephilia was cut short around 1930, and was not recovered until the postwar period; it then reached a peak in the 1950s with the increase in specialized film publications, foremost among them *Cahiers du Cinéma,* with its policy of auteurism.[11] The second stage saw film studies enter the academy, and also saw a dramatic shift in its critical focus. Though the issue of film authorship opened the academic door for film studies, it was distinguished as a discrete discipline by the post-'68 influence of continental theory (Marxism, semiotics and structuralism, psychoanalysis—all appropriated by film studies well in advance of literary studies). But crossing that threshold into scholarly legitimacy meant leaving the cinephilic spirit behind. What had been cinephilia's objects of obsession now became objects of suspicion. Scholars of this second period, Andrew writes, "did not appreciate films but rather conspired to 'read' them as symptoms of hidden structures."[12] The third stage, beginning in the mid-1980s, was marked by a turn away from this "grand theory" and a return to history, one whose focus also broadened beyond production to include issues of reception. These trends, Andrew explains, have been dominated by "the cultural studies approach, where, moreover, political urgency [race, class, ethnicity, gender and sexuality] frequently sets the research program."[13] Though grand theory may have been pushed aside, the anti-cinephilic spirit that it fostered had become deeply embedded in the discipline. "Is it any wonder," Andrew asks, that after three decades of institutionalization, with its concomitant standards of scholarly research and writing, "students today have difficulty crediting cinephilia and the florid writing that it inspired?"[14]

My own project, to quote Rivette, proposes "to reinject into contemporary methods the spirit and the theory of the first period, though without rejecting the contribution made by the third, but rather trying to cultivate one through the other." I do not intend a wholesale rejection of the second stage (though it has been the source of academic film studies' lingering anti-cinephilic streak), but rather I want to emphasize that my project will be working to remobilize the first stage's cinephilic spirit in the service of the third stage's primary interests: film history and reception studies. But carrying out this task means, on the one hand, restricting the focus of my historical investigation while, on the other, extending the ways in which scholarship in the areas of history and reception has been done.

A History of Cinephilia

De Baecque and Frémaux define cinephilia first and foremost as "a way of watching films," and only secondarily as a way "of speaking about them and then of diffusing this discourse."[15] It follows that their proposal places special emphasis on practices of spectatorship and reception. They offer a description of the ways in which the lives of cinephiles become organized around rituals and practices of moviegoing and movie watching:

The first object of cinephilic study is its cultural—we could almost say cultic—practices. The dark cinema has often been compared to a temple, and it is true that cinephilia, although it is carried out in the most secular of spaces, is marked by a great religiosity of its ceremonies. Cinephilia is a system of cultural organization that engenders rituals around the gaze, speech, and the written word. Here, undoubtedly, is the very identity of the practice: once "bitten by the cinema" (this is how cinephiles, somewhat rabidly, described themselves in the early 1960s), everything comes to depend on how one sees films, from where in the audience, in what position, according to which individual framing, on how a screening is brought to life, how the group gets around, how this intimate diary of the gaze is shared (by conversation, by correspondence, by published writing), and how, finally, the films become the site of symbolic battles through competing attitudes and writings.[16]

As this passage clearly suggests, the more historically conspicuous practices of critical debate and writing come only after the obsessive practices of the cinephile lifestyle. Even within like-minded groups, distinctive and individual spectatorial ceremonies emerge. *Cahiers* critic Jean Douchet has described his own viewing habits in detail.

I have to enter the auditorium by the right-hand stairway and aisle. Then I sit to the right of the screen, preferably in the aisle seat, so that I can stretch my legs. This is not just a matter of physical comfort, or the view: I have constructed this vision for myself. For a long time, at the Cinémathèque, I sat in the front row, in the middle, with no one in front to disturb me, in order to be completely immersed in the show, always alone. Even today, it's impossible for me to go to the cinema with anyone; it disrupts my emotion. But over the years and after many films, I've drawn back a bit, off to the right, and I've found my axis toward the screen. At the same time, I've positioned my spectatorial body with minute care, adopting three basic positions: stretched out on the ground, legs draped over the seat in front of me, and, finally, my favorite but the most difficult position to achieve, the body folded in four with the knees pressed against the back of the seat in front of me.[17]

While tracing the emergence of specialized journals and ciné-clubs or describing the development of a key critical position might be easily charted in a traditional history, an account such as Douchet's, with all its particularities and peculiarities, would seem to escape conventional historiographic practices. But if we are to embark on a history of cinephilia, such specifics must be faced—especially since so many cinephiles describe experiences that are similar, yet uniquely their own. As justification for their focus on the particularities of reception, de Baecque and Frémaux cite André Bazin, who, "in a stunningly prophetic vision, announced as early as 1948 that a complete accounting of the cinema would be a 'total art of the watching of films.'"[18] Bazin argued, "The future historian must pay greater attention to the stunning revolution which is in the process of unfolding in the consumption of films than in the technological developments during these same years."[19] The historian of cinephilia, then, should explore not only how films are seen (under what circumstances of distribution and exhibition), but also how they are *watched* (by groups and especially individuals, each with his or her own particular idiosyncrasies).

The "definitive essence of cinephilia," de Baecque and Frémaux explain, is organized around "a culture of the discarded," one that is inclined "to find intellectual coherence where none is evident, to eulogize the non-standard and the minor";[20] and the nascent history of cinephilia, they note, has generally followed suit, choosing "limited subjects that could be viewed as anecdotal, even derisory."[21] Not wanting to be excluded from this pattern, I will explore in this book one element of the cinephile's spectatorial experience, what Paul Willemen has dubbed "the cinephiliac moment": the fetishizing of fragments of a film, either individual shots or marginal (often unintentional) details in the image, especially those that appear only for a moment. Willemen argues that what persists in almost all cinephilic discourse is a celebration of the spectator's subjective encounter with "fleeting, evanescent moments" in the film experience.[22] Whether it is the gesture of a hand, the odd rhythm of a horse's gait, or the sudden change in expression on a face, these moments are experienced by the cinephile who beholds them as nothing less than an epiphany, a revelation. This fetishization of marginal, otherwise ordinary details in the motion picture image is as old as the cinema itself. Indeed, as the story goes, many viewers of a century ago who watched the first films of the Lumière Brothers were often delighted less by the scenes being staged for their amusement than by the fact that, in the background, the leaves were fluttering in the wind.

Chapter 2 provides a detailed definition of the cinephiliac moment, and also explores several related issues that are important for the consideration of these experiences. First of all, I argue that the cinephile spectator is characterized in part by a particular viewing strategy, what I call (borrowing a term from historian Wolfgang Schivelbusch) "panoramic perception": this is the tendency to sweep the screen visually in order to register the image in its totality, especially the marginal details and contingencies that are the most common sources of cinephiliac moments. Indeed, this spectatorial tendency increases the possibility of encounters with cinephiliac moments. Second, I argue that an encounter with a cinephiliac moment is not just a visual experience, but also a more broadly sensuous one; it is an experience that has been repeatedly linked in critical writing to the haptic, the tactile, and the bodily.

Chapters 3 and 4 focus, respectively, on writings by André Bazin and the young auteurists of *Cahiers du Cinéma*, which are, without doubt, the most famous critical statements of the great period of cinephilia. These chapters investigate the ways in which this critical writing functioned, at least in part, as critical rationalizations or justifications for a certain cinematic experience that is vividly marked by encounters with cinephiliac moments. But this investigation does not limit itself to the time and place of postwar France. It also looks back, to critical writings from France in the 1920s, an important period of proto-cinephilia, and forward, to writings from the period of overseas expansion of cinephilia in Britain and the United States in the 1960s. While film criticism is at the heart of this investigation, I also borrow freely from thinkers and disciplines outside of film studies in an effort to give the clearest possible sense of the nature of the cinephiliac moment and how it was accommodated by these film critics in their theories. These chapters do not offer a chronological history; rather, they are synthetic, selecting a variety of voices and positions from across specific times and places and drawing them together in the consideration of the cinephiliac moment. In addition, these chapters explore how encounters with cinephiliac moments are linked to certain film styles and, especially, to the very ontology of film.

It should be clear, then, that this book is not a history surveying the various forces (cultural, technological, economic) that combined to create a culture of cinephilia in postwar France or anywhere else. Rather, it is an intellectual history tightly focused on this one issue of cinephiliac reception. In contrast to much reception studies work of the past decade, which has regularly explored the ways in which specific identity groups make meaning of films or parts of films, this book considers an area of spectatorial experience that resists co-optation by meaning; indeed, if the cinephiliac moment is among the most intense of cinematic experiences, it seems to draw its intensity partly from the fact that it cannot be reduced or tamed by interpretation. This book instead explores the ways in which a variety of critics, most of them from the great period of cinephilia (1945–68), have responded to the cinephiliac moment—how they have described their experiences of it, how they have accounted for its existence, and how they have speculated about its implications.

A Cinephiliac History

In many important ways, this project responds to Geoffrey Nowell-Smith's call for a "history of subjectivities."[23] But writing such a history inevitably means rethinking the very practice of writing history. So while chapters 2 through 4 are largely *descriptive,* devoted to defining the cinephiliac moment and tracing how certain critics have written about it, chapters 5 and 6 are primarily *prescriptive.* Here, the emphasis is on finding a way to remobilize and reintegrate the cinephiliac spirit into contemporary film studies, and here the focus of my study affords an opportunity to do so. In creating a history of cinephilia focused around cinephiliac moments, we see that these experiences and the material of which they consist have profound implications for the very practice of historiography. In the 1930s, Walter Benjamin and his colleague Siegfried Kracauer came to see film as offering an impressive challenge not only to the older, established arts but also to dominant historiographic practice. Kracauer argued that historicism—that history, consolidated in the nineteenth century, whose discourse is marked by linearity, emplotment, clear cause-and-effect relationships, distinction between major and minor issues or events, and so forth—does not recognize anything from the past or present that it cannot employ for its purposes. Kracauer specifically located film's challenge to historicism in its vivid rendering of details, which he read as signifiers of a repressed, alternative, undeveloped history—"indexes of history in the making."[24]

Benjamin followed Kracauer's lead, first by restating the latter's argument in a variety of forceful ways, but then, more importantly, by experimenting with alternative historiographic forms, most famously in the *Arcades Project,* a history of nineteenth-century Paris that was to be composed largely of photographs. The link to my own project on cinephilia should be clear: the kinds of filmic details that are most often the occasion for cinephiliac moments are the sites of both a challenge to historiographic practice and an opportunity for its transformation. This new way of writing history is also the opportunity for the re-integration of the cinephiliac spirit into critical and historical writing. Chapter 5 reviews Benjamin's and Kracauer's positions in greater detail, and chapters 6 and 7 seek to explore the implications of their claims about the relationship between history and film by experimenting with a different form of historical writing about film: the cinephiliac anecdote—a form that is designed to produce unexpected and useful knowledge about the movies, the starting point being what our proprietary discipline might regard as an excessive or inappropriately zealous cinephiliac pleasure.

1 The Desire for Cinema

Andrew Sarris's 1973 collection of critical writings, *The Primal Screen,* contains an essay on *mise-en-scène* that begins, "The subject of this piece was suggested by a letter from Dr. Irving Schneider of Chevy Chase, Maryland." Dr. Schneider wrote in part:

> I've been asked to write a review of psychiatric documentary films, teaching and research ones, primarily from a phenomenological point of view. With respect to some of the ideas I'm working up, I need a good working definition or explanation of the notion of *mise-en-scène*. Like camp and several other terms, I think I know what it means but I am not sure. A search through theatrical dictionaries and film works yields no definition. Friends and I have used the term occasionally to refer to the sum of all the elements making up a film, and

at other times to the placement of the actors within a setting, but none of us can agree on what the most common or accurate usage is.

I would appreciate it greatly if you could find the time and inclination to explain to me your understanding of the term, and perhaps tell me something of its origin in film criticism.[1]

Ever since I first read this letter, more than twenty years ago, it has held enormous charm for me, in large part because of Dr. Schneider's somewhat naive optimism about both the films he's reviewing and the people who will read his review. Is a consideration of *mise-en-scène* really essential for an intelligent critical report on the professional usefulness of these films? Will the psychiatrists who read the review understand more (or be more confused) about whether or not these films fit their needs with Schneider's use of this term? And given that we generally think of *mise-en-scène* as having an expressive function, do films such as these even have *mise-en-scène*?

This letter is also a vivid indication of the cultural cinephilia famously eulogized by Susan Sontag, for it points to one of the essential characteristics of American cinephilia of the 1960s and 70s: it was a time when even non-cinephiles had an experience of cinephilia. Dr. Schneider would not fit the precise definition of "cinephile" offered by Antoine de Baecque and Thierry Frémaux (one whose life is "organized around films"),[2] but his letter evinces the way in which critical terms, concepts, and debates whose use would normally be limited to specialists had filtered down beyond cinephiles, in a way that they no longer do, to simple film enthusiasts. It is hard even to imagine how in our present context a comparable letter might read, because the gap separating film academics from the general population of movie enthusiasts, or from most practicing film critics for that matter, has increased so dramatically. Of course, Sarris was both an academic and a journalist/critic, teaching at Columbia University as well as writing a weekly column for New York's weekly alternative paper, *The Village Voice*, where he had the space and freedom to educate interested readers toward a connoisseurship of cinema. Dr. Schneider was clearly a reader who had signed on as a willing pupil. Indeed, Dr. Schneider's desire to incorporate the term *mise-en-scène* into his own review mimicked the way in which earlier film critics like Sarris had used it to serve themselves: the specialized concept brought a new kind of legitimacy to the films being reviewed, as well as to the reviews themselves. The term *mise-en-scène* had come to the United States from France, as part of the critical terminology that had emerged during that country's own intense period of cinephilia; and that cinephilia, though unique in many ways, mimicked characteristics and strategies of other historical moments of art appreciation in transformation.

Cinephilia and Connoisseurship

The two most famous and influential theoretical positions of postwar French cinephilia came from critics associated with the journal *Cahiers du Cinéma*. The first emerged in the critical writings of André Bazin, especially his essays "The Ontology of the Photographic Image" and "The Evolution of the Language of Cinema."[3] In the "Ontology" essay, Bazin, in contrast to critics like Rudolf Arnheim, sought to establish the photographic image's privileged link to the reality it represented as something not to be overcome, but to be embraced; for it was in the automatically produced objectivity of the film image, Bazin believed, that the cinema found both its defining characteristic and its unique power. In the "Evolution" essay, Bazin offered a strong rebuttal to prevailing notions about the cinema and its history. First, Bazin challenged the received opposition between the silent and sound periods—an opposition that reflected the belief that the cinema as an art form had reached its peak in the 1920s, just prior to being cut short by the advent of sound. He instead posited across that supposed break a continuity of aesthetic conception in the work of directors who sought to extend cinema's defining characteristic into a formal and stylistic practice. Focusing on directors as diverse as Jean Renoir, William Wyler, F. W. Murnau, Roberto Rossellini, and Orson Welles, Bazin similarly erased the European/American dichotomy (a corollary of the silent/

sound opposition), enabling him, as Thomas Elsaesser explains, "to acknowledge theoretically, and consequently to validate the historical development
which had pushed the cinema toward becoming a predominantly narrative
medium (the very development which had disaffected the intellectuals)."[4]
Bazin's commitment to popular education led him to work vigorously, both in
print and in public lectures, to deepen his and the audience's understanding
of cinema by considering not just its high art examples, but also its most common and popular manifestations, such as Hollywood genre films.

This serious consideration of Hollywood cinema had a profound effect on
the younger generation of critics at *Cahiers*. Frustrated by the current French
cinema's preoccupation with adapting major literary works in a dull, lifeless way, these young critics—Jean-Luc Godard and François Truffaut among
them—turned their sights to American films, which they believed displayed
the directness, unpretentiousness, action, and modern attitude that their own
national cinema lacked. They carried out their critical redemption of American cinema (and justified their obsession with Hollywood) via their infamous
editorial policy, *la politique des auteurs,* which was founded on the contention
that certain Hollywood directors, such as Howard Hawks and Nicholas Ray,
showed across their respective bodies of work consistencies of style, theme,
and worldview. Applied to a European director of art films—for example,
Ingmar Bergman, whom the *Cahiers* critics also admired—such an idea would
not even have raised an eyebrow. But applied to directors employed in the
assembly-line film factory of Hollywood, where directors often had at best
marginal input into scripts, casting, and the like, this "auteur theory" (as it
came to be known) was an outrageous provocation. The *Cahiers* critics further argued that, in spite of the fact that Hollywood directors did not have the
freedom that their European counterparts allegedly enjoyed, filmmakers like
Hawks or Ray expressed their unique view of the world through the visual
aspects that they did control, such as camera placement and movement, lighting, direction of performances, pacing, etc.—variables that, when combined,
went by the term *mise-en-scène.* Armed with these theories, the *Cahiers* critics
constructed a revised history of the cinema, one based not on individual films
or film movements, but on individual directors. No matter how problematic
or even contradictory it may have been at times, the auteur theory is no doubt
the main reason that cinephilia is associated with the *Cahiers du Cinéma* critics above all others.

Paul Willemen has argued that the *Cahiers* theory of authorship was "a
form of secondary elaboration, a rationalisation and social justification" for
the obsessive pleasures of the cinephile; it was an attempt to "make the pleasure of cinephilia productive instead of repressing it or reducing it to a secret
activity for initiates only."[5] This move of rationalization was crucial for the

success of cinephilia, for with it the cinephiles identified themselves not just as fanatics, but as specialists. Cinémathèque Française director Dominique Païni has emphasized the mixture of subjective obsession and objective specialization that was unique to cinephilia and crucial to its success: "To see a film was, for the cinephile of the years 1948–68, a contradictory act which revealed a very rational accounting of films as much as it did of *satori*" (a Japanese term designating a sudden, religious revelation, one that may be understood as marked by both fulfillment and a loss of meaning); it was both "a confirmation of taste" and "a constant monitoring of knowledge."[6] What this combination led to was the construction of an interpretive community that effected a profound rethinking of cinema. Païni concludes, "Incontestably, cinephilia was an original *idea,* one particularly innovative to the field of film criticism. It owed nothing to the Academy or art history."[7]

In fact, however, one can draw a clear comparison between cinephilia and the art critical discourse of connoisseurship, which, as S. J. Freedberg has defined it, is "the use of expert knowledge of a field (in this case, the history of art) to identify objects in it, determine their quality, and assess their character."[8] Taking as an example Bernard Berenson, one of the most famous of all connoisseurs, the similarity between connoisseurship and cinephilia becomes clearer. Working in the late nineteenth and early twentieth centuries, Berenson began his career as an art authenticator, trained in the methods of Giovanni Morelli. Focusing almost exclusively on internal evidence, Morelli had argued that, in assigning authorship to a painting, one must look past the obvious characteristics of a style or school and focus instead on marginal elements such as fingernails and earlobes, for these are details that the painter composes rapidly, without conscious intent, and it is thus here that his personality shows through most clearly. It was only through careful analysis and comparison by this method, Morelli argued, that authorship could be established with a high degree of certainty.

After attributing a significant number of unsigned works to their respective Italian masters, Berenson turned gradually to critical description and appreciation. Never a true theorist, Berenson's skill was instead "his gift for the perception and appreciation of particular experiences," for as it is with cinephilia, "the specific experience is the essence of connoisseurship."[9] These experiences, recounted in his writing, led to the establishment of a canon of the painters of this period that is largely taken for granted today. In a 1979 *New York Times* article, Hilton Kramer summarized Berenson's impact on the study of art:

It still comes as something of a shock to us, if we are not experts in the field, to discover how little was actually known about the early Italian masters as recently as a century ago. The revered names of Giorgione, Mantegna and Lorenzo Lotto, of Boticelli and Correggio and others in this fellowship of glory, are confidently taken for granted, and it seldom occurs to us to wonder how the exact authorship of the paintings now assigned to them actually came about. [. . .]

The study of art history, moreover, is now such a highly developed field of scholarship, with armies of specialists jealously standing guard over their arcane areas of expertise, that it taxes our credulity to be asked to believe that, as recently as the 1890s, an amateur . . . could establish himself as the world's leading authority on early Italian painting. Yet this, in effect, is what Berenson managed to do.[10]

One needs only to change a few specifics in the above paragraphs—replacing the 1890s with the 1950s, artists like Giorgione and Boticelli with directors like Hawks and Walsh, and Berenson with the young critics Godard and Truffaut—to make this an equally accurate description of the influence that the postwar cinephiles had on film history and criticism. Furthermore, in reassessing Hollywood cinema, Godard, Truffaut, and others had focused on the two key issues associated with connoisseurship: *attribution* and *taste*. While the issue of attribution is not exactly the same in filmmaking as it is in painting (except, perhaps, during cinema's earliest years, when many films went without directorial credit), the concern with identifying and valuing authorship is. Though the *Cahiers* position, *la politique des auteurs*, has often been criticized as reactionary Romanticism, one can understand that an important part of the success of their critical justification of Hollywood cinema was the appeal to a commonly held value: that of the work of art as the expression of an individual artist. This precedent was at least partly set by the discourse of connoisseurship, for as Freedberg notes, "where history has allowed to exist the evidence of single personalities, and even their names, the result of connoisseurship is the definition of an individual artist."[11] Again, the similarity to cinephilia and auteurism is notable. Before the cinephiles came on the scene, certain Hollywood directors (such as Ford or Wyler) may have been appreciated for their skill and talent, but the young *Cahiers* critics—with their enthusiasm for, and knowledge of, so much American cinema—were able to go further, seeing in the details of a film's *mise-en-scène* marks of distinctive, individual authorial presence. Attribution led to the establishment of a pantheon of film artists. Directors whose works showed consistencies of style, theme, and worldview were elevated to the status of *auteur*, while other directors were ranked as mere craftsmen (or *metteurs-en-scène*).[12] The *Cahiers* pantheon, like Berenson's, is one that is largely taken for granted today.

While the young *Cahiers* critics may stand as the film world's precise counterparts to the art world's connoisseurs, André Bazin's position is a bit more complicated. First of all, Bazin was never as preoccupied with the issue of authorship as were his protegés (indeed, he wrote the first critique of the auteur policy),[13] so it might indeed be more useful to classify Bazin, as David Bordwell has, as a historian of style.[14] Such a designation does not take us far afield, however, for as Freedberg notes, the relationship between the historian of style and the connoisseur is a close one.

There is an important distinction to be made between connoisseurship and the history of style, but one must nonetheless affirm the essential ground they share: a primary concern with the aesthetic substance of the object, which serves as an open bridge between these linked and reciprocally reinforcing disciplines.[15]

One way to further clarify the differences and similarities between Bazin and the younger *Cahiers* critics is to trace the influences on them of a commonly acknowledged figure in pre- and postwar French culture, one who was also a famous art connoisseur: André Malraux. Though perhaps best known as a novelist, filmmaker, Resistance hero, and, later, as de Gaulle's minister of culture, Malraux also spent much of his life in the study of art. His 1951 publication, *The Voices of Silence* (itself a revised and expanded version of his earlier, three-volume *Psychology of Art*), opens with the highly influential section "Museum without Walls," in which Malraux considers the influence of photographic reproduction on our experience and study of art. Rosalind Krauss has traced two key influences on Malraux's thinking.[16] First was the comparative method of Heinrich Wölfflin, who was one of the first art historians to use photographic reproductions of works of art to develop a complex argument about styles of different periods—in his case, comparing the classical and the baroque. The second was the German critic Walter Benjamin, whose essay "The Work of Art in the Age of Mechanical Reproduction" explored the profound impact that photography had on the history and function of art. Malraux took a position somewhere between the two influences. He argued that photographic reproduction—with its ability to alter scale and to focus on details, and with its power of radical recontextualization—had rendered the history of art a jumbled mass of images, a condition that permitted (even encouraged) a decontextualized comparison of the formal qualities of art consisting of quite different materials, uses, and geographic and temporal origins.[17] Unlike Benjamin, Malraux did not see these conditions as a potential means for transforming the role of art in society, but as a way of facilitating a comparative approach that would reveal in otherwise very different works a similar "spirit of art" that exceeded any cultural or historical context.

David Bordwell explains that this very "sense of history as simultaneous order presides over the 1950s and 1960s *Cahiers* writings. Griffith is a contemporary of Resnais; Feuillade, of Cukor. Mizoguchi's ties to Japanese culture are ignored because, according to Luc Moullet, masterpieces are outside time and place."[18] Further encouragement for this ahistorical comparative ap-

proach came at Henri Langlois's Cinémathèque Française, where the young
critics regularly saw double and triple features of films from very different
nations, styles, and periods (for example, Ingmar Bergman's *Smiles of a Summer Night* followed by Sam Fuller's *I Shot Jesse James* and Robert Flaherty's
Nanook of the North). Just as Malraux had argued that the museum preceded
photographic reproduction in the facilitation of the comparative approach,
Dominique Païni has written that it was "thanks to Langlois's museum of
cinema, to his way of hoarding films, to his practice of opening up a dialogue
between them" that the young *Cahiers* critics were led to their own comparative critical approach.[19]

Like Malraux, these young critics were clearly interested in works of all
stripes and colors, and they were interested in locating an analogous "spirit of
cinema" in what they saw. They found this spirit living in the works of certain
directors, and they focused especially on those films that most clearly expressed a given director's style and worldview, regardless of whatever faults or
limitations might otherwise mark it. Malraux's words could just as easily be
attributed to the *Cahiers* auteurists: "For we now know that an artist's supreme
work is not the one in best accord with any tradition—nor even his most complete and 'finished' work—but his most personal work, the one from which he
has stripped all that is not his very own, and in which his style reaches its
climax."[20] But as we have seen, in spite of their interest in individual artists
from the whole of cinema's short life, the *Cahiers* critics were not especially
concerned to trace order, succession, and influence; they were not interested
in "history" in the strict sense of that term.

Bazin, on the other hand, was. While his comparative approach, like Malraux's, was used to trace a stylistic tendency horizontally, across geographic
and generic boundaries, it was also used to track a clear vertical line through
cinema's history, especially the 1920s through the 1940s. While it is true that
Bazin's history of style encroached on connoisseurship in that it clearly privileged one stylistic tendency (realism) over others, that privilege was rigorously
justified in terms of film's ontology, and not just according to his individual
taste. Furthermore, though Bazin sometimes celebrated individual directors—
especially Welles and Renoir, whom his protegés also favored—it was not simply because their work had an identifiable personal style, but because, in spite
of their very different styles, their work showed a commitment to film's ontology. Together, Bazinian realism and *Cahiers* auteurism reinvigorated an interest in cinema, bringing it to an unprecedented level of appreciation.

The Death of Cinephilia

While the *Cahiers* critics' love for Hollywood cinema prompted them into establishing their policy of authorship, one negative motivation for these cine-

philes, and one of the most often overlooked influences during this period, was the emergence of another mass media entertainment: television. Dudley Andrew has argued that, while the cinephile's devotion to the movies was, on the one hand, a rebellious response to "the claustrophobic institutions of literature that had held the cinema and a genuine popular culture hostage," it was, on the other hand, also "a quiet, defensive war against another, less evident enemy: the disorganized, unaccredited, and unencumbered images beginning to pour out of television screens, in France and elsewhere."[21] But if television is an overlooked factor in the emergence of cinephilia, it has been a highly conspicuous factor in its transformation—and the cinephile's issue with television is not only one of aesthetics. In what follows, I would like to focus briefly on one of the defining factors of cinephilia, one in which television is deeply implicated. Not only is it an issue that helps effectively illustrate something about the life of the cinephile, but it further makes clear my own stake in this issue (personal testimony being a key feature of all cinephilic writing).

During its peak years, explains former *Cahiers* critic and filmmaker Luc Moullet, the cinephilic spirit thrived on "a fundamental dialectic between accessibility and inaccessibility."[22] Films were accessible in the sense that, compared with works of literature, their individual brevity and the relative brevity of film's history to that point made it possible for a cinephile to see and have a command of a great number of movies. "An individual could be familiar with almost everything," Moullet writes. "I could see, or believe I could see, all of Hawks, all of Hitchcock, while it would be impossible to have read all of Balzac (or Voltaire, or Hugo)."[23] This factor of accessibility was no doubt crucial for the successful dissemination of cinephilic ideas: the cinephile's ability to approach "coverage" of the field of cinema in so short a period of time—meaning that his ideas were applicable to an extraordinarily broad range of films and filmmakers—gave him an authority comparable to literary scholars who had labored for decades.

But in spite of this accessibility, catching up with individual films wasn't always an easy task. Moullet writes,

Reaching cinemas in the neighborhoods, the suburbs, the countryside or abroad was a very hazardous affair. . . . Until a short time ago all these difficulties gave me a feeling of being a pioneer, an explorer, a dare-devil, a hero. This victory over adversity gave me a naive pleasure, like that of someone who conquers a summit or discovers a virgin pass, a specific pleasure that was part of the quest. [. . .] Inaccessibility creates a sense of urgency, forces you to see films the moment they are shown. I bent over backwards to watch Autant-Lara's *Lucien Leuwen* (which, by the way, was a disappointment) when it was shown on television, because I knew there was a possibility that I'd never again have the chance to see it, while it took me twenty years to read Stendhal's remarkable *Leuwen*, because I knew I could always get it at the library.[24]

Marc Vernet has echoed Moullet's claim, arguing that cinephilia "came about in the context of scarcity" and that, in general, love for cinema has depended "to a great extent on its fugitive, evanescent character."[25]

This dynamic balance of availability and rarity did not end in the 1950s, but in fact lasted well into the 1970s and early 1980s, when the expansion of cable and pay television and, most importantly, home video brought it to an end. Robert B. Ray describes the scene prior to video, as well as the changes the new technology brought:

Prior to videotape, most movies were, in a very real sense, *rare*. The films that came to town, or a museum, or one's university—like, for example, *The Lady from Shanghai, Meet Me in St. Louis, Masculine-Feminine, The Seven Samurai*— might not come again. As a result, one made an effort to see them. Now, with almost everything available on tape, one may postpone indefinitely watching something like Rossellini's *The Rise to Power of Louis XIV.*[26]

As a result of the restricted availability in the pre-video days, the cinephile not only anticipated or recalled happily the times when one was able to see a rare film gem, but also let that anticipation or recollection seep into other aspects and areas of one's life. Even the most banal activities—the journey to the theater, standing in line for a ticket, where one went for dinner or a drink afterward—were intensified by their proximity to the movie itself, and they became threads that made up one's tangled memories of the film experience.[27] Films thus existed for people as *events*, but not in the commercial, promotional sense of that term. Rather, as Thomas Elsaesser has written, seeing movies (especially, perhaps, re-released "classics" at repertory cinemas) became, like other aspects of our lives, "events that have happened to us, experiences that are inalienably ours," ones that we revisit in our memory and make up who we are.[28]

In the period before video there was clearly a quasi-religious aspect of film viewing and filmgoing. That is, there was a decidedly "auratic" quality to the film experience, if we define "aura" as Walter Benjamin once did: as an object's "presence in time and space, its unique existence at the place where it happens to be."[29] That is, the aura of any work of art emerges out of specific conditions of reception. It is reasonable, then, to think of rarity and availability not simply as opposites, but as existing on a continuum. At the extreme of rarity are those conditions described by Benjamin in a world before mechanical reproduction: if you wanted to know what the *Mona Lisa* looked like, you had to travel to Paris to see it, for there were no facsimiles of it in existence. At the other extreme is the complete and total availability of works that are not in any way governed or defined by a unique existence in time and space (for example, perhaps, an Internet website featuring interactive multimedia artworks). The cinephile's experience of movies is somewhere in between: closer to the latter set of conditions, perhaps, but still retaining clear traces of the former because, for so long, availability had been determined by restricted conditions of distribution and exhibition. For the cinephile, the auratic experience of moviegoing was in an important way prompted by this restricted availability. The change of habits in film viewing that Ray describes—the increased availability, the increased likelihood of postponement—signals the end of the experiencing of a film as an event. The knowledge that a film can always be caught a few months hence on video makes movies subject to us rather than us being subject to them. Their existence as events is weakened.

My recognition of this state of affairs is clearly the result of my own experience of cinephilia. I was born in 1963 and became interested in movies in grade school. I vividly remember the early 1970s, that time before the boom in cable television and videotape made cinema's historical treasures accessible to me. Each weekend, I begged my parents or older siblings to drive me to the theaters to see the new releases, and I caught the previous year's films— censored and with commercial interruptions—on network television. Beyond that, the history of cinema seemed to me little more than a rumor. An ordinary Hollywood classic like Howard Hawks's *Only Angels Have Wings* was no less exotic to me than Jean-Luc Godard's *Le Mépris:* both were equally out of my reach. When such films did appear on television or at a local museum, the pleasure was for me as fleeting as it was intense. Even new releases were greeted with the feeling that their appearance was special. I can recall times when I was watching a movie and the pleasure became so great that I would consciously say to myself, "You'd better enjoy this now, take in all you can, because soon it'll be over and gone."

To extend the pleasure of the cinephilic experience, I turned, like many others, to reading criticism. Indeed, I fit comfortably into that final wave of cinephiles described by de Baecque and Frémaux, the ones who arrived just too late, after the most important battles of cinephilia had been fought. But rather than giving up, we broadened our cinephilic gaze. De Baecque and Frémaux summarize the shift:

For us, the pleasure of the reader often replaced the pleasure of the spectator. And since film's auteurs had already been consecrated, devouring film literature in journals, magazines, and books was for us another way of being cinephiles— the only way perhaps that could be ours alone. Our love for the cinema spread beyond films and filmmakers to embrace critics and spectators. It was a sort of second look at the state of cinema. Hence this fundamental difference: while our predecessors fetishized films and auteurs, we deplored the disappearance of movie-houses and of the cinephilic passion that our elders lived through. From that moment, everything changed: it was no longer a matter of sanctifying filmmakers but also critics; no longer only films but also texts; no longer only cinema but also cinephilia.[30]

Again, their account precisely describes my own experience. As an adolescent, I spent much more time reading about movies than actually watching them. To learn about film history, I scoured the library shelves and bookstores for volumes devoted to celebrating those great films that I half-guessed I would never see. I became an obsessive collector of film books, especially volumes of reviews by critics like Stanley Kauffmann, John Simon, Pauline Kael, and others, critics whose work was then appearing in book form with great regularity. I still have a half-dozen or so of these volumes that I swiped from my small community library—I was the only one who had ever checked them out. This criticism was a crucial factor in the consolidation and expansion of my experience of cinephilia. In the spring of 1999, when I visited my hometown of West Palm Beach, Florida, for the annual Society for Cinema Studies conference, the site I pointed out to friends with the most pride was Main Street News in Palm Beach. As much as any movie theater, that newsstand was my cinematic road to Damascus, for it was there, as a sophomore in high school, that I was first able to buy a copy of *The Village Voice*, an event that marked my introduction to the auteurism of Andrew Sarris, and through him to Bazin and *Cahiers*. This event has colored years of watching, reading, and thinking about the movies.

When I went away to college a few years later, still in a time of restricted availability, I did my best to mimic my forebears' experiences of tracking down films wherever I could. Several weekends each month, my roommate and I would make the long drive to Atlanta to catch whatever interesting films were playing at the city's half-dozen repertory and art cinemas. (I remember seeing, among many others, *Forbidden Planet,* the restored version of *Seven Samurai, Eraserhead, Singin' in the Rain,* plus lots of Hitchcock.) But this fun didn't last long. Before I graduated, the repertory cinemas had closed and the art cinemas were struggling. Television, pay cable, and home video, of course, had a hand in this change, which was by no means all bad. But the shift to accessibility occurred gradually. As early as 1974, I was able to see some of the previous year's releases uncut on cable, but one could never be absolutely certain which films would turn up on pay TV and which would disappear for good; further, the fact that VCRs were not commercially available until the late 70s meant that these television screenings were marked by a restricted accessibility. Similarly, in the early days of home video, the Hollywood studios seemed to regard releasing films on video as roughly the equivalent of the publishing practice of remaindering books (though at a much higher price); thus, video releases of most films came long after their initial theatrical exhibition, if at all. Soon, however, the studios were seeing video release as the second phase of distribution, one which often would ultimately result in a higher gross than the theatrical release, and new films were hurried into video stores before they could be forgotten. More importantly, the studios began releasing videotapes of thousands of films from their archives, thus for the first time making available the history of cinema—at least, Hollywood cinema.

For me and for many others like me, then, television, video, and cable were able to nurture our already established cinephilic relationship to movies. This "new cinephilia"[31] stimulated by home video was, Adrian Martin writes, one which "opened up new intensities, new streams for the circulation and appreciation of cinema." He explains:

Video consumption completely altered the character of film cultures all over the globe: suddenly, there were self-cultivated specialists everywhere in previously elite areas like B-cinema, exploitation cinema, and so-called cult cinema. Where I live, directors including Abel Ferrara, Larry Cohen, and even far-left-fielders like the forgotten erotomaniac Walerian Borowczyk, figure as video-shop directors, to be ferreted out and perpetually rediscovered by termite-like connoisseurs.[32]

But for the most part, this new kind of cinephilia was enjoyed by those like myself, who had some experience with the old kind, and who thus knew how to navigate what was now available to them; furthermore, the backlog of films came onto the market relatively slowly, or at least slowly enough that it felt manageable. For the younger generations who have never known cinephilia in its "pure" state, the situation is in many ways more difficult. While there is surely no shortage of young people who are interested in movies or who want to become filmmakers, there is, as Stanley Kauffmann has noted, a dearth of students with a real interest in the history of cinema, and by this I mean an interest in any film made before *The Godfather.* "Bright university students," Kauffmann writes, "whose predecessors cared about the best films of the present and past, now don't even know that they haven't seen those films."[33]

But my sense is that this is not simply a matter of laziness or lack of interest. Rather, this reluctance on the part of so many young students to seek out the broad range of films that the history of cinema has to offer seems to mimic the change of habits in perception brought on by the conditions of modernity: faced with an abundance of stimuli—or in this case, an abundance of availability, of choices—one closes down, sets up boundaries where none seem to exist, retreats into what one already knows instead of seeking out what is new. People like myself, who had lived through the transition to video availability, did not have to start with virtually the entire history of cinema before them the way today's students do. Further, the critics to whom we devoted ourselves had already alerted us to what to seek out. In my own case, Sarris's *The American Cinema,* barely ten years old when the video boom began, functioned just as he hoped it would—as a way to begin to sift through and prioritize viewing of the mass of films (American films mostly) from the classical period.[34]

For the post-cinephile generations, this shift to virtual accessibility has resulted, quite paradoxically, in a certain loss of history due to the "televisualization" of cinema. A number of scholars have argued that, instead of constantly alerting us to the past, to the continuum of history and time, as photography and cinema so urgently do, the televisual image seems to trap us in a perpetual present, in part because the televisual has become synonymous with the always available, the always present.[35] Thomas Elsaesser has noted the profound effect this loss has had on our individual and collective identities:

If the cinema came into being as a way of recording the real and preserving time, its marriage with television and video has begun to bleed also into the sense of ourselves as creatures existing in a single spatio-temporal extension. [...] Characteristic of our time is the feeling that [the] idea of history has entered a deep conceptual twilight zone, affecting all its traditional signposts and markers: our notion of temporality and causality, our notion of agency and veracity. [History] now appears to exist in suspended animation, neither exactly "behind" us, nor part of our present, but shadowing us rather like a parallel world which is real, hyper-real, and virtual, all at the same time.[36]

This change occurred along with the waning of cinephilia and the increase in availability. In the 1950s and 60s, and even well into the 70s, cinema saw television as its rival and fought its opponent by offering spectacles and subject matter that television could not meet or contain. By the 1980s, however, once the cable and video boom was well under way, the movie industry began to see television not as its competition, but as its cohort. On the one hand, of course, movie theaters still offer what television cannot: scale, both in image and sound. But because today the vast majority of a movie's life will be lived on television, films must be shot in such a way that they will also play effectively on the small screen. Changes have thus been made in cinematic style to accommodate a film's being shown on television sets with much smaller screens, dramatically reduced contrast range, and, oftentimes, incorrect aspect ratios (resulting in the cropping of up to 15 percent of the right and left sides of the image). Filmic images are now composed in a shallower depth-of-field, there are more close-ups than ever before, and visual information is more clearly centered in the frame. Spectators are not required to scan the frame in the way required by widescreen or even Academy ratio cinematic images, but they can instead watch in the distracted manner of the television viewer, confident that they can get the essential information from the image with just a glance.[37] This overall decreased complexity results in film images that are unencumbered by any ambiguity; these are images that are, to quote Roland Barthes, "impoverished"—his term for advertising images whose components are totally arranged and thoroughly dominated by cultural coding. Due largely to television, film images have reached a similar point of simplicity.

Nowhere have the changes in film style wrought by the cinema's relationship to television been described more pointedly than in the writings of the French critic Serge Daney, editor of *Cahiers du Cinéma* from 1973 to 1981. When, in 1987, Daney left film reviewing to write a regular column of media criticism in the daily paper *Libération,* he did so not because he had given up his cinephile convictions, but rather (as Malcolm Imrie has explained) because he wanted "to see what happened to films, and life, as television embraced them."[38] What he observed was not reassuring. In his last essay to be translated into English before his death—a review of Jean-Jacques Annaud's 1992 film, *The Lover*—Daney designated Annaud as "the first non-cinephile robot in the history of cinema."[39] We now have, he wrote, "the prototype . . . of a new breed of filmmaker: the 'post-film-maker,' in other words, one who knows nothing of what the cinema once knew"; indeed, he continued, Annaud makes films "in complete ignorance of the fact that there had *been* any cinema before him."[40]

This ignorance of history has effects on film style. Daney goes on to describe the new approach, in which a film is no more than "a series of orphan images, images which must, *one by one,* be seen, recognised and, so to speak, *ticked off* by the spectator-consumer. In this aesthetic, an image never finds its sequel, its mystery, or its elucidation in another, more or less continuous image." What we have instead is "a run-through of visuals" where "the spectator is trapped by his own feeble status as consumer-decoder. He hasn't time to understand anything which he didn't already 'know'—which leaves him with nothing, with the already-seen or the scarcely seen at all, with ads and logos, visuals and kitsch, in short, with banalities and platitudes."[41]

What this simplified style prevents is the possibility of the *projection* of the spectator into the film image in any substantive way. In *Art and Illusion,* E. H. Gombrich provides not only a detailed consideration of "the beholder's share" in the mimetic experience, but he also insists that the viewer's role is largely projective—that is, that, to some extent, the viewer recognizes in the art encountered things that he or she has encountered in experience. In this way, the viewer makes the art his or her own, participating not only in meaning or experience, but in production itself.[42] But the style employed by much contemporary cinema offers little space for such projection because so much contemporary cinema does not ask us to consider our experience of the world, but only of other films, other audiovisual images. The absence of this space for spectatorial projection in movies is crucial for cinephilia because, as Christian Metz has acknowledged, the cinephile's relation to films, especially those that are loved or highly valued, is "broadly projective" in nature.[43] In a cinema that does not allow for this kind of projective relationship, Daney writes, "something essential . . . has disappeared."[44]

It is, of course, possible to restrict the existence of pure cinephilia, as Paul Willemen does, to a time and place when one's relationship to the cinema was still largely "uncontaminated by a relationship to television."[45] But while this may account for the death of cinephilia in its broad cultural sense, it does not explain the death of cinephilia in the more narrow, specialized region of professional film scholarship (both popular and academic). For the answer to that, explains Dominique Païni, we must look to the Langlois affair and the events of May '68. First, he argues, the Langlois affair marked a crisis in the history of cinephilia—one that was, perhaps paradoxically, both its ultimate success and the beginning of its end. The Langlois affair began in February 1968, when the French government, which had long provided subsidies to the Cinémathèque Française, but which had maintained a hands-off stance, decided to take control by removing the volatile, secretive Langlois and replacing him with someone more sensitive to bureaucratic procedure and order. Cinephiles immediately poured into the streets to protest Langlois's dismissal, and great filmmakers from around the world sent telegrams refusing the Cinémathèque the right to show their films unless Langlois was reinstated. The protests succeeded, and a few weeks later, Langlois was back in charge.

On the face of it, this was cinephilia's finest hour. But Païni sees it a bit differently. He argues that the state's identification of interest in what had formerly been an operation of marginal cultural worth was an acknowledgment of legitimacy, both for the cinema as an art form and for cinephilia, which had been nurtured more richly at the Cinémathèque than anywhere else. In these events, Païni writes, cinephilia went from being "a 'deviant' form of behavior (we should recall the stigma still attached to heavy film-going even in the 1960s, which Truffaut has described) [to being] integrated into cultural policy."[46] With this validation, cinephilia lost the clandestine, countercultural energy on which it had thrived for so long.

From there, the situation worsened. The Langlois protests spiraled into a nationwide expression of anger at the de Gaulle administration's policies, culminating in the intense cultural and political unrest of May '68. In those five months, many formerly diehard cinephiles increasingly became politically minded, as well as suspicious of the now-official culture of cinephilia. In the years immediately following 1968, film scholarship in many important quarters (including *Cahiers du Cinéma*) committed itself to a decidedly anticinephilic position. Focusing on ideology rather than aesthetics, film scholars of the period worked to show the ways in which film grammar and even the cinematic apparatus are determined by dominant class and gender interests, and that the pleasure that results in the cinematic experience is itself a product of those oppressive forces.[47] A clear example of this shift into anti-cinephilia can be found in the influential writings of Christian Metz. With his commitment to semiotic and psychoanalytic theories, Metz deemed it necessary to willfully repress a memory of the cinephilic experience. In the section entitled "Loving the Cinema" in *The Imaginary Signifier*, Metz wrote,

To be a theoretician of the cinema, one should ideally no longer love the cinema and yet still love it: have loved it a lot and only have detached oneself from it by taking it up again from the other end, taking it as the target for the very same scopic drive which had made one love it. Have broken with it, as certain relationships are broken, not in order to move on to something else, but in order to return to it at the next bend in the spiral. Carry the institution inside one still so that it is in a place accessible to self-analysis, but carry it there as a distinct instance which does not over-infiltrate the rest of the ego with a thousand paralysing bonds of a tender unconditionality. Not have forgotten what the cinephile one used to be was like, in all the details of his affective inflections, in the three dimensions of his living being, and yet no longer be invaded by him: not have lost sight of him, but be keeping an eye on him. Finally, be him and not be him, since all in all these are the two conditions on which one can speak of him.[48]

Regardless of the extent to which one may disagree with Metz's position, it is possible to see in the work of the finest theorists of this period precisely the balancing act, the "deliberate ambivalence," between cinephilia and anti-cinephilia that Metz prescribes.[49] More often, however, it felt in the 1970s as though the majority of scholars saw their love of the cinema as something to be cast off or outgrown in the way one outgrows adolescence.[50] Even some scholars committed to the semiotic enterprise saw this attack on cinephilia as a loss. For example, Peter Wollen (in the guise of his alter ego, Lee Russell) recently remarked, "I was attracted by the element of cinephilia [in the early days of academic cinema studies] and that's precisely what got lost with the relentless expansion of theory over the face of academe."[51]

Although the anti-cinephilic critical position has lost center stage in the past decade, traces of it still remain, and the suspicion of cinephilia holds firmly enough that, in recent years, the field of academic cinema studies has been largely silent on the topic. Many film scholars seem to be embarrassed at the idea that one might publicly acknowledge that one's own research, or for that matter the choice of a career, might be motivated by an intense love for cinema. For what the politicization of 1970s film theory erased was the fascination with what Paul Willemen has described as "the revelatory powers . . . of the image-in-movement."[52] At the 1995 Lyon conference on cinephilia, Sylvia Harvey remarked that the ideological/semiotic project's "extreme mistrust of the fruits of the camera's labors" has resulted in a secularism that has no place for the cinephile's belief in a "sense of the special, even 'sacred' nature of the photographic image."[53] Though she openly acknowledges that we cannot return to some supposedly Edenic world before the linguistic turn (nor should we want to), she nevertheless identifies it as "one of the challenges of current secular criticism to reconstruct or re-invent a sense of the sacred and the immortal, and perhaps to find other words than these to refer to the constant presence of the extraordinary within the ordinary, to foreground significance which is present without words"—precisely the recovery of some sense of the cinephilic within cinema studies.[54] This book attempts to do just that.

2 The Cinephiliac Moment and Panoramic Perception

Near the beginning of his delightful autobiography, *My Life and My Films,* Jean Renoir recounts his first visit to the cinema, in 1897, when he was just two years old. Renoir and his beloved older cousin, Gabrielle, were paying a visit to the Paris department store Dufayel when, Renoir reports, a man asked them if they wanted to see the "cinema."

> Scarcely had we taken our seats when the room was plunged into darkness. A terrifying machine shot out a fearsome beam of light piercing the obscurity, and a series of incomprehensible pictures appeared on the screen, accompanied by the sound of a piano at one end and at the other end a sort of hammering that came from the machine. I yelled in my usual fashion and had to be taken out.[1]

Renoir then comments, quite appropriately, on the irony that his first encounter with the medium that would become the love of his life was a complete failure. But before leaving the scene, Renoir notes, "Gabrielle was sorry we had not stayed. The film was about a big river and she thought that in the corner of the screen she had glimpsed a crocodile."[2]

While this scene may at first seem merely amusing, it could be argued that Renoir's story is about an encounter with early *cinephilia*, for in this anecdote a marginal filmic detail exemplifies the most basic of cinephilic experiences, the *cinephiliac moment*; furthermore, it perfectly characterizes the cinephile's defining mode of vision: *panoramic perception.*

The Cinephiliac Moment

In a 1994 dialogue with Australian scholar Noel King, Paul Willemen noted that, in the varied body of critical writings associated with cinephilia, there exists a recurring preoccupation with an element of the cinematic experience "which resists, which escapes existing networks of critical discourse and theoretical frameworks."[3] Noel King clarifies that this "something" emerges in the cinephile's "fetishising of a particular moment, the isolating of a crystallisingly expressive detail" in the film image.[4] In these "subjective, fleeting, variable" moments, Willemen writes, "What is seen is in excess of what is being shown."[5] The cinephiliac moment is "not choreographed for you to see"—or rather, if it is, it is not choreographed for the viewer to dwell on excessively. "It is produced *en plus*, in excess or in addition, almost involuntarily."[6] Willemen cites his own fascination with "the moment when the toy falls off the table in [Douglas Sirk's] *There's Always Tomorrow*,"[7] while Noel King, citing the famous dropped glove scene from *On the Waterfront*, writes, "I tend to notice the number of times Eva Marie Saint tries to retrieve the glove and the things Brando does to delay this happening."[8] Other cinephiles have their own cherished moments. Of director Nicholas Ray, critic David Thomson writes, "it is as the source of a profusion of cinematic epiphanies that I recall him: Mitchum walking across an empty rodeo arena in the evening in *The Lusty Men*, the wind blowing rubbish around him; that last plate settling slowly and noisily in *55 Days at Peking*; . . . the CinemaScope frame suddenly ablaze with yellow cabs in *Bigger Than Life*."[9]

The American critic Manny Farber regularly devoted space in his reviews to such privileged moments. In an essay on the work of action genre directors like Howard Hawks, Raoul Walsh, and Anthony Mann, Farber wrote that, although these directors' films "are filled with heroism or its absence, the real hero is . . . the unheralded ripple of physical existence, the tiny morbidly lifeworn detail."[10] Indeed, far more than plot or character, these marginal bits are what stick in his memory. Years after seeing these films, Farber writes, one most vividly "remembers the way a dulled waitress sat on the edge of a hotel bed [or], the weird elongated adobe in which ranch hands congregate before a Chisholm Trail drive."[11] In the course of celebrating Howard Hawks's *The Big Sleep*, a film that "ignores all the conventions of a gangster film to feast on meaningless business and witty asides," Farber provides what is perhaps an extreme example of a cinephiliac moment: "One of the fine moments in 1940's film is no longer than a blink: Bogart, as he crosses the street from one bookstore to another, looks up at a sign."[12] As Greg Taylor put it, if American auteurist Andrew Sarris offered in his criticism a connoisseurship of lists, Farber offered in his a connoisseurship of details.[13]

Roger Cardinal, another critic who has written suggestively about the fascination with marginal filmic details, argues that the identification of these privileged moments is a subjective, even "self-reflexive" act. In "Pausing over Peripheral Detail," he explains, "What I notice, or elect to notice, is necessarily a function of my sensibility, so much so that a list of my favorite details will equate to an oblique mirror-image of myself, becoming more noticeably idiosyncratic the longer it extends."[14] He continues,

Who else but I will have taken note of the black glasses worn by the man who sounds the curfew horn in Robison's *Warning Shadows* (1923); Lauren Bacall's hand clutching and unclutching at the back of the chair in the background in a tense scene in Huston's *Key Largo* (1948); the painting on A's bedroom wall of the mad Ludwig II of Bavaria out for a nocturnal sleighride, in Resnais's *Last Year at Marienbad* (1963); and of the author's name ("Juan Luis Echevarria") on the pink book shown to the camera at the climax of Ruiz's *Letter from a Library Lover* (1983)?[15]

It is, of course, possible that one or more of a viewer's privileged moments may be shared by another. For example, James Naremore has noted that a number of other people have remarked in print on one of his own favorite cinephiliac details: the color of Cary Grant's socks in the cropduster sequence from *North by Northwest*.[16] But even held in common with others, such details remain one's own, no doubt in large part because the initial encounter was a private one, even though it occurred in the public space of a darkened theater. Cardinal notes, "While any one of these collector's items could figure in someone else's inventory, the fact of their being grouped by me implies a characteristic angle of vision governed by my individual tastes and fetishes."[17] Willemen similarly notes the subjective nature of each cinephile's chosen moments.

I can't detect any consistency among cinephiles, beyond a broad selection of "good objects." [. . .] What is being revealed is not the same to all critics. All critics do not select the same privileged moments to which they attach their cinephilia. The moments are different but each is talking about a pleasurable relation to that particular film. The difference in selection is less important than the fact that you are signalling the relationship of pleasures generated between you and the screen.[18]

Indeed, at its very basis, Willemen argues, the cinephiliac moment "has something to do with what you perceive to be the privileged, pleasure-giving, fascinating moment of a relationship to what's happening on the screen."[19] Put another way, the cinephiliac moment may be understood as a kind of *mise-en-abyme* wherein each cinephile's obsessive relationship to the cinema is embodied in its most dense, concentrated form.

In the past, academic film studies has explained these experiences by classifying their material under the heading of "excess." In *Narration in the Fiction Film*, David Bordwell defines excess as whatever cannot be assigned meaning or relevance in relation to the broadest sense of a film's narrative. This excess includes "colors, expressions, and textures" that "become 'fellow travelers' of the story."[20] But as David Ehrenstein has argued,

If films were only their narratives, only their stories, such things [like a viewer's fascination with the color of Cary Grant's socks] wouldn't be possible. And the fact that they *are* possible isn't something to be swept under the rug or ignored as irrelevant, but rather investigated in as thoroughgoing a manner as possible. For what's at stake is the relationship between the relative autonomy of the spectator on the one hand, and the actual process of his intellection of the elements on the other—something that diagesis-bound [*sic*] semiotic studies (such as Stephen Heath's on *Touch of Evil*) haven't really been willing to come to grips with.[21]

Though we may locate qualities of excess at every turn in a motion picture, not every point of excess provokes the epiphanic *frisson* marking the experience as being of that special class of excess, cinephiliac moments. Ultimately, it is less the quality or nature of the image itself that is excessive than the cinephile's response to it. Lesley Stern, describing one of her cinephiliac moments in detail, provides another good example.

There is an extraordinary moment in *Blade Runner* when Pris, like a human missile, comes somersaulting straight toward us. One moment she is immobile (in a room full of mechanical and artificial toys she appears to be a wax doll); the next moment she is galvanized into life, her body moving at the speed of light. The force of her somersault charges the air; reconfiguring space and time, her bodily momentum is transmitted and experienced in the auditorium as bodily sensation. My stomach lurches. It is always surprising this moment, this movement, always and without fail it takes me aback. Yet what can it mean to yoke these incommensurate terms—*always* and *surprising*? Let me just say, at this point, that I am both surprised and haunted by this cinematic moment. I can't quite put my finger on the feeling it evokes, though there is a phrase of [Jean] Epstein's that resonates: "On the line of communication the static of unexpected feelings interrupts us."[22]

While it is clear that the moment Stern identifies is not accidental, but rather carefully designed and choreographed, the emphasis she places on it is greater than its visual quality or narrative importance would normally provoke. In true cinephiliac fashion, Stern has assigned to this filmic moment what Roger Cardinal has described as a "wholly 'unreasonable' priority and value."[23] It is thus important to make a distinction between Willemen's cinephiliac moments and the more commonly occurring memorable filmic moments, such as the ones described famously by Walker Percy in his novel, *The Moviegoer:*

Other people, so I have read, treasure memorable moments in their lives: the time one climbed the Parthenon at sunrise, the summer night one met a lonely girl in Central Park and achieved with her a sweet and natural relationship, as they say in books. I too once met a girl in Central Park, but it was not much to remember. What I remember is the time John Wayne killed three men with a carbine as he was falling to the dusty street in *Stagecoach,* and the time the kitten found Orson Welles in the doorway in *The Third Man.*[24]

While I would not want to deny for a second the extraordinary pleasure that filmic moments such as these bring to both the cinephile and the ordinary movie fan, they do not qualify as "cinephiliac moments" as I am using that term because they are precisely designed to be memorable; and they are memorable because they are both visually striking and narratively important (the climax in *Stagecoach,* an important turning point in *The Third Man*). The moments in which I am most interested are those that achieve this level of memorability—especially if only subjectively—even though they are not designed to. Lesley Stern, echoing Cardinal's argument about self-reflexivity, further links the feeling produced by cinephiliac moments to the euphoric experience of the uncanny, identifying them as "a strange and unexpected meeting with yourself."[25]

For both Willemen and Cardinal, an important precedent for the fascination with marginal details in film images is found in Roland Barthes's "The Third Meaning" and *Camera Lucida.* In both these works, Barthes attempted to identify that element of photographic representation that exceeds semiology's capacity to assign meaning. In the former work, he dubbed these points of excess "third" or "obtuse" meanings and argued that, "It is at the level of the third meaning, and at that level alone, that the 'filmic' finally emerges. The filmic is that which cannot be described, the representation which cannot be represented. The filmic begins only where language and meta-language end."[26] In the latter work, making a clearer distinction between public and private, objective and subjective, Barthes chose a different term: the *punctum*. The *punctum* is a site that, for Barthes, disturbs or punctures the unity of the *studium,* which he defines as the culturally determined meaning communicated in a photo (a combination of denotation and connotation), one shared by the photographer who snaps a picture and the public who receives and recognizes it. The *punctum* is a detail that attracts him, that reaches out beyond the *studium* and pricks him: a boy's bad teeth in one snapshot and a woman's strapped pumps in a studio portrait. Specifying its status as objectively present, but only subjectively provocative, Barthes wrote that the *punctum* "is what I add to the photograph and *what is nonetheless already there."*[27] This statement—and Cardinal's claim about self-reflexivity—confirms something of the projective nature of encountering such details.

In the context of Barthes's overall critical project, the third meaning and the *punctum* can be understood as eruptions of figuration in a text otherwise dominated by representation. In *The Pleasure of the Text,* Barthes contrasted representation to figuration, arguing that while the former is an organization of cultural and ideological meanings, resulting in *plaisir* (pleasure), the latter is beyond such generalizable meaning, marked by *jouissance* (bliss)—the individual's fetishistic, bodily experience of pleasure. (Indeed, as Gregory Ulmer has argued, the late period of Barthes's critical work is guided in large part by fetishism.[28]) Placing figuration on the side of fetishism, and setting representation against it, Barthes wrote, "That is what representation is: when nothing emerges, when nothing leaps out of the frame: of the picture, the book, the screen."[29] In spite of his stated resistance to it, the cinema, he argued, is one privileged site of the figurative. He wrote, "Even more than the text, the film will always be figurative (which is why films are still worth making)—even if it represents nothing."[30] That is, more than written texts, the cinema affords the possibility for the kind of fetishistic projection that results in the experience of cinephiliac moments.

While Barthes's privileged moments are found in still images, the cinephile most often locates his or hers in motion. But, as Raymond Durgnat points out, "Time and time again people imply that movement entails a narrative. Yet movement often isn't even action." He further explains, "All the leaves moving around on a tree don't constitute as many narratives as there are leaves."[31] It seems the subjectivity that marks encounters with cinephiliac moments has prevented film theorists from attempting to consider them in any thoroughgoing way beyond their role as elements that may exceed the system under consideration. Willemen writes that the individual cinephile's encounter with the figurative moment of subjective revelation "may be different from the person sitting next to you, in which case you may have to dig him or her in the ribs with your elbow to alert them"; nevertheless, he concludes, "There is a theory of the cinema implicit in the dig of the elbow into the ribs just as much as there is in Metz's work."[32]

But before we get to that, it is worth noting that, even with the fetishization of fragments or moments, cinephilia is not completely unique—at least, not exactly. For at roughly the same time that Giovanni Morelli was locating the evidence of authorship in the marginal details of paintings, the English connoisseur/critic Walter Pater was focusing attention on this other kind detail, one existing less in the work of art itself than in the spectator's epiphanic experience of it. In his most famous work, *The Renaissance: Studies in Art and Poetry* (1873), Pater explained that, if the goal of art and art criticism is, as Matthew Arnold claimed, "To see the object as in itself it really is," then in his own critical approach, "aesthetic criticism," the first step toward this goal is to "know one's impression as it really is."[33] In other words, the aesthetic critic should ask, "What is this song or picture, this engaging personality presented in life or in a book, to *me*? What effect does it really produce on me? Does it give me pleasure? and if so, what sort or degree of pleasure?"[34] Though *The Renaissance* is organized largely around great artists, the cornerstone of Pater's critical approach was a commitment to the perceptual capabilities of the viewer or critic.

Even more specifically, as Harold Bloom explains, Pater founded his critical position "upon privileged moments of vision, or 'epiphanies.'"[35] That is, rather than mobilizing his greatest critical praise for an artwork in its totality, or for certain periods or styles, Pater celebrated most of all his intense experiences of details of works. In an essay on Renaissance poet Joachim Du Bellay, Pater wrote, "A sudden light transfigures a trivial thing, a weathervane, a windmill, a winnowing flail, the dust in the barn door; a moment—and the thing has vanished, because it was pure effect; but it leaves a relish behind, a longing that the accident may happen again."[36] Elsewhere, in his essay on Giorgione, Pater writes of "profoundly significant and animated instants, a mere gesture, a look, a smile, perhaps—some brief and wholly concrete moment" that becomes the focus of his experience of beauty.[37]

Importantly—and in stark contrast to predecessors Matthew Arnold and John Ruskin—Pater never sought to justify his privileged experiences by recourse to any social or moral argument. He valued the sensuous experience of artworks as an end in itself, the fruits of keen perception. "It is with movement, with the passage and dissolution of impressions, sensations, images, that analysis leaves off," Pater wrote; and he was most preoccupied with these sensual experiences that were beyond any interpretation.[38] Thus, in Pater's writing there is little in the way of critical analysis; his writings are mostly an account of his experiences of works (or fragments, moments of works) of art. He was "more a master of reverie than of description," Harold Bloom explains ("let alone analysis, which is alien to him").[39] Pater continued, "Every moment some form grows perfect in hand or face; some tone on the hills or the sea is choicer than the rest; some mood of passion or insight or intellectual excitement is irresistibly real and attractive for us,—for that moment only. Not the fruit of experience, but experience itself, is the end."[40] Bloom concludes, "Pater remains the most honest recorder of epiphanies, by asking so little of them."[41]

It is hard not to read into Pater a certain unconscious desire for cinema, for although he was writing about works of art that are not time-based (e.g., painting and poetry), his epiphanic experience of certain details of those works has a clear temporal dimension. But this can be understood only if we remember that it is not simply the works themselves, but the *experience* of them that is at issue, for the experience of anything exists *in time*.[42] Out of the flux of sensations produced by a work of art, any one of them can intensify—momentarily—to the point of sublime experience. But Pater also saw these privileged moments he encountered as being bound up with the specificity of a particular work's given medium. He maintained that each art form has characteristics that are specific to it, and individual works in a given form achieve their greatest force within those specific characteristics. The beginning of "all true aesthetic criticism," Pater wrote, is the understanding that "the sensuous material of each art brings with it a special phase or quality of beauty, untranslatable into the forms of any other, an order of impressions distinct in kind."[43] Furthermore, and because of this fact, each art has its own "special responsibilities to its material," and "one of the functions of aesthetic criticism is to . . . estimate the degree in which a given art fulfils its responsibilities to its special material."[44] These remarks from Pater precisely sum up André Bazin's position, for it was he who most explicitly spelled out the specific nature of cinema's "material." Furthermore, it is with this point that we can see a clearer justification for a focus on cinephiliac moments.

Why the Cinephiliac Moment?

1. *Ontology.* Willemen claims that he cannot find in theatrical or other criticism any discourse that fetishizes "the non-coded or slippage out of the code" in the way that cinema criticism so persistently has.[45] He concludes, then, that the cinephiliac moment is linked to the specificity of cinematic representation, and thus is in solidarity with the basis of André Bazin's theoretical position as laid out in "The Ontology of the Photographic Image." There, Bazin empha-

sized the photographic image's status as an objective, automatically produced representation. Willemen summarizes:

The ontology of cinema, as voiced by Bazin, claims that, because a mechanical reproduction is involved, there is a privileged relationship between cinema and the real. That is to say, there is something which is being reproduced and therefore there is an unfilmed world before the camera came along and pointed to it, some of which (and the more the better, as far as Bazin is concerned) transpires into the recorded and projected image. And what people like Bazin want you to relate to in their polemic is precisely the dimension of revelation that is obtained by pointing your camera at something that hasn't been staged for the camera.[46]

The cinephiliac moment is the site where this prior presence, this fleeting experience of the real, is felt most intensely or magically.

This general experience of the real in film images has been described by another word: "indexicality." The term, which comes from American polymath Charles S. Peirce's classification of the different kinds of signs, was introduced to film studies by Peter Wollen in his *Signs and Meaning in the Cinema*.[47] Peirce, Wollen explained, divided all signs into three categories—icon, index, and symbol—with classification depending on the way in which the sign referred to the thing it represented. An icon is a sign that refers by similarity to what it represents; for instance, a portrait of a person resembles him or her. A symbol has an arbitrary relationship to what it represents, with reference secured by social conventions and codes; the three colored lights of the traffic signal, for example—red, green, yellow—are symbols alerting us respectively to stop, go, or proceed with caution. An index is a sign "by virtue of the existential bond between itself and its object"; the sign has been produced by the very thing it refers to.[48] The most common examples are fingerprints or shadows, but Peirce himself identified photographs as belonging to the indexical class of signs (even though photos generally possess iconic properties) because the image was produced by a "physical connection" between the thing represented and its representation.[49]

Though Bazin did not use this word, he was clearly referring to this property of indexicality when he compared a photograph to a death mask, and when he wrote, "One might consider photography . . . as a molding, the taking of an impression, by the manipulation of light."[50] Film's indexical status gives it a unique advantage over other representations that are primarily iconic, as Bazin explained: "A very faithful drawing may tell us more about the model but despite the promptings of our critical intelligence it will never have the irrational power to bear away our faith."[51] For the indexical quality of the film image is the mark or trace of a prior presence, and this trace can suddenly and unexpectedly make itself felt to the viewer. This experience, Willemen stresses, in part relates to something that is dead but alive, past but present; thus his choice of the term "cinephiliac" over "cinephilic," because of "the former's overtones of necrophilia."[52] While it is possible to fetishize that which has been carefully stylized, as so much is in the films of a director like Max Ophuls, Willemen explains, the cinephiliac moment exists outside of or beyond what has been intentionally aestheticized, even though it may be a deliberate part of the film's design. "You can value Ophuls because he does something else (fetishizes the frame, screens off the real) or you can fetishize that dimension of the real which shines through."[53] The cinephiliac moment can be described as the sudden eruption of the real (or the indexical) in a text dominated by iconic and symbolic properties. This is not to argue the flawed nature of the symbolic system, but rather, and perhaps paradoxically, its necessity. As Willemen argues,

it is no accident, indeed, it is highly necessary, that cinephilia should operate particularly strongly in relation to a form of cinema that is perceived as being highly coded, highly commercial, formalised and ritualised. For it is only there that the moment of revelation or excess, a dimension other than that which is being programmed, becomes noticeable. If that in itself is the system of the film, as, say, in a Stan Brakhage film, you don't have a cinephiliac moment because it's no longer demarcatable . . . because the whole film tries to be it.[54]

Lesley Stern's description of cinephiliac moments as uncanny experiences seconds this argument, for as Freud wrote, experiences of the uncanny are most likely to appear in situations that are familiar, structured, or, in the narrative arts, when the status of the real is at its strongest. Furthermore, Laura Mulvey has addressed indexicality's links to the uncanny, as well as to the experience of time—two issues that I will return to in later chapters.[55]

2. *Movies as Fragments.* This emphasis on the fragmentary image-moment is a reminder that films are themselves made up of fragments: framing that shows us only a portion of the real space of an action, and editing that does likewise with time, allowing us to see only what the director deems necessary. Jean-Luc Godard has described the activity of directing in precisely these terms—as questions of space (what is shown) and time (for how long): "The problem which has long preoccupied me, but which I don't worry about while shooting is: why do one shot rather than another [and] . . . What is it ultimately that makes one run a shot on or change to another?"[56] Classical Hollywood's continuity system, with its linchpin formal devices of centering and matching, was designed to efface the inherently fragmented nature of filmic narration by focusing only on what was relevant to the plot and eliminating anything superfluous.[57] By fetishizing certain shots or certain actions within

shots, the cinephile reminds us of, and asks us to consider anew, the fragmented quality of all films, also reminding us of the inherently fragmentary nature of the filmmaking process.

Though the most common understanding of this dominant filmmaking practice is that all the fragments are selected more or less in advance, through meticulous scripting and storyboarding, some filmmaking practice seizes on what is accidentally captured during the filming process, using it as the starting point for a new, unexpected narrational pattern. Noël Burch has described Sergei Eisenstein's strategy in just this way.

The accidental provides far more subtle and more complex cutting possibilities than any filmmaker can foresee. . . . In the scene in *October* where the buxom bourgeois women in their rustling laces poke out the young sailor's eyes with the tips of their umbrellas, Eisenstein brings the camera right up to the action and follows it very closely, aware that, in addition to the intrinsic beauty of the shots thus obtained, this kaleidoscopic flurry of dancing silhouettes, whirling cloth and dripping blood will result in a cascade of images, visible in all their detail only in the developed film, for the cameraman himself will not even have seen them as he views the action through his small eyepiece (a feather boa visible on screen for a few fractions of a second, a flare frame only a few inches long), aware that these "accidents" will later afford him the possibility of cutting to another shot in a visually interesting way at almost any frame.[58]

In locating cinephiliac moments—that is, in selecting (or being selected by) certain image-moments over others—the cinephile mimics this filmmaking practice in particular, that one that is mobilized by discovery of what has been captured unexpectedly.

3. *Critical Writing.* As Christian-Marc Bosséno has explained, the cinephile, unlike members of most specialized audience groups, "left us, in writing, a record of his experience, recounting in detail his pleasures and dislikes in the manner of an herbalist; these Confessions were then freely published. We have a large quantity of articles, interviews, lists and notes which allow us to retrace, from its origins, the life and work of the *cinémane.*"[59] The existence of this critical writing as a record of cinephiliac encounters is important in itself, but it also has another, more important historical value—that of being a crucial bridge between individual and cultural cinephilia.

As de Baecque and Frémaux note, cinephilia begins with the individual film lover and the idiosyncrasies of his or her relationship with the cinema. But cinephilia extends from there into a network of other like-minded people, and at its strongest moments, this sharing has grown into a cultural force as well. The cinephiles's dialogue, which leads ultimately to revaluation and reassessment of cinema, is legitimized in large part through critical writing. In addition, the cinephiliac moment is one aspect of the individual cinephile's relationship to cinema that is intimately linked to this critical writing practice, and therefore with the dissemination of cinephilic ideas. Paul Willemen argues that one can easily trace a preoccupation with cinephiliac moments through much of the criticism written during the important historical periods of cultural cinephilia. Cinephiliac moments, he argues, have regularly been moments which, "when encountered in a film, spark something which then produces the energy and the desire to write, to find formulations to convey something about the intensity of that spark."[60]

4. *Phenomenology.* It would be possible to address the phenomenon of cinephiliac moments through any number of theoretical frameworks. What little has been written in depth about the subject has usually opted (as Willemen does) for a psychoanalytic approach, and though my study will occasionally refer to the discipline of psychoanalysis, it will, for the most part, privilege a phenomenological framework, for several reasons. First, it is difficult to overstate the influence of the philosophy of phenomenology on postwar European culture, including cinephilia. Even when not explicitly cited, it is clear that the discussions of phenomenology—in both its transcendental and existentialist variations—deeply influenced postwar cinephilic thinking about cinema.[61] But while the writings of those cinephile critics were crucial in gaining film studies a foothold in the Academy, by the time film studies enjoyed a secure place (in the late 1960s), phenomenology had been succeeded by structuralism, and that theory's vocabulary and concepts dominated serious discussion of film. So in spite of its historical importance in the establishment of academic film studies, phenomenology remains, to use Dudley Andrew's term, a largely "neglected tradition."[62] A consideration of phenomenology is crucial to recovering an important cultural factor in the development of historical cinephilia.

In addition, focusing as it does on the conscious experience of phenomena and the world as it is lived and experienced by individuals, phenomenology offers a fruitful approach for the film scholar investigating the individual, subjective experiences of the cinematic event. While the theoretical approaches of structuralism, semiotics, and Marxism address patterns, structures, and schema, they do not address the singular experiences—such as cinephiliac moments—that escape such schema. Phenomenology does, however, and two of its tenets will be of particular importance for this study. First, in contrast to gaze theory, which posits a passive spectator, phenomenological theory insists on what Vivian Sobchack has described as an "active eye," one that is "introceptively, *subjectively busy:* at work prospecting its world, actively making— and visibly marking—the visual choice to situate its gaze again and again."[63] Second, phenomenology's contention that "the phenomena of our experience

are always correlated with the mode of our experience"—that is, that what we perceive depends on our perceptual posture—is crucial, as we will see, for a discussion of cinephiliac moments.[64] While my study claims no position in phenomenological debates, it will occasionally return to the concepts of phenomenology to further articulate its object of study and that object's implications, both for criticism and history.

5. *Historiography.* Because of its status as the mark of a prior presence, a photographic image enjoys a certain privileged relationship to what it represents, and thus an apparently privileged relationship to history. At the same time, however, such details reveal the limits of traditional historiographic practice. Siegfried Kracauer and Walter Benjamin argued that film was a dramatic challenge to history, for the particularities and contingencies in photographic images mark what traditional, realist historiographies cannot contain. That is, not only are cinephiliac moments one place to begin a history of cinephilia but also they have important implications for the very practice of historiography—as we will see in chapter 5.

The Cinephile and Panoramic Perception

In order to extend the discussion of cinephiliac moments by Willemen (and others), I would like to place them into the context of recent discussions of the cinema's relationship to the general conditions of modernity and, in particular, to habits and changes in visual perception. For it is my contention that the cinephile has a particular perceptual/spectatorial posture that facilitates the experience of these moments.

The encounters that I am defining as cinephiliac moments depend in large part on an alternative spectatorial practice, one that stands in some contrast to the spectatorial posture assumed by dominant cinema. But giving up this more traditional posture for an alternative demands effort, for dominant cinema so thoroughly guides the spectator's gaze that it has created habits of viewing that are hard to break. Roger Cardinal explains, "Our competence as readers of film language has established a kind of *fixation on congruity* which regulates our assessment of detail and ensures that we do not get it wrong and stumble into alternative, incongruous readings. Above all, the coherence we identify tends to reinforce our sense of the intentionality and relevance of the details in question."[65]

In contrast to this disciplined viewer, Cardinal writes, is the viewer who possesses a "wilfully perverse gaze," a viewer who actively resists the congruity forced on images by the continuity system and instead seeks out the details not categorizable as *studia*.[66] Cardinal explains:

A distinction thus emerges between two divergent strategies of viewing. The first is the "literate" mode in which a single-minded gaze is directed towards the obvious *Gestalt* or figure on offer; where the artist has centred or signalled his image in accordance with the conventions of representation, the viewer's gaze will be attuned to the focal message and will ignore its periphery. [. . .] The second mode is one which focuses less narrowly and instead roams over the frame, sensitive to its textures and surfaces—to its ground. This mode may be associated with "non-literacy" and with habits of looking which are akin to habits of touching. The mobile eye which darts from point to point will tend to clutch at fortuitous detail or to collect empathetic impressions of touch sensations.[67]

Kaja Silverman, writing about Roland Barthes's fascination with filmic details, has dubbed this alternative method of watching a "productive look." While culture works to determine how subjects can look and what can be seen or shown, the productive look attempts to see independently of these controlling processes. Driven by "an appetite for alterity," Silverman writes, productive cinematic lookers are drawn to those moments or places that lie outside of, exceed, or are marginal to the "given-to-be-seen" of the film at hand.[68]

This activity of productive looking and the discoveries it makes are similar to what Wolfgang Schivelbusch, in his book *The Railway Journey*, calls "panoramic perception."[69] Prior to the railway, Schivelbusch explains, the fastest and most common method of long-distance travel had been the horse-drawn coach; but with the development of the railroad, it became possible to triple the amount of distance traditionally covered in a given period of time. This dramatic increase in the speed of travel had a profound effect not only on people's concepts of space and time but also on their habits of visual perception. While the slowness of pre-rail travel enabled full visual and sensory experience of a landscape, the speed of the train meant a transformation in visual perception. The only alternative was for the passenger to "acquire a mode of perception adequate to technical travel"—a mode of perception Schivelbusch calls "panoramic."[70] On the one hand, Schivelbusch uses this term to evoke comparison to the perceptual experience of visitors to nineteenth-century panoramas;[71] but in his use of the term "panoramic," Schivelbusch has something even more specific in mind. He explains that when a rail traveler gazed out the window of his compartment, as a landscape from which he was disconnected rolled past, he would fix on some object or detail in the tableau—something that, under different circumstances, might have gone unnoticed—and he would follow it for the brief moment that it was in his field of vision. Schivelbusch cites the nineteenth-century travel journalist Benjamin Gastineau, who wrote that this "novel ability," this capacity "to perceive the discrete, as it rolls past the window indiscriminately," was best described as "la philosophie synthétique du coup d'oeil ('the synthetic philosophy of the glance')."[72]

Numerous film scholars have explored the link between Schivelbusch's description of the rail traveler gazing out the window and the experience of the viewer before the cinema screen.[73] One of the earliest and most influential statements came from Mary Anne Doane, who explored the implications for film theory of Schivelbusch's point that, due in part to the "frame" of the railcar window, train travelers experienced an odd feeling of separation from the landscape they observed, and that this separation provoked a different perceptual posture. Schivelbusch writes, "Panoramic perception, in contrast to traditional perception, no longer belongs to the same space as the perceived objects: the traveler sees the objects, landscapes, etc. *through* the apparatus which moves him through the world."[74] Doane argues that, through its "regularization of vision and the subject's relation to the screen," classical cinema "reasserts and institutionalizes the despatialization of subjectivity" that is experienced by the rail traveler.[75] Furthermore, she writes, the radical reorganization of the experience of space and time effected by rail travel is "entirely compatible" with that of "filmic narrative," for both activate "the spatial and temporal ellipsis, the annihilation of the space and time 'in-between' events."[76]

Doane's argument is quite suggestive, but I would like to point out two things as a partial corrective. First, it overlooks a crucial fact about the composition and arrangement of dominant cinema's images and their contrast with the rail traveler's visual experience. As John Ruskin complained, with the development of rail travel, a sense of the wholeness of a journey was lost, and substituted for it was a journey of parts, of fragments.[77] While cinema, too, consists of image fragments, dominant cinema's formal grammar sews together those fragments into a new, seemingly continuous whole. So, while the cinema's succession of images suggests comparison with the "loss of continuity" Schivelbusch describes as a typical experience during rail travel, the continuity system makes it seem as if we've taken the journey by coach, for we feel as if we've seen it all, or at least all that is of consequence. In addition, though the comparison of the separating effect of the train window with the cinema screen may seem apt in some cases, classical cinema's continuity system works to increase the viewer's involvement with the drama she is observing, focusing her attention on certain details rather than others, thus reducing a sense of separation from what is viewed.

Furthermore, while Doane's analogy between the rail traveler's panoramic perception and cinema spectatorship remains a suggestive one—for it points to a spot where two different technologies of modernity and the effects they produce find sudden convergence—her application of it overlooks a specific and important component of Schivelbush's definition. "What, exactly," Schivelbusch asks, "did this new perception that we are referring to as 'panoramic' consist of?" His answer is clear: "*the tendency to see the discrete indiscriminately.*"[78] While Doane and other film scholars have been inclined to articulate the general analogy between the viewing circumstances of the rail traveler and the movie viewer, they have focused less energy on exploring what Schivelbusch himself clearly identifies as this defining feature of panoramic perception: the inclination to fix on marginalia in the images or landscape that pass before the viewer's eyes. Because the continuity system organizes film images so that they are perceived by the viewer not as random, but as related and thus legible, "panoramic" does not necessarily describe the perceptual habit of the ordinary film viewer but, I would argue, only that of a select viewer—one best exemplified by the cinephile.

Unlike the rail traveler, the cinephile does not simply forsake the primary, attentive viewing mode Roger Cardinal describes for its alternative, the panoramic. Rather, like that prototype of the modern spectator, the *flâneur*, the cinephile engages in both modes simultaneously.[79] Tom Gunning has explained that, "As an observer *par excellence*, the *flâneur* attempted to assert both independence from and insight into the urban scenes he witnessed."[80] Similarly, the cinephile is, on the one hand, focused in the way that the film's makers would want him or her to be; but, as the most "literate" of film viewers, the cinephile is able to "read" what is on offer with comparatively little effort and thus has a certain amount of perceptual energy left over. This energy is then devoted to a posture that facilitates the panoramic scanning of the image (in the same way that the *flâneur* employed it for a panoramic scanning of the city).

Writing about his viewing of films from the transitional teen years, Cinémathèque Française director Dominique Païni states that he found himself in just this divided position. "I installed myself in a *flânerie* comparable to that posture that has been well known since Baudelaire, one between lassitude and perception in a state of alarm . . . between being captive and distanced." Partly distracted from the narrative, Païni found himself noticing "the micro-events of existence recorded on film," such as "reflections of crowds in store windows, 'veduta' [Italian for "views" or "sights"] of a street in the background."[81] My own position is that, even once the filmic grammar that encourages absorbed attention was in place or understood, the cinephile retained the supplemental glance, in part because his skills as an absorbed viewer were so sharp and efficient. As David Ehrenstein says of Gilbert Adair's fascination with the color of Cary Grant's socks in *North by Northwest*'s crop-duster sequence: "what it proves isn't that Adair is nodding at the switch—not paying attention during one of the most famous set pieces in movie history—but rather that he's really on the ball."[82]

Jean Douchet has offered confirmation of the cinephile's glancing tendency, saying that he "began to sit off to the right" in the theater in order to be able to "sweep the screen with my eyes quickly." He explains, "I find that this position to the right allows for an oblique angle which facilitates this sweeping vision. It also gives rise to an involvement in the shot—not a critical distance, which would be pretentious and stupid and would destroy the place of the spectator, but rather, sometimes, a certain ambivalence."[83] This ambivalence is the desire, on the one hand, to be absorbed in the image and, on the other, to retain a spectatorial autonomy that allows for the free scanning of the screen.

Christian-Marc Bosséno has written that the cinephile's spectatorial posture is marked by an oscillation, between "a simultaneous immersion and distancing,"[84] and a confirmation of the desirability of this tension—as well as of the cinephile spectator's visual scanning habits—can be found in the *Cahiers* critics' positive response to widescreen formats. François Truffaut's essay on CinemaScope, "A Full View," opens with three short paragraphs that alert us to several characteristics of the cinephile spectator.

If he had been with us that morning, our greatly missed friend Jean-George Auriol would have been the first to express his enthusiasm; he was the one who always said, as he took his place in the front row of the stalls: "When you're at the cinema you have to make sure you get a full view."

Admirable sentiment, admirable maxim, completely justifying Cinema-Scope. The more one goes to cinemas, the more one feels the need to get close to the screen in order to mitigate the hateful critical objectivity induced by a habit that turns us into a blasé audience and therefore a bad audience. Here we have

the closeness, still refused by some, coming to us of its own accord, demolishing the arbitrary boundaries of the screen and replacing them with the almost
ideal—with panoramic vision.[85]

First, Truffaut acknowledges that the appeal of a larger image size—
achievable either by increasing the size of the screen or reducing the physical
distance between oneself and the screen—is motivated by the cinephile's desire
to reduce the space of "critical objectivity" that prevents total involvement in
the film, and to achieve instead a greater "closeness" with the image. But this
desire for closeness does not mean that these cinephiles wanted to be totally
dominated by what they observed. Rather, the *Cahiers* critics celebrated the
fact that an increased image size also increased the visual freedom they had
before the film image. André Bazin argued that, with widescreen formats, one
was "physiologically unable to synthesize all the elements of the image: one
must exercise one's look, not only by turning one's eyes, but by moving one's
head," an activity that resulted in the increased freedom and " 'participation'
of the spectator."[86]

In contrast to their praise of 'Scope, Truffaut and Jacques Rivette derided
3-D processes during these same years in large part because they did not allow
the viewer this visual freedom; indeed, one was forced to sit nearly immobile
in order to get the desired effect. Rivette saw the two technologies as standing
in direct opposition to one another, in both aesthetic and moral terms. He
wrote that the

use of depth, where the distorted perspective imposes on the protagonists an
often arbitrary variation in scale, dominated by disproportions, incongruities,
ridicule, is surely allied to a sense of the absurd; while the use of breadth surely
goes with intelligence, equilibrium, lucidity, and—by the very openness of its
relationships—with morality.[87]

This claim shows a concern for an aesthetic/moral position that involved a
certain equanimity of treatment not only of the subjects of a film but also of
the spectators; for unlike 3-D, CinemaScope showed respect for viewers by giving them a greater measure of freedom in their spectatorial activity. Finally, it
is worth noting that, in his sharply critical review of the 1953 3-D film *Man in
the Dark,* Truffaut claimed that "the only effective scene from the point of
view of subjectivity is the scenic railway, shot with an ordinary camera with
the help of a transparency."[88]

Writing at the same time as the *Cahiers* critics, Roland Barthes, too,
praised the CinemaScope format for the visual freedom it gave him.

Until now, the look of the spectator has been that of someone lying prone and
buried, walled up in the darkness and receiving cinematic nourishment rather

in the way that a patient is fed intravenously. Here . . . I am on an enormous balcony, I move effortlessly within the field's range, I freely pick out what interests me, in a word, I begin to be surrounded.[89]

Like Truffaut, Barthes not only appreciated 'Scope as a cinema of choice, he celebrated its engulfing quality, and this led him to speculate about the possibility of a 'Scope *Potemkin*. What he does not seem to be alert to, Jonathan Rosenbaum points out, is that Eisenstein's fragmented, rapid-fire editing severely restricts one's freedom to scan the image in the way Barthes desires.[90] This point—along with the variety of examples about 'Scope, and the analogy between the film spectator and the rail traveler gazing out the window—might lead us to the conclusion that a viewer might employ panoramic perception only when viewing wide shots, long takes, or sequence shots—what Béla Balázs called "panoramic shots."[91] But while certain technologies (such as 'Scope) or techniques (such as sequence shots) might seem to facilitate panoramic perception, and other techniques (such as "dialectical" or even analytical editing) might seem to restrict it, this may not be strictly the case. For example, it is possible to view a whole film panoramically, laying emphasis not simply on details of shots, but on certain shots in their entirety, especially close-ups. In a section from his *Theory of the Film*, Balázs wrote of the close-up's extraordinary revelatory capability.

The close-up has not only widened our vision of life, it has also deepened it. In the days of the silent film it not only revealed new things, but showed us the meaning of the old. [. . .]

The close-up can show us a quality in the gesture of a hand we never noticed before when we saw that hand stroke or strike something, a quality which is more often expressive than any play of features. The close-up shows your shadow on the wall with which you have lived all your life and which you scarcely knew; it shows the speechless face and fate of the dumb objects that live with you in your room and whose fate is bound up with your own.[92]

The close-up's ability to animate, to reveal the physiognomic aspects of inanimate objects, makes these shots, too, potential sites for the cinephile's experience of cinephiliac moments. Indeed, it may be precisely because the object seen in close-up is removed or separated from the larger context of a scene that makes these shots radiate this potential.

But, Balázs argued, more powerful than close-ups of objects are close-ups of faces. In "Defense and Illustration of Classical Construction," an essay rebutting André Bazin's critique of analytical editing, Jean-Luc Godard wrote, "In *The Magnificent Ambersons*, it is not the famous kitchen scene which I find shattering [a lengthy sequence shot seemingly designed for panoramic perception] but, in this atmosphere of the twilight of the gods, the little face clutching at happiness which Welles has secured from Anne Baxter."[93] The shot to which Godard seems to be referring is a close-up of Baxter's character, Lucy Morgan, her hat perched awkwardly atop her head, after she has bid a sad farewell to her true love, George Minafer (Tim Holt). In fact, André Bazin had himself seen the unique potential of close-ups to reveal reality, and in his review of Dreyer's *Passion of Joan of Arc,* he seized on Balázs's point.

Seen from very close up, the actor's mask cracks. As the Hungarian critic Béla Balázs wrote, "The camera penetrates every layer of the physiognomy. In addition to the expression one wears, the camera reveals one's true face. Seen from so close-up, the human face becomes the document." Herein lies the rich paradox and inexhaustible lesson of this film: that the extreme spiritual purification is freed through the scrupulous realism of the camera as microscope.[94]

Here, Bazin looks past the face of the character to the face of the human actor playing him, for it is there that film's privileged relationship to the pro-filmic reality it records registers with greatest force. Paul Willemen made a similar point about Noel King's fascination, mentioned earlier, with Brando in the scene from *On the Waterfront:* "In the case of Brando and the gloves, the main point is that at that moment he does something which allows you to glimpse Brando incarnating a character. There is a moment of doubling, of ghosting, as they would say in photography, . . . suddenly there is a bit of Brando the person."[95] King confirms that his cinephiliac moments regularly consist of "dialogue performed via bodily gesture, a mixture of vocality and *mise-en-scène.* [. . .] As a cinephile," he notes, "I could as readily fetishise to name some favourites, Jean Arthur's voice, Henry Fonda's way of walking in *My Darling Clementine,* Barbara Stanwyck's performance in *The Lady Eve.*"[96]

The emphasis in these examples on the face and body of the actor is one realm of cinematic excess that, as Bill Nichols has noted, has been largely ignored by modern film scholarship, and it is an issue of particular importance for a consideration of cinephiliac moments.[97] In an essay on Robert Aldrich, Adrian Martin wrote,

The Angry Hills is a decidedly minor Aldrich film, disliked both by its star (Robert Mitchum) and its maker because of studio interference. But there are details in it which haunt me, and all of them bear . . . on matters of the human form, and the human body. In fact, I am struck by the way people's filmgoing souvenirs of Aldrich tend to be memories of strange and grotesque body presentations.[98]

This insight leads Martin to a consideration of the French critic Nicole Brenez's recent work on what she calls, in an echo of Roland Barthes, "figuration."[99] Martin explains that, in contrast to traditional film analysis,

Figural analysis . . . is less concerned with lenses and depth of field than with mobile arrangement, displacement, and pulsation of screen particles. Shot divisions, even scenes or sequences are less pertinent for this work than analytic "ensembles," slices of text and texture that demonstrate the economy and logic of a film's ceaseless transformation of its elements.[100]

Figuration finds its most conspicuous site in bodies and their movement, and the cinephiliac moment, so often linked to the body on screen, might be thought of as the smallest possible element of a given figural ensemble. Bodies—especially stars' bodies—have, of course, long been the sites of spectatorial fascination and fetishization. But beyond performance or even beauty is the sheer pleasure of watching someone—a specific body—moving on screen. David Thomson argues that this is a "vital principle" of the cinema:

it is often preferable to have a movie actor who moves well than one who "understands" the part. A director ought to be able to explain a part, but very few men or women can move well in front of a camera. In *The Big Sleep*, there are numerous shots of Humphrey Bogart simply walking across rooms: they draw us to the resilient alertness of his screen personality as surely as the acid dialogue. Bogart's lounging freedom captures our hopes.[101]

This constant process of movement is a field of potential cinephiliac moments from which we can select (or be selected by) one that strikes us. Manny Farber singled out the earlier-cited moment of Bogart glancing at a sign as he crosses a street in *The Big Sleep*. Though cinephiliac moments are by no means limited to appearances of or in the human body, such appearances enjoy a special place in defining and understanding the cinephiliac moment and its effects.

The Recovery of Sensuous Experience

In detailing the effects of rail travel on perception, Schivelbusch explains that all the senses, not just vision, were affected. He writes, "Smells and sounds, not to mention the synesthetic perceptions that were part of travel" in pre-rail times "simply disappeared."[102] But panoramic perception was also a spontaneous and, more importantly, a *productive* response to the perceptual challenge provoked by this modern technology, for it was a way to recover the loss of sensuous experience that so marked the individual's experience of the modern world. This assault on sensory perception and the loss of sensuous experience has been described in different ways.

In *Techniques of the Observer*, for example, Jonathan Crary explains that, in the late eighteenth and early nineteenth centuries, a transformation occurred in the philosophical consideration of perception that separated off and privileged vision as a higher-functioning bodily system, one intimately linked

to knowledge and power because it was the sense most clearly under the individual's control. This shift was mirrored (and fueled) by developments during the same period in the science of physiology, which was engaged in a project investigating "the division and fragmentation of the physical subject into increasingly specific organic and mechanical systems."[103] Crary explains:

Physiology at this moment of the nineteenth century is one of those sciences that mark the rupture that Foucault poses between the eighteenth and nineteenth centuries, in which man emerges as a being in whom the transcendent is mapped onto the empirical. It was the discovery that knowledge was conditioned by the physical and anatomical functioning of the body, and perhaps most importantly, the eyes.[104]

Crary argues that this splitting off and privileging of the visual is a historical condition that provoked a variety of other technological and cultural developments, including the invention of photography (rather than the other way around, as has commonly been the contention), as well as a host of other visual entertainment forms commonly associated with the nineteenth century.

A variation on this scenario of the splitting of vision and sensuous experience has been offered by Walter Benjamin in his account of the characteristics and effects of modernity. Benjamin wrote that the individual who is subjected to the barrage of stimuli that characterizes modernity develops an anesthetic shell, or what Freud called a "stimulus shield," to protect himself from the repeated perceptual "shocks" to his neurological system.[105] This individual—who sees, but protects himself from bodily stimulation—lives in a state in which ordinary sense experience is cut off from cognition. This condition, Benjamin believed, must be corrected. Susan Buck-Morss has explained that, for Benjamin, the key task facing the individual—especially the artist—in modernity is "to undo the alienation of the corporeal sensorium and *to restore the instinctual power of the human bodily senses for the sake of humanity's self-preservation,* and to do this, not by avoiding the new technologies, but by *passing through* them."[106]

Rail travelers engaged in panoramic perception, Schivelbusch suggests, have found a way to do just this. He writes that the "intensive experience of the sensuous world," which had been so thoroughly dulled by the excessive stimuli of modernity, "underwent a resurrection" in the rail traveler's development of a panoramic style of perception.[107] Schivelbusch further notes that, around the same time, this recovery of sensuous experience also found a site in photography. Making an explicit link between panoramic perception and the perceptual idiosyncrasies of those in the mid-nineteenth century who gazed at the first photographs, Schivelbusch cites Hans Buddemier, who wrote that the public was at first fascinated "not by the taking of a picture of any specific object, but by the way in which any random object could be made to appear on the photographic plate."[108] Describing "how intensely the first photographs were scrutinized, and what people were looking for," Buddemier writes:

For instance: looking at a picture of a building across the street from one's own window, one first started counting the roof shingles and the bricks out of which the chimney was constructed. [. . .] Tiny, until then unnoticed details are stressed continuously: paving stones, scattered leaves, the shape of a branch, the traces of rain on the wall.[109]

These photographic details recall Barthes's *punctum* and third meaning, especially in the way that the experience of them extends beyond the realm of the "visual-metaphoric" and into what Roger Cardinal described as "a tactile-metonymic dimension."[110] The encountering of cinephiliac moments marks another such recovery—or retention—of sensuous experience resulting from a passage through the technologies of modernity. Indeed, crucial to Cardinal's comparison of the two types of viewers is that the individual who views panoramically experiences what he or she encounters not just visually, but in a bodily manner—tangibly or haptically. Lesley Stern underscores the "sensory affect" produced by the moment she describes,[111] and Cardinal reminds us that "what is strongest in Barthes's response is its physical aspect. The recognition is an event which 'stings' and engages his entire body."[112]

It is in these moments of revelation that the cinema achieves that doubling effect so valued by Walter Benjamin.[113] As Michael Taussig has explained, for Benjamin, mimesis in its most desired form involves not only a visual copying or imitation, but also "a palpable, sensuous, connection between the very body of the perceiver and the perceived."[114] These two features in combination—"copy and contact," iconicity and indexicality—are, of course, what characterize the photographic image. Like Bazin, Benjamin linked modern mimetic machines to ancient or "primitive" mimetic practices, both in process and effect. A representation bears a certain visual similarity to its model, but is also produced by physical contact with it (e.g., Bazin's "death mask"); this combination of features, in turn, provokes an analogous set of responses in the viewer: recognition of visual copy and stimulation of sensuous response, as if by physical contact.

These characteristics result, Benjamin wrote, in the photograph's ability to give "its products a magical value such as a painted picture can never again have for us."[115] Noting that "the distracting element of [film] is . . . primarily tactile,"[116] Benjamin gave special attention to details that bore the strongest physical sense of the indexical mark of the referent: "No matter how artful the photographer, no matter how carefully posed his subject, the beholder feels an irresistible urge to search the picture for the tiny spark of contingency, of the Here and Now, with which reality has seared the subject."[117] Drawing a comparison with the new discipline of psychoanalysis, he described these details and the experience they provoke as evidence of an "optical unconscious," one revealed by the photographic machine. For Benjamin, then, this eruption of the indexical, material quality in film images is also an eruption of the haptical or the tactile in a technological product ostensibly derived from and devoted to the separating off of vision from other bodily experience. Emphasizing the subjectivity of these encounters, Taussig explains that the optical unconscious revealed by photography "bespeaks a newly revealed truth about objects as much as it does about persons into whom it floods as tactile knowing."[118] Finally, Taussig concludes, it is Benjamin's view that "it is precisely the property of [modern mimetic] machinery to play with and even restore this erased sense of contact-sensuous particularity animating the fetish."[119]

With this point, we return to the cinephiliac moment's status as a fetish, a term whose meaning I want to make clear, borrowing as I do what Laura Marks has described as "a recuperative notion of fetishism," one borrowed from the etymological and historical research on that term conducted by William Pietz.[120] The term "fetish," Peitz explains, was coined in the sixteenth century by Portuguese traders in West Africa, who were puzzled by the Africans' valuation of objects that, in European economic and cultural systems, had no discernible value. Adding to the confusion of the Portuguese was the fact that these fetishes were important not just because of what they referred to, but because of the way in which they referred. Marks explains, "Fetishes get their power not by *representing* that which is powerful but through *contact* with it, a contact whose materiality has been repressed."[121] In much the same way that the fetish reanimates repressed materiality, the cinephiliac moment—an excess of exchange between a film's makers and its viewers—reanimates the repressed materiality of the film image.

It was this sensuous, material quality of film that Bazin was so fascinated with, and he regularly celebrated—indeed, fetishized—those filmic moments in which such materiality erupted with great force. For example, in an often-cited passage from his review of Vittorio De Sica's *Umberto D.,* Bazin describes the scene in which the maid wakes up and comes into the kitchen to make coffee. This sequence, he explains, gains its realistic force from the fact that it consists of simply a "succession of concrete instants of life, no one of which can be said to be more important than another."[122] Offering an example, Bazin writes, "We see how the grinding of the coffee is divided in turn into a series of independent moments; for example, when she shuts the door with the tip of her outstretched foot. As it goes in on her the camera follows the movement of her leg so that the image finally concentrates on her toes feeling the surface of the door."[123] Even here, then, among these events of alleged equality, he locates one that seizes him above all others, a moment of material contact: the toes feeling the door. This detail is valued first for its natural, realistic quality and then for the unforced, objective manner of its presentation; but beyond these critical justifications, it holds an especial force and gains extra value for Bazin because of its physical quality. It is the best of cinephiliac moments: a sensuous experience of materiality in time.

3 André Bazin and the Revelatory Potential of Cinema

Cahiers du Cinéma was not alone among the film journals contributing to France's culture of cinephilia in the postwar years. *Positif,* the chief rival of *Cahiers,* as well as the MacMahonist *Présence du Cinéma,* were crucial voices in the ongoing public discussion about cinema. But if we think of this period as experiencing the rebirth and full flowering of cinephilia, it is without question due primarily to *Cahiers,* for several related reasons. First is the spectacular success of the French New Wave, whose most famous directors had, of course, been longtime critics for *Cahiers.* The success of Godard, Truffaut, Chabrol, and others not only brought international attention to *Cahiers* but also helped to legitimize their critical agenda of auteurism, a position that had been attacked and even ridiculed in both French and Anglo-American circles. Other magazines had no such specific critical agenda, and even if they had, they had no band of critics-turned-directors to bring fuller attention and legitimacy to it.

Furthermore, *Cahiers du Cinéma* owed its very existence to the individual who, more than any other, was responsible for nurturing the rebirth, growth, and transformation of cinephilia in the postwar years: André Bazin. Colin MacCabe has forcefully stated Bazin's importance:

If the beginning of the twentieth century saw the creation of art forms through cinema, recorded music, the popular press and radio (later joined by television), which reached audiences on a scale which even the most popular of national literatures could never dream of, it was a long time before these forms (because they addressed themselves to the unlearned) received the kind of cultural and historical analysis which is the unearned right of their contemporary traditional arts—literature, music, painting.

If there is a single individual who by his own efforts altered this state of affairs, it was the French thinker and activist André Bazin.[1]

If this seems like hyperbole, we need only remember the cultural climate in which Bazin began his labors as a critic. In his biography of Bazin, Dudley Andrew writes that, in 1942, when Bazin began committing himself primarily to the cinema and started his ciné-club with Jean-Pierre Chartier, serious consideration of film and other such popular forms was virtually nonexistent.

It is difficult for us in our age to feel the depth of contempt in which cinema was generally held in the period. There had been a flowering of ciné-clubs in the late twenties and early thirties in France, but by the time of the invasion, there were literally no ciné-clubs or any serious journals devoted to the art. Once the sound film came into use, most intellectuals placed the cinema beside the circus as a popular art not warranting reflection. The cult of stars and the dominance of Hollywood in the thirties solidified this view. Nor was there any support for film at the university. Indeed, the snobbist attitude was strongest at the Sorbonne.

The zero point from which Bazin and Chartier built their film society couldn't have been more absolute.[2]

But Bazin was not deterred. Firm in his conviction that cinema was a popular art form of vital importance for contemporary cultural life, Bazin committed himself to creating a public environment in which cinema would be treated with all the seriousness of the established arts.

But if we associate cinephilia, as so many do, primarily with the young Turks of *Cahiers du Cinéma,* with their obsessive, proclamatory writing style and their provocative, often outrageous celebration of Hollywood films and directors, it is strange to think of André Bazin as a cinephile.[3] While Bazin's love for the cinema must go unquestioned, that love expressed itself in critical writings that, while affirming the emotional power of the movies, defended the cinema through a set of arguments that were carefully and logically constructed. François Truffaut has described Bazin's method:

While he had a heart as big as a house he was also logic itself, a being of pure reason and a superlative dialectician. He had complete faith in the power of argument. [. . .] He would expose a dishonest argument by first taking over his adversary's thesis, developing it better than had the man himself, and then demolishing it with rigorous logic. Only in the articles of Sartre, whom Bazin particularly admired, does one find a comparable intelligence and similar intellectual honesty.[4]

Furthermore, Truffaut reminds us, Bazin's passions were not restricted to film. "He loved the cinema, but still more he loved life, people, animals, the sciences, the arts."[5] Both these characteristics—rigorous, critical logic and breadth and depth of interest outside film and the other arts—place Bazin outside the official circle of cinephilia. Following the analogy between cinephilia and connoisseurship, we must count Bazin less as a film connoisseur than as a historian of style, and we can add to this his commitment to cultivating an understanding of film—and thus, nurturing a film culture—in the broadest possible reaches of society, far beyond the limits of specialized connoisseurship of the young cinephiles. Although as MacCabe has noted, the more elitist approach of the young critics (with their rarefied concepts like *auteur* and *mise-en-scène*) saw wider acceptance than Bazin's more cultural approach, his influence on those younger critics cannot be overstated. A consideration of Bazin's ideas is crucial to any history of cinephilia.

Bazin, who had trained to be a teacher before turning to film criticism, believed that it was the responsibility of the educator both to uphold and to destroy tradition, and this is precisely what he did with his writings on cinema in the immediate postwar years, by rethinking both the very basis of cinema and its history. Bazin began this process with "The Ontology of the Photographic Image," an essay which originally appeared in a volume devoted to painting. There, he focused on two tendencies or ambitions in the history of painting: "one, primarily aesthetic, namely the expression of spiritual reality wherein the symbol transcended its model; the other purely psychological, namely the duplication of the world outside."[6] Bazin wrote that while the history of the plastic arts is often thought of only in aesthetic terms, the psychological issue is equally crucial, for it points to the deep need that representations satisfy for individuals and for culture in general. He specifies what is at stake in the psychological tendency: "If the history of the plastic arts is less a matter of their aesthetic than of their psychology then it will be seen to be essentially the story of resemblance, or, if you will, of realism."[7] In an acknowledged oversimplification, Bazin associates painting's aesthetic tendency with "true realism," which is the attempt "to give significant expression to the world both concretely and in its essence," and he associates the psychological tendency with, at its worst, "pseudorealism," which is nothing more than "a deception aimed at fooling the eye."[8] Bazin regarded pseudorealism, made possible by the development of perspective, as marking painting's fall, for it brought to painting a total preoccupation with appearances at the expense of any concern for the expression of essence. Photography, Bazin argued, redeemed painting, for it freed it from the burden of being the medium whose responsibility it was to offer perfect resemblances.

But photography not only redeemed painting, it also transformed the status of the realist burden it accepted. With film, the definition and experience of realism was radically changed, not because the camera offers more perfect representations than painting (it doesn't necessarily), but because of the way in which photographic representations are produced. In a famous and much-debated passage, Bazin argued that the defining factors in photographic representations are their essential objectivity and the fact that they are automatically produced.

Originality in photography as distinct from originality in painting lies in the essentially objective character of photography. For the first time an image of the world is formed automatically, without the creative intervention of man. The personality of the photographer enters into the proceedings only in his selection of the object to be photographed and by way of the purpose he has in mind. Although the final result may reflect something of his personality, this does not play the same role as is played by that of the painter. All the arts are based on the presence of man, only photography derives an advantage from his absence. Photography affects us like a phenomenon in nature, like a flower or a snowflake whose vegetable or earthly origins are an inseparable part of their beauty.[9]

That is, our knowledge of how the photographic image is produced is crucial in our response to it. Film's solution to the problem of realism, Bazin wrote, "is to be found not in the result achieved but in the way of achieving it."[10]

As was noted in chapter 2, Bazin argued that the photographic image possesses a privileged relationship to what it represents in part because of its status as an indexical mark. Bazin compared the photograph to a fingerprint and a death mask, and described it as "a kind of decal or transfer"[11]—that is, a representation produced by direct physical contact with the object represented. Several scholars recently reconsidering film's ontology have emphasized this aspect as definitive.[12] Furthermore, I want again to emphasize the other properties of the film image that Bazin explicitly identified and that many recent commentators overlook or underemphasize: automatism and objectivity. Both these concepts challenge traditional assumptions about the practice of artmaking. The mechanical apparatus functions to intervene, offering objectivity where one expected subjective expression, and automatism where one expected intentionality. Automatism and objectivity brush up against and even embrace the irrational aspects of mechanically reproduced images in ways that are of especial importance for this study.

The automatically produced image becomes a means of revelation about the world, and the cinema is an instrument facilitating such encounters, for it allows us to locate what it transfers. In Bazin's words,

The aesthetic qualities of photography are to be sought in its power to lay bare the realities. It is not for me to separate off, in the complex fabric of the objective world, here a reflection on a damp sidewalk, there the gesture of a child. Only the impassive lens, stripping its object of all those ways of seeing it, those piled up preconceptions, that spiritual dust and grime with which my eyes have covered it, is able to present it in all its virginal purity to my attention and consequently to my love. By the power of photography, the natural image of a world that we neither know nor can see, nature at last does more than imitate art: she imitates the artist.[13]

In other words, photography does naturally what it had previously been the role of artists in one tradition to do: show us aspects of the world that we see everyday, but that escape our tired view. Often, as Bazin's remarks make clear, what is revealed most forcefully are the marginal details of the image on display, and his writings show a consistent appreciation of such details, whether they are present by chance or design (or both). In his review of Jean Renoir's *La Chienne*, for example, Bazin writes: "Lulu's rooms are strikingly detailed (the porcelain bibelots). The importance of the street is emphasized by a realistic set, which is defined and concretized by sharp details (the slope) and by pictorial effects such as reflections in shop windows or automobile mirrors."[14] Bazin's attention to these details—both the programmed and the unprogrammed —is evidence of a highly active and perceptive film viewer, registering the image in all its aspects, not merely its centered figures and action.

For Bazin, these details are crucial for a full realistic effect, for as Dai Vaughan has explained, it was not simply moving pictures that gave early cinemagoers such a strong impression of reality, it was motion in combination with the capturing of contingent details. For this reason, Thomas Edison's shorts, filmed as they were against the dark backdrop of the Black Mariah, did not have the forceful realistic effect so effortlessly and magically achieved in the films of the Lumière Brothers, which were shot in the open air and teemed with details. Vaughan writes:

We need look no further than [Georges] Sadoul's *Histoire général* [*du cinema*] for ample evidence of the fact that what most impressed the early audiences were what would now be considered the incidentals of scenes: smoke from a forge, steam from a locomotive, brick dust from a demolished wall. Georges Méliès, a guest at the first Paris performance (who was soon to become a pioneer of trick filming), made particular mention of the rustling of the leaves in the background of [the Lumières' film] *Le Déjeuner de bébé*. . . . The movements of photographed people were accepted without demur because they were perceived as performance, as simply a new mode of self-projection; but that the inanimate should participate in self-projection was astonishing.[15]

It is in these details that the camera's essential objectivity, and its automatic production of an image that is also an indexical mark, registers most powerfully. No longer is the viewer moved by the pseudorealism of appearances, but now by the knowledge that the image viewed is an objective, automatically produced imprint of the objects it represents.

But as Philip Rosen has explained, the objective–subjective opposition that the camera seems to resolve in favor of the former term is, in fact, maintained in a dynamic relation in Bazin's theory. Bazin's phenomenological disposition shows through clearly for Rosen, who writes that, although "one must always be aware of [Bazin's] emphasis on the pre-givenness of the concrete, objective real," one must be equally aware that "the processes by which human subjectivity approaches the objective constitute the basis of his position."[16] Emphasizing "the primacy of the *activity* of the subject" in Bazin's phenomenologically influenced theory, Rosen explains that "Bazin can almost always be read as analyzing the status of the objective *for* the subject. That is, 'objective' here can be put in quotes with greater clarity, for the 'objective' is always inflected by the 'subjective,' never available except through the processes of the latter."[17] With this reading, Rosen offers a corrective to the various critiques of Bazinian realism, which commonly proceed from a simplistic understanding of Bazin's argument about the camera's objectivity. Rosen sums up: "Ontology proceeds from the subject's desire rather than [from] a supposedly direct relation between apparatus and filmed object."[18] That is, the desire of the subject—the obsession with realism that Bazin traces throughout the history of the plastic arts—makes crucial the film image's status as an automatically produced, objective image.

Rosen's argument squares with Paul Willemen's claim that the encountering and identification of cinephiliac moments is a subjective experience, but a subjective experience of the objective real shining through what has been aestheticized. Bazin readily acknowledged that the cinematic realism he favored was itself an aesthetic, but it was an aesthetic that made space for whatever was undesigned or unprogrammed to shine through. To use Bazin's terms, encounters with these unprogrammed elements—what we are calling cinephiliac moments—are psychological, not aesthetic experiences.[19] Indeed, Willemen not only rejects the idea that cinephiliac moments can be equated with aesthetic experiences but also argues that they are specifically opposed to them.

There is a form of stylisation in the cinema which is actually the equivalent to academicism in critical discourses. The whole new wave and the discourse of cinephilia, in France at least, was quite specifically against the academic notion of "the aesthetic," of what was thought to be a beautiful image, from Autant-Lara to Cayette, the whole cinéma de papa. A whole tradition of quite self-consciously aestheticized French art cinema was explicitly opposed to the discourse on cinephilia, with its predilection for things which did not appear to be stylized or aestheticized. In a sense, cinephiliac discourse appeared to privilege absence of aestheticization, where something shines through beyond the aestheticized. And this is . . . mystically designated in terms of the real coming through.[20]

In what follows, I will explore the implications of Bazin's writings for the encountering of cinephiliac moments: first, through a discussion of the similarities between Bazin's ontological theory and the theories and practices of the Surrealists; and second, through a consideration of a style—what I am calling the "sketched film"—in the privileged tradition of films that put their faith in reality.

Bazin and the Legacy of Surrealism

If one were to make a list of the "received ideas" circulating in film studies, near the top would be the discipline's most conspicuous and long-running conflict: the montage/*mise-en-scène* debate with its respective, representative figures, Sergei Eisenstein and André Bazin. The arguments for each side have usually been explained in roughly the following terms. For Eisenstein, fragments of film are mere mechanical reproductions of reality that need to be shaped and transformed through the process of montage. On the first page of his *Film Form*, Eisenstein explained:

Primo: photo-fragments of nature are recorded; *secundo:* these fragments are combined in various ways. Thus, the shot (or frame), and thus, montage.

Photography is a system of reproduction to fix real events and elements of actuality. These reproductions, or photo-reflections, may be combined in vari-

ous ways. Both as reflections and in the manner of their combination, they permit any degree of distortion—either technically unavoidable or deliberately calculated.[21]

In other words, whatever "meaning" is to be communicated resides not in
the shots themselves, but in what is suggested by their arrangement and juxtaposition. Though Eisenstein insisted that montage was the basis of filmic art,
he acknowledged important examples of it elsewhere. "We cannot deny," he
wrote, "that this process is to be found in other art mediums" such as painting,
ideograms, and literature.[22] Bazin, on the other hand, wanted a system of aesthetic standards that were indeed grounded in the central distinguishing characteristics of the film medium. I have noted Bazin's identification of a key
characteristic as the photographic image's power to "lay bare the realities" of
the physical world it represents.[23] "The image," he further argued, should be
evaluated "not according to what it adds to reality but what it reveals of it."[24]
Bazin thus criticized Eisensteinian montage, for that practice shifts emphasis
away from the objective content of the images and instead treats those images as raw material to which a clear, unambiguous meaning can be assigned
through editing. Among the techniques by which filmmakers might effectively
reveal reality are the long take and the sequence shot, for these respect the in-
tegrity of visual space and foreground the temporal element cinema adds to
still images. Further, such techniques are more "democratic," for rather than
dictating what the viewer should look at, they allow the viewer's eye to actively

engage with the image and wander, scanning for relevant dramatic information or, as Bazin's earlier remarks about *La Chienne* suggest, for whatever details the viewer chooses.

In fact, however, the montage/*mise-en-scène* opposition was in place well before Bazin came on the critical scene—and Bazin criticized both approaches. By the early 1920s, *mise-en-scène* practice was best exemplified by the other dominant cinematic movement of the period, German Expressionism. Bazin explained that, in films such as *The Cabinet of Dr. Caligari* (1919), meaning is communicated not via the juxtaposition of images, as in montage, but by the contrived arrangement and inflection of objects within the frame through camera placement, lighting, set design, and so on. Importantly, it is this definition of *mise-en-scène,* even when not in the services of an expressionist aesthetic, that is the generally accepted definition in film studies, and it is the one regularly associated with Bazin. In fact, however, Bazin had criticized this notion of *mise-en-scène* as being essentially in league with montage when he grouped them together as approaches that "put their faith in the image" rather than "in reality."[25] Bazin explained:

By "image" here I mean, very broadly speaking, everything that the representation on the screen adds to the object there represented. This is a complex inheritance but it can be reduced essentially to two categories: those that relate to the plastics of the image [*mise-en-scéne*] and those that relate to the resources of montage, which, after all, is simply the ordering of images in time. Under the heading "plastics" must be included the style of the sets, of the make-up, and, up to a point, even of the performance, to which we naturally add the lighting and, finally, the framing of the shot which gives us its composition.[26]

Thus, the institutionalized definition of *mise-en-scène,* the one usually associated with Bazin, was in fact roundly criticized by him. Indeed, he argued elsewhere that the "the highest level of cinematic art coincides with the lowest level of *mise-en-scéne*."[27] For as with montage, excessive *mise-en-scéne* betrays cinema's special potential by bending and distorting reality, seeking to eliminate ambiguity through carefully composed, "readable" images.

While Bazin's was the valued position in the 1950s and early 1960s, by the end of the latter decade, the pendulum had swung to the other extreme, back toward Eisenstein and others, and the preferred terms for identifying the opposing ideas were no longer *mise-en-scène* and montage, but were now "realism" and "modernism." Bazin's realist theories, it was now argued, were naive; he did not understand that "realism"—now often pejoratively dubbed "illusionism"—was itself a construction, a discourse determined by ideological interests and values. Representative of these critiques was Annette Michelson's discussion of Bazin in her 1968 review of the English translation of Bazin's *What Is Cinema?*, and in her introduction to the 1973 translation of Noël Burch's *Theory of Film Practice*, where she argued that Bazin's critical writings belie a sensibility that is "fundamentally antipoetic, resolutely antimodernist." [28] In spite of some reassessment of his theoretical writings, this attitude toward Bazin is very much in force today, some thirty years later.

While the terminological shift from montage/*mise-en-scène* to modernism/realism was in some ways productive, broadening the discussion of cinema to include concepts and criteria that cut across the arts, the shift often moved consideration away from specifically cinematic concerns, even to the point of eliding significant, constitutive differences between cinema and the other arts. Important among these was the issue of *automatism*, which Bazin had identified as one of the key features of filmic representation. This position led Bazin to argue that a profound shift in the history of representation had occurred with photography and cinema, and that the production of artwork in these new media had to be rethought according to these facts.

According to this schema, Bazin's position places him in league with a variety of other theorists and art movements that are generally aligned with modernism, and whose practices might seem, at first thought, to be sharply at odds with his own. It is my hope that this argument will run counter to the received idea of Bazin's theories, which are indisputably subtle and complex, and in need of some serious reconsideration. In support of my claim, I will trace some points of contact between Bazin and several of these other indisputably "modern" theorists and art movements, in particular, the theories and practices of the Surrealists—a movement whose values were, in contrast to Michelson's claim about Bazin, fundamentally poetic, resolutely modern. In entertaining this claim, one might keep in mind several things. First, as Surrealism is perhaps the most influential avant-garde movement of the century, one whose legacy extends into the present, it is unlikely that, only a decade after its peak of activity, a young Frenchman like Bazin, with a keen interest in the arts, would not in some way feel its influence on his thought. Indeed, Dudley Andrew's biography of Bazin reports that, for a time in the early 1940s, Bazin was "a fanatic surrealist, a follower of Cocteau, and an energetic practitioner of automatic writing." His companion at the time recalls "a long weekend at her parents' country home in which Bazin spent each morning scribbling madly in an effort to catch the flow of his unconscious." [29] The connection to Jean Cocteau remained: when Bazin's film society, Objectif 49, organized the Festival du Film Maudit at Biarritz, Cocteau officially presided over the proceedings.

Second, one should recall Bazin's affection for the films of Louis Feuillade, which were also favorites of the Surrealists. Henri Langlois once stated: "I am persuaded that Surrealism first existed in the cinema. You've only got to look at *Les Vampires* to understand that the cinema, because it was the expression of the twentieth century and the universal unconscious, carried Surrealism within it."[30] In *Sight and Sound*'s first Top Ten poll in 1952, Bazin selected *Les Vampires* as his choice for the greatest film ever made.

Third, while it is true that Bazin rarely wrote about Surrealist films, and that he probably would have assigned most to his unfavorable category of works that distort or "add to" reality, it would also be good to remember that Bazin's pantheon included the filmmaker perhaps most immediately associated with Surrealism: Luis Buñuel. Bazin championed Buñuel because he believed the director's sensibility emerged not through manipulation of the world, but through acute observation of it. He regarded Buñuel's *Un Chien Andalou* and *L'Age d'Or* as "the only cinematic productions of major quality inspired by surrealism," and he praised *Las Hurdes,* claiming that "Buñuel's surrealism is no more than a desire to reach the bases of reality."[31]

As a place at which to gather some points of contact between Bazin's theories and the concerns of Surrealism, I would like to use Bazin's description of the final scene of Jean Renoir's 1932 film, *Boudu Saved from Drowning*. This passage reveals several interests of Bazin's that were also primary concerns for André Breton and the Surrealists. Bazin wrote:

Boudu, newly wed, throws himself into the water. Dramatic or psychological logic would demand that such an act have a precise meaning. [. . .] But Renoir, like his character, quickly forgets the act in favor of the fact, and the true object of the scene ceases gradually to be Boudu's intentions and becomes rather the spectacle of his pleasure and, by extension, the enjoyment that Renoir derives from the antics of his hero. The water is no longer "water" but more specifically the water of the Marne in August, yellow and glaucous. Michel Simon floats on it, turns over, sprays like a seal; and as he plays we begin to perceive the depth, the quality, even the tepid warmth of that water. When he comes up on the bank, an extraordinarily slow 360-degree pan shows us the countryside before him. But this effect, by nature banally descriptive, which could indicate space and liberty regained, is of unequaled poetry precisely because what moves us is *not* the fact that this countryside is once again Boudu's domain, but that the banks of the Marne, in all the richness of their detail, are intrinsically beautiful. At the end of the pan, the camera picks up a bit of grass where, in close-up, one can see distinctly the white dust that the heat and wind have lifted from the path. One can almost feel it between one's fingers. Boudu is going to stir it up with his foot. If I were deprived of the pleasure of seeing *Boudu* again for the rest of my days, I would never forget that grass, that dust, and their relationship to the liberty of a tramp.[32]

1. Automatism and the Work of the Artist

One of the most influential critical statements from a writer associated with *Cahiers* was Alexandre Astruc's 1948 essay "The Birth of a New Avant-Garde: *La caméra stylo.*" In a famous proclamation, Astruc wrote that

> the cinema is quite simply becoming a means of expression, just as all the other arts have been before it, and in particular painting and the novel. After having been successively a fairground attraction, an amusement analogous to boulevard theatre, or a means of preserving the images of an era, it is gradually becoming a language. By language, I mean a form in which and by which an artist can express his thoughts, however abstract they may be, or translate his obsessions exactly as he does in the contemporary essay or novel. That is why I would like to call this new age of cinema the age of caméra-stylo (camera-pen).[33]

Although Bazin was in deep sympathy with Astruc's statement, the latter's argument distracts from an element of filmic representation that was crucial for Bazin: in addition to being an instrument for writing, the camera is also—indeed, perhaps first and foremost—an instrument for *recording*. That is, Bazin understood, the cinema is a technology that writes even in the absence of an author. But rather than apologizing, as many early film theorists had, for cinema's unique ability to record reality, or treating it as something to be overcome, Bazin believed that the cinema's singular ability to automatically reproduce the world was precisely what had to be reckoned with. This acknowledgment then demanded a concomitant rethinking of the role of the artist in producing work.

In the "Ontology" essay, we have seen, Bazin addressed both automatism and the revised role of the artist working in a mechanically reproducible medium: "For the first time an image of the world is formed automatically, without the creative intervention of man. The personality of the photographer enters into the proceedings only in his selection of the object to be photographed and by way of the purpose he has in mind."[34] In photography and cinema, then, unlike painting or sculpture, the artist does not compose or create things so much as he *chooses* them; a machine carries out the process of representation, not the hand of the artist himself. An embracing of film's inherent automatism means opening oneself to those fortuitous, chance encounters that are regularly *captured* by the camera in spite of the operator's intentions, and that form the basis of cinephiliac moments. Bazin's recording–writing opposition did not demand an either/or commitment; indeed, his preferred filmmakers were those who worked the productive tensions available in the opposition, those who attempted always to hold the two possibilities in place at the same time. Certain key elements were, of course, to be composed, but once these were in place, Bazin believed, the filmmaker should adopt a posture of patient watchfulness and wait for the world to reveal itself.

Often what the filmmaker and his camera captured was, for Bazin, more important than the primary subject of the shot or scene. For example, in the review of *Boudu*, Bazin actively resists reading the final scene according to the common, academic concept of *mise-en-scène*, which would focus on what is interpretable or translatable (the shot "could indicate space and liberty regained"); indeed, Bazin argues that such "meaning" is precisely *not* what makes this scene effective (the scene is "banally descriptive"). Rather, it is the attention given to particular, realistic detail—the grass, the dust—especially their physical, sensuous quality: "One can almost feel it between one's fingers," he writes.

For Bazin, it is in part Renoir's clear understanding that the camera automatically captures the specificity of such details that marks this as a memorable filmic moment. Bazin argued that, in this scene, what counts for the director "is not verisimilitude but accuracy of detail."[35] Renoir's camera "does not simply record the dramatic relationships and underline the main lines of the plot; on the contrary, it focuses on what is original and irreplaceable in the scene."[36] In doing so, Renoir appropriately balances the recording and writing aspects of cinema.

While Renoir, Rossellini, and a few others are regularly cited as quintessentially Bazinian filmmakers, it is often overlooked that, in the "Ontology" essay, Bazin identified the Surrealists as exemplary users of mechanical reproduction. For as much as any art movement, Surrealism embraced the automatic recording capabilities of film technology, especially as it challenged traditional, Romantic notions of authorship and self-expression. Bazin made this explicit in an essay celebrating the work of Jean Painlevé, a director of nature and science films:

What inspired choreographer, what delirious painter, what poet, could imagine these patterns, these forms, these images? Only the camera possesses the key to this universe where supreme beauty is at one with both nature and chance simultaneously; that is to say with everything that a certain traditional aesthetic considers the opposite of art. Only the Surrealists had a presentiment of this existence, in their search for the secret of an image factory through the virtually impersonal automatism of their imagination.[37]

The debt Surrealism owed photography is well known. In his 1924 "Manifesto of Surrealism," André Breton defined Surrealism as "Psychic automatism in its pure state,"[38] and he made explicit the movement's debt to photography when he defined the Surrealist practice of automatic writing as "a true photography of thought."[39] Even when not explicitly engaged with photographic machines, the Surrealists sought to simulate their functioning and effects.

One of the most astute appreciators of Surrealism was Walter Benjamin, and the play on words available in English in the title of his essay "The Work of Art in the Age of Mechanical Reproduction" explains what the Surrealists understood: that in a medium of mechanical reproduction, what is changed is the *work* of art. That is, one no longer needs to labor in the same way to make art the way one did before. "Forget about your genius, your talents, and the talents of everyone else," Breton wrote in his demand for a different concept of art and the artist.[40] Indeed, through such Surrealist practices as automatic writing and the Exquisite Corpse, one was freed from the burden of invention and creativity. The automatic method did the work for the artist.

Bazin believed that the camera was primarily an instrument for recording and only secondarily an instrument for writing, and the Surrealists conceived of their project in an analogous way. For Surrealism was primarily a strategy of reception, a means of attending to the world differently; or, as Adrian Martin has described, it was "a theory of experience—a set of suggestions about how to perceive the world in a suitably intoxicated manner."[41] One of the best-known examples of how the Surrealists perceived the world differently was in their moviegoing habits. Man Ray regularly watched the screen through his fingers in order to isolate parts of the image, and Breton preferred to drop in on the cinema, unaware of and uninterested in what was playing, and watch only until the narrative began to take hold.[42] These activities mark the extreme of what I have described as panoramic perception, a spectatorial posture that resolutely resists submission to what is prescribed.

Extrapolating from the understanding that, as Hubert Damisch has put it, "photography's contribution . . . is less on the level of *production*, properly speaking, than on that of *consumption*," it was only secondarily that the Surrealists produced works, and these were sometimes re-composed records of their experiences with their alternative methods of reception.[43] Understood in this way, then, Joseph Cornell's *Rose Hobart*, a landmark of Surrealist-influenced cinema, is simply a record of the way in which Cornell himself watched the 1931 Hollywood potboiler *East of Borneo*, fascinated and distracted as he was by its B-grade star. Breton's own *Nadja*, too, can be understood as a record of the author's accidental encounter with a young woman and the ten days they spent together in Paris in 1926, perceiving the world through Surrealist eyes. "We do not have any talent," Breton wrote, "[but have instead] made ourselves into simple receptacles of so many echoes, modest recording instruments."[44] Like the film scenes Bazin valued, these Surrealist

works compose and arrange elements, to be sure, but this "active" compositional element is preceded by the more "passive" element of pure reception.

This embracing of automatism and the attendant shift in the role of the
artists was not, for the Surrealists or for Bazin, an end in itself. They believed
that automatic means could do what conventional artmaking practices were
losing their capacity for: revealing what Breton called "the marvelous" embodied in the everyday.

2. Things in the World

In many ways, Surrealism was brought into being, and into action, by a specific
state of affairs in the early part of this century that André Breton described
urgently as a "fundamental crisis of the object."[45] In the opening paragraph
of his first Surrealist manifesto, Breton wrote, "Man has trouble assessing the
objects he has been led to use, objects that his nonchalance has brought his
way, or that he has earned through his own efforts."[46] Put more simply, the
Surrealists believed that objects in the world possess a certain but unspeci-
fiable intensity that has been dulled by everyday use and utility. Given what
they saw as the failure of more traditional doctrines to effectively deal with
such problems presented by the modern era, the Surrealists initiated a plan of
their own to reanimate this dormant intensity, and bring their minds once
again into close contact with the matter that made up their world.

This "crisis" that the Surrealists identified was being simultaneously diag-
nosed by others. One important example is the philosopher Martin Heidegger,
who held that the essence of modernity was found in a certain technological
orientation he called *Gestell,* or "enframing."[47] This tendency encourages us to
see the objects in our world only in terms of how they can serve us or be used
by us. The task Heidegger identified was to find ways to resituate ourselves
vis-à-vis these "objects" so that we may see them as "things," pulled into relief
against the ground of their functionality. Heidegger believed that art had the
great potential to counter the technological orientation of enframing and reveal the "thingness" of objects.

One of the primary methods the Surrealists employed in their attempt to
counter what Heidegger called "enframing" was a radical *reframing.* Thus, André
Breton's maxim, appropriated from Lautréamont, "Beautiful as the chance encounter of a sewing machine and an umbrella on an operating table," is an
expression of the belief that simply placing objects in a context with which
they are not normally associated reinvigorates their mysterious qualities, rais-
ing them to a realm where they are both commonplace and foreign, banal
and perplexing, objects and "things." Walter Benjamin's celebration of the
Surrealists suggests clearly that it was at precisely this level that the movement

most thoroughly succeeded. Describing the effect of Breton's *Nadja*, Benjamin wrote,

Breton and Nadja are the lovers who convert everything that we have experienced on mournful railway journeys (railways are beginning to age), on godforsaken Sunday afternoons in the proletarian neighborhoods of great cities, in the first glance through a rain-blurred window of a new apartment, into revolutionary experience, if not action. They bring the immense forces of "atmosphere" concealed in these things to the point of explosion.[48]

What the Surrealists realized about photography and cinema was that it could carry out this reanimating process automatically; the process of framing objects in a lens was often enough to create precisely the magical charge they sought. Describing the effect, Walter Benjamin drew a comparison between the photographic apparatus and Freud's psychoanalytic methods. Just as Freud's theories "isolated and made analyzable things which had heretofore floated along unnoticed in the broad stream of perception,"[49] Benjamin argued, the photographic apparatus similarly focuses on "hidden details of familiar objects," revealing "entirely new formations of the subject."[50] Writing about his experiences at the cinema, Louis Aragon further explained the effect:

Poets without being artists, children sometimes fix their attention on an object to a point where the concentration makes it grow larger, grow so much it completely occupies their visual field, assumes a mysterious aspect and loses all relation to its purpose. . . . Likewise on the screen objects that were a few moments ago sticks of furniture or books of cloakroom tickets are transformed to the point where they take on menacing and enigmatic meanings.[51]

As his review of *Boudu Saved from Drowning* shows, André Bazin, too, was fascinated by the cinema's curious power to make the most ordinary objects seem suddenly inflated. The festival of concrete details he perceives in the final scene of *Boudu* is a clear indication for him that Renoir is a filmmaker who "forgets the act in favor of the fact." In "An Aesthetic of Reality," one of his numerous essays on Italian neo-realism, Bazin argued that the "unique cinematic narrative in *Paisà* is not the 'shot,' an abstract view of reality which is being analyzed, but the 'fact.' A fragment of concrete reality in itself multiple and full of ambiguity."[52] It was this level of ambiguity that Bazin wanted to see reanimated in objects alongside any function they possessed in the narrative. Describing a hypothetical scene in which the opening of a door is of dramatic significance, Bazin suggests that, for the director of "shots," the doorknob is "less a fact than a sign brought into arbitrary relief by the camera, and no more independent semantically than a preposition in a sentence." For such a director, "the color of the enamel, the dirt marks at the level of the hand, the shine of the metal, the worn-away look are just so many useless facts, concrete parasites of an abstraction." For the director of "facts," however, these concrete characteristics would be as conspicuous as the doorknob's dramatic significance.[53] As Peter Wollen explains, it is Bazin's desire for objects in film "to have a residual being beyond the pure instrumentality demanded of them by the plot" that results in his fascination with details like the dust on the riverbank in *Boudu,* especially their sensuous quality (the dirt marks and the shine of the metal).[54] This "residual" is evidence of the "thingness" of objects being reawakened.

During the immediate postwar years when Bazin was formulating his theories, France was itself experiencing a new "concern with things."[55] Part of this interest was due to the Americanized modernization of Europe, but part of it can also be attributed to the last gasp of phenomenology, a philosophy that was soon to give way to the paradigm of structuralism and a turn away from the individual and toward the general. This phenomenological interest in things, which was formed in Bazin during the interwar years, is strongly apparent in his essay on Charlie Chaplin. In a section called "Charlie and Things," Bazin, sounding a great deal like Heidegger, describes Chaplin's unique gift for reanimating the thingness of objects. "The utilitarian function of things relates to a human order of things itself utilitarian and which in turn has an eye to the future. In our world, things are tools, some more some less efficient, but all directed toward a specific purpose. However, they do not serve Charlie as they serve us."[56] On the other hand, Bazin notes, "things which refuse to serve him the way they serve us are in fact used by him to much better purpose because he puts them to multifarious uses according to his need at the moment."[57] That is, Charlie reanimates the thingness of objects by what Bill Brown has deemed to be the best way possible: by exploring their "misuse value."[58] In a conflation of Marxist and Surrealist philosophies (he cites Walter Benjamin at length), Brown argues that if our regular encounters with objects ask us to attend only to their use value, and the commodification of objects undermines that, then the only way to recover the thingness of objects is by "irregular reobjectifications" that would "deform the object, however momentarily, into a thing" and free the object "from the systems to which [it has] been beholden."[59] Further, this misuse reanimates the sensuous characteristics of things, their materiality, their individuality. Indeed, Brown argues, this resignifying praxis—like that carried out by the Surrealists—is inextricably bound up with the recovery of sensuousness.

For Bazin, the goal is not to erase use value, but only to bring it into balance with the thingness of the object being used. Describing the technique of Rossellini's *Paisá,* Bazin employed one of his famous analogies, that of someone using stones to cross a river. "Actually, it is not the essence of a stone to allow people to cross rivers without wetting their feet any more than the divisions in a melon exist to allow the head of the family to divide it equally. Facts are facts, our imagination makes use of them, but they do not exist inherently for this purpose."[60] Though he was writing here about narrative, Bazin's analogy sums up his commitment to an aesthetic that balances the two, a cinema that would show us both: the object and its thingness, the stone-as-bridge and the stone-as-stone. This balancing, Bazin argues, is at the heart of Renoir's greatness, "his feeling for the appearances of things," his attention to the "physical, tactile reality of an object."[61]

3. REALISM, THE UNCANNY, AND OBJECTIVE CHANCE

It is with the concrete tactility of realistic details that, for Bazin, the photographic/cinematic image achieves the ultimate of becoming an "asymptote of reality."[62] As an asymptote (a straight line that is approached but never met by a moving point on a curve as the point moves into infinity), the cinematic image comes as conceivably close as an image can to truly reproducing reality. That it doesn't fully achieve it, however, is not a shortcoming. Indeed, as the line and the point—that is, reality and its representation—move close together, a spark leaps for the amazed viewer.

At its peak, Bazin's sense of realism in details is like Freud's description of what provokes that feeling called the "uncanny": "a repetition of the same thing" where such a repetition would not normally occur; "the phenomenon of the 'double'"; a startling or striking resemblance between two things.[63] Freud described the uncanny as producing an unsettling effect, but Lesley Stern has written that the uncanny—which is above all "a *sensation* . . . a certain bodily knowing"—can provoke not only a sense of the fateful, but also a feeling of euphoria, and this is closer to Bazin's experience.[64] Freud links the experience of the uncanny both to psychologically striking visual representations and to automatism. Good instances of the uncanny include "doubts whether an apparently animate being is really alive; or conversely, whether a lifeless object might not be in fact animate," and the impressions made by "wax-work figures, ingeniously constructed dolls and automata."[65]

Thus, the new context of the object, in a photographic representation, provokes the double status of things Bazin desired: in the film frame, objects are both themselves and something new, living and not living, real and magical; but the actual differences, though certain, are scarcely perceptible. William Paul has suggested that the return of the repressed that marks the uncanny also marks these charged points, for here, the irrational, magical quality Bazin associated with ancient representational practices reappears in a technologically sophisticated form.[66] Bazin wrote that one may describe this doubling experience as akin to "'poetry,' or 'surrealism,' or 'magic'—whatever the term that expresses the hidden accord which things maintain with an invisible counterpart of which they are, so to speak, only an adumbration."[67]

Bazin's invocation of Surrealism in this passage is perhaps itself uncanny, for I would argue that Bazin's experience with details in the cinematic image is a rough approximation of André Breton's experience with what he called "objective chance"—a phenomenon that Margaret Cohen has described as a quintessential experience of the uncanny.[68] For Breton, objective chance was, quite simply, coincidence. "I intend to mention," he announces early in *Nadja*,

only the most decisive episodes of my life *as I can conceive it apart from its organic plan,* and only insofar as it is at the mercy of chance, temporarily escaping my control, admitting me to an almost forbidden world of sudden parallels, petrifying coincidences, and reflexes peculiar to each individual, of harmonies struck as though on a piano.[69]

From his first meeting with Nadja, itself the result of coincidence, Breton attends to and describes a number of such uncanny encounters. For example, walking the streets of Paris together one night, the couple finds they have wandered from the Place Dauphine to a bar called Le Dauphine, an animal with which Breton was most regularly associated in one of the Surrealists' games.[70] Louis Aragon, too, was sensitive to such moments of coincidence, but in contrast to Salvador Dali and his "paranoiac-critical method," which gave the paranoid's sense of an ultimate order to the universe, these privileged moments provoked in Aragon the opposite reaction. Attending to such moments was a way of "pushing back the frontiers of logical reality and revealing the infinite possibilities within the scope of the concrete world."[71] It was, then, precisely in attending to certain particulars that this effect was produced.

Explaining his preoccupation with these coincidences, Breton claimed, "I am concerned with facts which . . . present all the appearances of a signal, without our being able to say precisely which signal, and of what."[72] These signals appeared to him, of course, because he was open to them, that is, because he had committed himself to a project of attending to the world and his experiences in it differently. Thus, for Breton, objective chance was revealed simply by *watching differently*—by panoramically scanning the city as he encountered it, looking past what was on offer to see what was not explicitly so. Further, as with Bazin's response to the scene from *Boudu,* Breton resisted interpreting these encounters, explaining that "in such matters the right to bear witness to me seems all that is granted."[73] He watches differently, takes note of certain concrete details, and, like Bazin, registers with great pleasure their effect upon him.

But are the details Bazin locates—the doorknob, the dust—merely "his

own projection, a reverie almost which has little relevance" to the scene or film in question, as Peter Wollen has claimed?[74] Perhaps, but this only again emphasizes the extent to which encounters with cinephiliac moments are not merely subjective, but what Rosen describes as "subjective projections." Such powerful experiences of the real mark for Bazin "a subjective striving, the subject projecting itself, a subjective investment in the image precisely as 'objectivity.'"[75] E. H. Gombrich has noted that this kind of projection is a basic component of the "beholder's share" in the encounter with art, perhaps especially those works whose effect of realism is quite high.[76]

The Sketched Film

Earlier, I remarked on Bazin's argument that the psychological experience of "realism" provoked by the film image in turn forms the basis of its aesthetics. That is, Bazin proposed that a cinematic aesthetic of realism is one that would mobilize the unique psychological effect of film images—one that would increase the viewer's sense of the film as an objective, automatically produced, indexical mark. We cannot be reminded often enough that, in Bazin's theory, realism is an aesthetic. This was an issue that he addressed repeatedly, including in his essay on William Wyler's *The Best Years of Our Lives*.

To want one's film to look true, to show reality, the whole reality and nothing but reality, may be an honorable intention. As it stands, however, this does not go beyond the level of ethics. In the cinema, such an intention can result only in a *representation* of reality. The aesthetic problem begins with the means of that representation.[77]

Furthermore, any number of very different aesthetic approaches can show faithfulness to film's ontology and achieve the goal of realism. "Wyler's method," Bazin wrote, "is completely different from Welles's and Renoir's. [...] The sadism of Welles and the ironic anxiety of Renoir have no place in *The Best Years of Our Lives*." But in each of these cases, the director shows a concern with "integrating into the overall structure and the individual image a maximum of reality."[78] In what follows, I want to address one aesthetic approach—one that is not specific to just one filmmaker or one school—that Bazin regularly celebrated; it is furthermore an aesthetic that is to be valued in part for its facilitation of cinephiliac moments.

While Alexandre Astruc's *caméra-stylo* analogy compared the director to the novelist, Bazin often saw the filmmaker as wielding a different camera-pen: that of the sketch artist. Throughout Bazin's writings on Italian neo-realist cinema, he favorably compared the style of those films to that of a sketch. He wrote of certain Italian films that they possess "a naturalness nearer to the spoken than to the written account, to the sketch rather than to the painting";[79] and of neo-realism's greatest director, Roberto Rossellini, he wrote, "several of his films make one think of a sketch: more is implicit in the line than it actually depicts."[80] Crucial to these observations is the fact that the sketch-like quality Bazin discussed was found not in the films of some minor cinematic style, director, or movement, but in a movement that Bazin privileged as exemplifying a "modern" cinema. To more fully appreciate Bazin's analogy, we should note that the most conspicuous characteristics of the sketch as a form are remarkably similar to what Bazin saw as forming the ontology of the photographically produced image.

Like a photograph, a sketch communicates a sense of immediacy-of-composition, something a classical painting does not. Indeed, it gives the impression that it has been composed automatically, instantaneously, out of a desire to register the image as near as possible to the moment of its existence. The artist has seen something—a gesture, an arrangement of elements, a play of light—and, with the sketch, has halted the flow of time, capturing that specific moment with his pen. Semiautomatically, the sketch artist quickly puts on paper visual approximations of what is seen. This speed of registration is one way that sketches can affect viewers in a manner similar to photos.

The sketch has an indexical quality as well, unlike classical paintings, which work primarily at an iconographic level. That is, the sketch retains a sense of physical connection to its production that classical paintings ordinarily do not, and this can provoke an effect similar to the one that, Bazin has noted, photographs have on their viewers. Both sketches and photographs flaunt that they are records produced by physical contact; the crucial difference is that in a photograph the indexical mark consists of what is being represented, while in a sketch the indexical mark is that of the artist. For example, upon seeing the *Mona Lisa,* one may appreciate the extraordinarily composed image, but upon seeing Leonardo's sketchbooks in a museum case, one cannot help but also marvel, "He touched this!"

Through the sketch, the artist further emerges as something approaching the objective recording device of the camera. Unlike the "licked surface" of classical-style paintings, sketches alert us not only to what is represented but also to the point of view of the artist who witnessed it and acted to register what was witnessed. Gombrich notes the psychological effect of these characteristics—especially the artist as objective recorder—when he writes that the sketch provokes our belief that what we see "must be nearer to what the artist saw . . . than [any] finished work," the latter carefully and painstakingly composed over a number of days or weeks.[81] The reference here to "what the artist saw" returns us to Philip Rosen's point that "the processes by which human subjectivity approaches the objective constitute the basis of [Bazin's] position," and that, for Bazin, "the 'objective' is always inflected by the 'subjective.'"[82] What is achieved is not total objectivity, but a nearness to or appearance of objectivity from a given point of view. Bazin never denied the presence or point of view of the artist, but in the "Ontology" essay's passage on objectivity, he de-emphasized it, writing, "The personality of the artist enters into the proceedings only in his selection of the object to be photographed and by way of the purpose he has in mind."[83] Bazin's *confrère,* Amédée Ayfre, who penned an important essay on neo-realism and phenomenology, stated the issue of point of view more problematically: "The mere fact that [the artist] positioned his camera in a particular spot, started or stopped filming at a particular moment . . . was enough to establish an inevitable gap between the representation and the real."[84] This gap might be significantly attributed to the limitations of point of view. As a corrective, both Bazin and Ayfre valued a cinematic technique that effaced itself in the presence of what was being observed. Ayfre, associating this approach with phenomenological realism, called for "an ascesis of the means." "In phenomenological realism," he wrote, "art is therefore established within the very act by which it seeks to destroy itself."[85]

Gombrich sums up the similarities between the sketch and the film image—and points to others—when he argues that, if "the hallmark of the medieval artist is the firm line that testifies to the mastery of his craft," then that of the postmedieval artist is not facility, which he avoids, but constant alertness. Its symptom is the sketch, or rather the many sketches which precede the finished work and, for all the skill of the hand and eye that marks the master, a constant readiness to learn, to make and match and remake till the portrayal ceases to be a secondhand formula and reflects the unique and unrepeatable experience the artist wishes to seize and hold.[86]

Crucial to Gombrich's summary is his description of the artist's "constant alertness," for it not only reminds us of point of view but also points to specific modes of perception and looking—both for the artist and the spectator—that are important for Bazin's analogy. Rossellini himself attested to this alertness when, in an interview with *Cahiers,* he remarked, "I have no fixed plan. What I do have, rather, is a particular speed of observation, and I work according to what I see."[87] Moreover, Peter Galassi has argued that this way of looking itself has a historical background that is bound up with that of the sketch. In the late eighteenth and early nineteenth centuries, Galassi explains in *Before Photography,* the sketch began to take on a value that it had not previously enjoyed. Whereas it had generally been regarded as nothing more than a preliminary draft for a larger, more detailed, and complex work, the sketch during this time was itself offered up as a completed work. Galassi explains that, in this period,

Artists and theorists distinguished among several types and two basic categories of the sketch: first, the compositional sketch (*ébauche* or *bozzetto*), meant to translate the painter's first idea for a composition into initial and then more elaborate form; second, the study from the model or from nature (*étude*), meant as a record of observation. Unencumbered by public duty, all sketches shared an informal, personal character, which was increasingly prized. But the two kinds of sketches—the *ébauche* and the *étude*—served opposite functions. The former was a record of imagination, the latter of reality.[88]

As film theorist Jacques Aumont explains, the registering of reality that the *étude* provides is dependent on a conception of the world as "an uninterrupted field of potential tableaux, scanned by the gaze of the artist who, exploring as he travels through the world, will suddenly stop in order to cut it up and 'frame' it."[89] Galassi goes on to argue that this visual procedure represented an anticipation of the camera, for it functioned according to a "photographic" sensibility: a certain style of looking, selecting, and registering an image or moment that would be normalized by the late 1800s. This perceptual shift was part of "the Neoclassical principle of artistic renewal, which sought to replace the fantasies of the eighteenth century with a more sober art, based in part on careful visual observation."[90] The invention of photography, Galassi argues, should then be understood as result of this shift in values (and not, as has commonly been held, with initiating it), and as intimately linked to a "deeply modern sense of art as exploratory rather than didactic."[91]

Furthermore, in contrast to classical paintings, which were commonly organized to present an essential moment—that is, a careful pose from which some narrative could be inferred—the sketch, a product of an alternative perceptual posture, focuses on registering the in-between, those ordinary moments when nothing of particular importance may be occurring. As we have seen, it is details captured by the camera—not only concrete *things* or *beings,* but also specific *moments*—that have so fascinated viewers since photography's inception. Gombrich has described the sketch as offering an image of "not the lasting but the transient," and he quotes Constable as writing that the goal of his sketches was "to give 'one brief moment caught from fleeting time a lasting and sober existence.' "[92] In *Camera Lucida,* Roland Barthes celebrates precisely this tendency of the camera: to capture for posterity what he calls the "any-moment-whatever" that then becomes a potential *punctum*—his photographic equivalent of a cinephiliac moment.[93]

With the sketch, then, the artist composes only those in-between elements that register with particular force. Unlike the painting or more detailed drawing, the sketch is not filled out; rather, it gives the viewer "just enough" to see what is being represented. Often times, sketched figures are removed from their context because that context is left uncomposed; or else only a single crucial element of that context is included as part of the sketch. Thus, a sketch of a woman bent over her needlework may present only the vaguest outline of the posture of the woman, for that is what has piqued the artist's eye and it is what he wants to share with his viewer; to render the scene more fully, in all its detail, would risk distracting the viewer from the specific element in which the artist is interested. Bazin described these values and methods as Renoir's:

For Renoir, what is important is not the dramatic value of a scene. Drama, action—in the theatrical or novelistic sense of the terms—are for him only pretexts for the essential, and the essential is everywhere in what is visible, everywhere in the very substance of the cinema. Of course, drama is necessary—that is what we go to the movies to see—but the story can get along easily by itself. It is sufficient to sketch just enough of it so that the audience has the satisfaction of understanding.[94]

We can compare these words of Bazin's with those cited earlier, that Renoir is a director who "does not simply record the dramatic relationships and underline the main lines of the plot; on the contrary [he] focuses on what is original and irreplaceable in the scene."[95] In the passage above, then, "essential" should not, I think, be read as referring to some Platonic notion of essence, but as a synonym for "most important," and as referring to "what is original and irreplaceable in the scene." Eric Rohmer, discussing Bazin's theories, linked this value to the issue of ontology: "The essential part is not in the realm of language but in the realm of ontology."[96] This essential is revealed most effectively via a narrative and visual style that does not compose things completely, but instead only sketches the main points, leaving room for the appearance of the irreplaceable concrete element, the marker of film's privileged relationship to the reality it records.

Renoir himself offered evidence in support of Bazin's conclusions. In his autobiography, Renoir wrote that, by his third or fourth film, he "was beginning to realize that the movement of a scrubwoman, of a vegetable vendor, or of a girl combing her hair before a mirror frequently had a superb plastic value. I decided to make a study of French gesture as reflected in my father's paintings."[97] But these "essential" elements Renoir identifies are not forced on the viewer by such formal means as restrictive, heavy-handed framing and editing. Rather, Renoir employs a visual style that encourages the viewer to encounter her own essentials, and this leads us to an important distinction between sketches and photographed images. While a filmmaker like Renoir may select or arrange only certain elements in the frame, the remainder that is left uncomposed is not blank, as it would be in a sketch on paper, but is instead "filled in" naturally by whatever else happens to occur in the frame at that moment the image is registered; and because the camera captures these details with just as much clarity as the ostensibly important ones, it is often this "filler" that imposes itself most powerfully on the viewer, but against any specific intentions. As Truffaut has put it, Renoir's desire is to have his film stand as a "semi-improvisation, a deliberately unfinished 'open' work that each viewer can complete for himself."[98]

André Malraux made precisely this argument in his "Sketch for a Psychology of the Moving Pictures." In this article, which was clearly an important model for Bazin's "Ontology" essay, Malraux first argued that the emergence of sound did not destroy cinema, but changed it, or rather, returned it to its original function, in league with the descriptive tradition in painting and with photography.[99] Cinema finds its place in this tradition most firmly, Malraux argued, when in addition to the presentation of some "suggestive, significant, vitally 'artistic' element," there exists a "memorable factor or remark"— that is, a memorable, often marginal detail. He writes:

True, there are highlights in every chaos, but they are not necessarily the same highlights for every art. When Robespierre's voice is failing, the crucial fact for the radio may be that failing voice; for the cinema it may be, for instance, the gestures of a sentry intent at that moment on bundling some children out of the room, or fumbling for his tinder-box.[100]

But such details register powerfully only if the viewer is allowed to discover them for himself, and this discovery is facilitated most effectively by the looser, more open style of the sketched film. Noël Burch has identified the "open" work as being one in which "the sudden intrusion of more or less 'natural' contingencies' into the totally artificial world of the work of art, in which in principle they are completely out of place," is quite welcome.[101] Clarification of this open style and its effects may be achieved by discussing a scene from Rossellini's *Paisà,* an exemplary sketched film.

In the film's final sequence, several American soldiers come upon a house in the marshlands of the Po River Valley, where they are welcomed and fed a dinner of polenta and eels. At one point, upon noticing that the family's baby has a number of mosquito bites on his head and neck, one of the GIs offers a bottle of medicine to the mother, instructing her to apply it to the bites. Rossellini films this entire exchange in a loose medium shot with both the mother and the soldier in the frame, and he uses a somewhat short focal length lens so as to provide maximum depth of focus without distortion. The setup is such that our attention is directed to these two characters, but the shot is not so close or soft that we lose a clear view of the bustling activity of the other soldiers and peasants both behind and in front of them. Importantly, Rossellini never moves in for individual close-ups, for this would not only remove the characters from their environment, forcing our attention exclusively on them, it would abstract the meaning of the scene, subordinating the exchange of concrete goods to the generalized theme of "generosity."

Further, cut-ins would have also created an artificial pause in the flow and flux of the activity around them, any part of which might at some point claim our attention. As it is written, staged, and shot, Rossellini directs our attention loosely, confident in his belief that by sketching in only a sufficient amount, the viewer will be encouraged to actively engage with what she's watching, and will have the satisfaction of coming to an understanding rather than being explicitly told. In the process, this active viewer may have the satisfaction of much more—an encounter with a memorable, revelatory detail, one both discovered and projected. Indeed, Gombrich argued that "the untidy sketch" allows for greater projection, both on the part of the artist as he sketches what he beholds, and on the part of the viewer encountering the work.[102]

Bazin was not the only *Cahiers* critic to compare Rossellini's films to sketches. Jacques Rivette wrote that, in films such as *Stromboli* or *Germany, Year Zero,* "the indefatigable eye of the camera invariably assumes the role of the pencil, a temporal sketch is perpetuated before our eyes."[103] Rivette also praised Rossellini as possessing cinema's "most active" look, one that is concerned not "with some transfiguration of appearances, . . . but with their capture,"[104] and argued his open style in turn encouraged the spectator to engage actively with the image, precisely the kind of visual activity Bazin so valued, one that led to epiphanic discoveries.

Positif's Gérard Gozlan once ridiculed Bazin's position on objectivity and spectator freedom, asking whether Bazin would value the visual activity of a spectator who "wants to look at the flies buzzing around the room or at the colour of the walls."[105] Though perhaps an extreme, such a practice may not be totally out of bounds, even for Bazin. After all, who does not retain as a primary impression from Renoir's *The River* the moths constantly fluttering around the evening lights and occasionally even settling on the characters in mid-dialogue. Perhaps even more extreme, Eric Rohmer confessed that, during his first viewing of Rossellini's *Voyage to Italy,* he found himself at one point "trying to read the time on a [wrist]watch that one of the actors on the screen [was] wearing."[106] But it is precisely in encounters with these kinds of marginal, even despised details that cinephiliac moments are experienced, and the looser, open style facilitates the panoramic scanning of the image that those cinephiles so loved.

Gilbert Adair has described this open style as "minimalist" for, in a paradoxical way, by giving too little it gives too much. He explains:

The problem with "minimal" art is not that it's minimal but that it's not. The eye strays. Inside a cinema it's been trained to do so, often with aberrant results. (Although I doubt that I could coherently relate the plot of *North by Northwest,* a movie I must have seen four or five times, I believe I shall remember to my dying day the colour of Cary Grant's socks as he flees from the crop-dusting plane.)[107]

This minimalist cinema is of the kind that "purposely offers the spectator less than what has come to be considered (but why and by whom and since when?) a normative amount of audiovisual information."[108] The eye is thus not just able, but prompted, to wander, and in wandering it makes discoveries. For example, Adair argues that "what matters" in Straub and Huillet's *The Death of Empedocles* (1987) is not so much Holderlin's poetry, the ostensible subject of the film, but rather "the physical presence of the text, of the speaker, of his gestures as he delivers Holderlin's lines, of the way in which his body moves in relation to the landscape and the frame, even of the impeccable cut of his toga as seen against the magnificence of the natural settings."[109] In contrast to the widely held notion that their films are essentially "difficult" cerebral exercises, Adair suggests that the texts performed are in fact also pretexts:

occasions for a reorientation of the spectator to the physical reality captured by the camera.

Even films by directors very different from Straub and Huillet yield images that—when removed from their context in a containing narrative—offer similar encounters with physical reality. As in Roland Barthes's "The Third Meaning" or *Camera Lucida,* the recontextualized image offers a *punctum,* what Adair defines as "one of those ostensibly peripheral details with which one finds oneself just as fascinated as with any of the film's characters and which may remain lodged in one's memory longer than most of the codified parameters (plot, character psychology, camera movements) by which the medium is supposed to communicate its fund of meanings."[110] In a still from Renoir's *A Day in the Country* (1936), in which the seductive Henri (Georges Darnoux) gently but passionately kisses the shy Henriette (Sylvie Bataille), the detail Adair lingers over is a still-lighted cigarette held in Henri's hand; in a shot from *Los Olvidados* (1950), it is the "saw-toothed corrugation of the hat brim" worn by one of Buñuel's street urchins.[111] Bazin argued that these aleatory elements form the basis of the cinema's greatness as an art form, for as he put it, "Chance and reality have more talent than all the world's filmmakers."[112]

4 *Cahiers du Cinéma* and the Way of Looking

There can be little doubt that, at least among the younger critics, *la politique des auteurs* was "the undisputed system" on which almost all critical writing at *Cahiers du Cinéma* was based.[1] Unlike Bazin, who balanced questions of authorship with a thoughtful consideration of a variety of other factors—genre, the star system, technology, economics, the industrial structure of the motion picture industry, and so on—Godard, Truffaut, and the others were concerned above all else with making a case for the auteur status of certain favored directors. But this explicit program did not always result, as one might expect, in an orthodox critical writing practice of evaluation marked by a careful presentation of evidentiary support. In reviews of films by privileged directors, emphasis was usually laid less on evaluation than on an articulation of the director's recurring theme or an attempt at a description of his style.

But Paul Willemen argues that even such apparently crucial issues as consistency of style and theme were, in *Cahiers* writing, often given less emphasis than a simple recounting of certain memorable scenes or moments. He explains,

> If you read the early *Cahiers* stuff that Truffaut and Godard were writing, you see that they were responding to films. They were not doing criticism but were doing written responses to films. [. . .] What they were writing at that time was a highly impressionistic account; in T. S. Eliot's terms, an "evocative equivalent" of moments which, to them, were privileged moments of the film. These are moments which, when encountered in a film, spark something which then produced the energy and the desire to write.[2]

Jean-Luc Godard was the critic perhaps most inclined to this practice of merely describing—but with great verve and excitement—a film's "privileged moments." For example, in his review of Samuel Fuller's *Forty Guns,* three of the four paragraphs are given over to such descriptions. Here are two:

> Gene Barry is courting ravishing young Eve Brent, making her charming début before the camera in an eye-shade borrowed from Samuel. Eve sells guns. Jokingly, Gene aims at her. The camera takes his place and we see Eve through the barrel of the gun. Track forward until she is framed in close-up by the mouth of the barrel. Next shot: they are in a kiss.
>
> The best scene lasts only three seconds. Gene Barry and Eve Brent are posing for their wedding photograph. Barbara Stanwyck's brother gallops up on a horse. A shot rings out. Gene Barry sinks into Eve Brent's arms, and she collapses and falls backwards under his weight. One has no idea which of the two lovers has been hit. In the next shot we find out when we see Eve, alive, lying under Gene Barry, dead. Three seconds, yes, but worthy of *Tabu.*[3]

Again, the description of these scenes is not justified according to some "objective" criteria of evaluation, especially as it relates to character, narrative, or theme. Indeed, there is no justification or rationale given whatever. These scenes are recounted simply because they were particularly striking, and thus memorable, in their conception and execution—at least for Godard. While simple pleasure alone may seem fair justification, one rarely finds such gratuitous recounting of scenes in contemporary film criticism. Even those critics who have space, knowledge, and a reasonably engaged and informed readership, rarely recount scenes in such detail, and when they do, it is only as evidence supporting a reading or critical evaluation. Godard's review reminds us of de Baecque and Frémaux's point that cinephilia begins with the individual who has a passionate love for the cinema, and extends from him or her to other like-minded individuals; for the recounting of privileged moments in such detail is a key feature of the dialogue about movies carried out among cinephiles.

In other reviews, Godard's focus on moments of sensuous, realistic detail—such as in his review of Jean Renoir's *La Nuit du Carrefour*—reminds one of Bazin's similar appreciation for fine detail, both designed and fortuitous.

Gunshots shattering the darkness: the purr of a Bugatti setting off in pursuit of the traffickers (a sublime subjective tracking shot through the streets of the sleeping village); the air of confusion, craziness or corruption about the villagers wandering on the main road; Winna Winfred with her English accent and the curious eroticism of her drug-addicted, philosophizing Russian; Pierre Renoir's lazy eagle eye; the smell of rain and of fields bathed in mist: every detail, every second of each shot makes *La Nuit du Carrefour* the only great French thriller, or rather, the greatest French adventure film of all.[4]

These details in combination create a powerful and intoxicating atmosphere, the experience of which extends beyond the visual and into the physical. Elsewhere, the moment as a record of reality—even the reality of the filming process—is valued for itself: "I love the moment in *Fallen Angel* when the camera, in order not to lose sight of Linda Darnell as she walks across the restaurant, rushes so fast through the customers that one sees the assistants' hands seizing two or three of them by the scruff of the neck and pulling them aside to make way for it."[5]

Truffaut, too, regularly singled out privileged segments for description in his reviews, and his selections were often justified by the claim that they epitomized something uniquely cinematic. Sometimes the selected segment or scene was a sequence of shots that were particularly striking or imaginative. Nearly half of his two-paragraph review of Howard Hawks's *Scarface* is given over to the following:

The most striking scene in the movie is unquestionably Boris Karloff's death. He squats down to throw a ball in a game of ninepins and doesn't get up; a rifle shot prostrates him. The camera follows the ball he's thrown as it knocks down all the pins except one that keeps spinning until it finally falls over, the exact symbol of Karloff himself, the last survivor of a rival gang that's been wiped out by Muni [Scarface]. This isn't literature. It may be dance or poetry. It is certainly cinema.[6]

Most often, however, Truffaut focused on details, little bits of business, specific moments. He wrote, for example, of the films of Jean Vigo, "Nothing that has been seen for the past thirty years has equalled the professor's fat paw on the tiny white hand of the child in *Zéro de Conduite,* or the physical embraces of Dita Parlo and Jean Dasté as they prepare to make love [in *L'Atalante*]."[7] Elsewhere, he delighted in "the little cries of Celia Montalvan when Blavette licks her back after she is stung by a bee" in Renoir's *Toni*.[8] It is these little moments, more than editing or calculated visual design, that marked for Truffaut the high points of cinematic experience. As Truffaut wrote in a 1951 letter to his friend Eric Rohmer, "Cinema is the art of the little detail that does not call attention to itself."[9]

But the spark that prompted the *Cahiers* critics' desire to write did not stop at descriptions. Rather, as Willemen argues, in their descriptions was an attempt "to find formulations to convey something about the intensity of that spark"; ultimately, this intensity was "translated and, to some extent, rationalised, secondarised, in the writing, into a *politique*."[10] The *politique*, too, worked on privileged moments and previously unacknowledged details, but here the focus was on those details that were signifiers of a director's consistent style, theme, and worldview. In effect, then, the young cinephiles' encounters with one set of privileged moments—subjective, fetishistic, à la Berenson— was displaced onto another set of moments that were, like the details Giovanni Morelli located in paintings, held up as objective evidence of authorship.

However, Willemen is quick to point out that this "rationalisation into theory did not make the sparks [of those privileged moments] go away. On the contrary: the theory gave us a keener sense of the dimensions the theory was gesturing towards but which kept escaping it."[11] That is, for those who were keen to it, auteurism was as much about what the theory could not contain as it was about the theory itself. The fact that, like those examples offered above, "cinephiliac discourse tends to work on scenes, on moments of gesture, on looks,"[12] was perhaps one of the ways in which the *Cahiers* critics attempted to serve both interests—the moment as evidence of authorship, and the moment as revelatory encounter for the spectator. This dual interest was most apparent in the writings on those films and directors that led the critics through consideration of a particular auteur and around again to their primary experiences, or, as Jim Hillier explains it, through a consideration of authorship back to a consideration of the cinema itself. The *Cahiers* critics balanced this dual interest with a single term—"*mise-en-scène*"—and perhaps no auteur allowed greater consideration of this mysterious concept than Nicholas Ray.

In spite of the *Cahiers* critics' moniker, "Hitchcocko-Hawksiens," Ray was perhaps the American director most important to them in the 1950s. As Hillier explains, Ray embodied "a particular conception of the filmmaker working within the system, always rebellious, often doomed, and a particular response to the modern world, as well as a particularly affecting style."[13] In the *Cahiers* writings on Ray's films of the 1950s, we can clearly see the prioritization of their critical concerns. First, traditional critical evaluation may be present, but it is subordinated to a reaffirmation of Ray's status as an auteur. In his review of *Johnny Guitar*, for example, Truffaut states up front that it is "by no means its *auteur*'s best film," but he gives little space to elaborating on its specific weaknesses or strengths; instead, he offers a fine summary of the way in which the film is consistent with Ray's other works:

All his films tell the same story, the story of a violent man who wants to stop being violent, and his relationship with a woman who has more moral strength than himself. For Ray's hero is invariably a man lashing out, weak, a child-man when he is not simply a child. There is always moral solitude, there are always hunters, sometimes lynchers.[14]

Similarly, Godard's conclusion that *Hot Blood* is only a "semi-successful film" with a "badly handled" plot is justified not by specific references to weak elements, but by the critic's conclusion that the director was "semi-uninterested in it."[15] Nevertheless, Godard notes, Ray's main theme is to be found, and this consistency confirms the film's value: "Always, in a Ray film, the leading character returns to something he once abandoned or scorned."[16] Jacques Rivette's review of *The Lusty Men* follows suit by glossing the film's weaknesses and offering another take on Ray's consistent theme:

Everything always proceeds from the simple situation where two or three people encounter some elementary and fundamental concepts of life. And the real struggle takes place in only one of them, against the interior demon of violence, or of a more secret sin, which seems linked to man and his solitude. It may happen sometimes that a woman saves him; it even seems that she alone can have the power to do so; we are a long way from misogyny.[17]

Beyond this elaboration of consistency of theme, much space is given to a detailed consideration of Ray's style and to the specific visual qualities of the film in question. All three critics compare Ray to Roberto Rossellini, and both Rivette and Truffaut single out the awkwardness of Ray's visual style, which they see as evidence (as with Rossellini) of the most direct and urgent attempt at expression, and thus evidence of sincerity and lack of pretension. "All his films are very disjointed," Truffaut writes, "but it is obvious that Ray is aiming less for the traditional and all-around success of a film than at giving each shot a certain emotional quality."[18] Rivette goes further, invoking the comparison of filmmaker to sketch artist discussed in the previous chapter: "In *The Lusty Men*, you can see how the idea of a role, or a scene, hurriedly sketched, can sometimes prevail over its realization, whether good or bad."[19] This urgency is further a sign for Rivette that, unlike so many others, Ray is a director with ideas, with an imagination.

Nicholas Ray is lavish with ideas . . . and when I talk about ideas, I really mean ideas of *mise-en-scène* or—if I were to be shocking about it—of framing or the way shots are put together, which these days are the only ideas whose profundity I wish to recognize, and the only ones which can reach the secret form which is the goal of every work of art.[20]

On the one hand, these comments seem to confirm the conventional understanding of *mise-en-scène*—that it refers to the formal means by which the director expresses himself. This definition of *mise-en-scène* was perhaps most clearly articulated several years later by one of the second generation of *Cahiers* critics, Fereydoun Hoveyda.

The originality of the *auteur* lies not in the subject matter he chooses, but in the technique he employs, i.e. the *mise en scène*, through which everything on the screen is expressed on the screen.

As Sartre said: "One isn't a writer for having chosen to say certain things, but for having chosen to say them in a certain way." Why should it be any different for cinema? . . . the thought of a *cinéaste* appears through his *mise en scène*. What matters in the film is the desire for order, composition, harmony, the placing of actors and objects, the movements within the frame, the capturing of a movement or a look; in short, the intellectual operation which has put an initial emotion and a general idea to work. *Mise en scène* is nothing other than the technique invented by each director to express the idea and establish the specific quality of his work.[21]

For Rivette, these "ideas" of *mise-en-scène* are, in Ray's films, particularly striking and imaginative. But as we read on, we get a clearer and more complex picture of Rivette's notion of Ray's imagination: "The imagination of each moment is only the concern to reveal, with each fresh blow of the chisel, the one and only hidden statue."[22] With this analogy, we find a profoundly Bazinian notion of *mise-en-scène*, one in which the director's responsibility is not to impose himself too strongly, but rather—again, as with Rossellini—to create a context for things to happen on their own, for reality to make an unexpected appearance.

With this definition of *mise-en-scène*, we return to Hillier's point that the *Cahiers* critics were particularly interested in those directors whose films led them through issues of authorship, into issues of cinematic language (framing, editing), and, finally, to issues of the cinema itself—that is, to ontological issues. Hillier stresses the influence here of Bazin, whose "earlier work on realism had become *Cahiers* orthodoxy. Bazin's assumptions about the nature of film, his thinking about transparency and narrative" are present throughout the writings of these younger critics.[23] For Rivette, the ontology issue manifests itself in Ray's films most powerfully in the director's "dilation of expressive detail," in his "search for a certain breadth of modern gesture,"[24] and even in the realm of objects and things themselves. Godard wrote in his review of *Bitter Victory*, "One is no longer interested in objects, but in what lies between objects and becomes an object in its turn. Nicholas Ray forces us to consider as real something that one did not even consider as unreal, something one did not consider at all."[25] The revelation of reality might just as readily come about unintentionally, for in Ray's films, Rivette wrote, "ideas . . . are scattered everywhere by the accidents of imagination."[26]

But this understanding of *mise-en-scène*, which includes both issues of authorship and issues of filmic ontology, is quite different from the academically institutionalized definition of that term, which has focused almost exclusively around authorship, or around the ways in which cinematic images are coded and can be deciphered or "read." But if *mise-en-scène* is only what's "written" or designed, then there is no room in it for a consideration of cinephiliac moments. It is my contention, however, that the *Cahiers* critics' concept of *mise-en-scène* involved both issues of authorship and issues of ontology. In this way, these critics were able to account not only for those details linked to authorship and expression but also for those details linked to spectatorship and fetishism. As film studies became institutionalized, however, the possibility of the latter was gradually eliminated. Exploring the changes in the definition of the term *mise-en-scène* will be helpful in better understanding the *Cahiers* definition, and in understanding how it could accommodate the experience of cinephiliac moments.

The Evolution of the Language of *Mise-en-Scène*

Hillier rightly notes that, in the auteurist polemic, *mise-en-scène* "established itself as a—perhaps *the*—central and essential concept in *Cahiers* and in later criticism influenced by *Cahiers*."[27] But he also points out that, "Whereas ideas about authorship were relatively easily admitted," especially in the academy, where film studies soon became a field of study, "the ideas about *mise-en-scène* proved more problematic."[28] Because the first film studies courses sprang up in association with literature or drama departments, film study was taught according to the prevailing values and assumptions of that academic context. Thus, while certain elements of movies were easily accommodated (narrative, character, and, most importantly, authorship), other elements, particularly *mise-en-scène*, presented serious difficulties. Because *mise-en-scène* refers to properties that are uniquely cinematic—that is, non-verbal, non-literary, non-linguistic—in the institutions that propagated film studies, institutions whose base of knowledge is rooted in language, there was simply no place for the issue of *mise-en-scène* as it was originally conceived. Where issues of authorship were concerned, emphasis moved to theme and identifiable visual

style at the expense of any consideration of automatism and its links to the revelatory power of the cinema. This critical approach remains largely in force. In *Film Art,* one of the most widely used introductory film texts, David Bordwell and Kristin Thompson define *mise-en-scène* in the following way.

Film scholars . . . use the term to signify the director's control over what appears in the film frame. As you would expect from the term's theatrical origins, mise-en-scene includes those aspects of the film that overlap with the art of the theater: setting, lighting, costume, and the behavior of the figures. In controlling the mise-en-scene, the director stages the event for the camera.[29]

Louis Giannetti's *Understanding Movies,* another popular introductory text, goes a bit further, including in its definition of *mise-en-scène* certain cinematographic elements, such as framing, focus, and shot duration: "Cinematic mise en scène encompasses both the staging of the action and the way that it's photographed."[30] Neither of these definitions implies a link between *mise-en-scène* and the notion of authorship such as that held by the auteur critics, but then the dilution of the concept of *mise-en-scène* did not wait for auteurism or even the more general issues of authorship to be pushed aside. Indeed, it began almost immediately, with the second wave of auteurist critics in the 1960s—Andrew Sarris in the United States, and the *Movie* critics in Britain. We can trace this dilution or evolution by looking at the critical writings on the films of an important auteur, Otto Preminger.[31]

Though committed to a cinema of directors, the critics at *Movie* were quick to point out that they did not take their beliefs to the farthest extremes of *la politique des auteurs,* and they sought a more systematic critical method that worked to understand the meanings in a given director's work. In their analytical approach, the *Movie* critics—Ian Cameron, V. F. Perkins, Robin Wood, and Mark Shivas among them—focused their attention closely on a film's *mise-en-scène,* which they then worked to interpret as a visual representation of character, theme, and ultimately, the director's attitude to his subject. For example, in his essay on Otto Preminger, "From *Laura* to *Angel Face,*" *Movie* contributor Paul Mayersberg writes about two key scenes in *Fallen Angel:*

Sitting on the deserted beach one night Linda [Darnell] listens to [Dana] Andrews telling stories of his past and the sea-scape seems to embody her desire for the adventure that will bring her all the material things she wants out of life. In the same setting two nights later Andrews spins the same line to Alice Faye, but this time the sea takes on quite a different significance: "One shouldn't set a limit on what one can do," she says idealistically. The parallel is there: the material possibilities of life are very limited, the spiritual possibilities (man's capacity for the development of himself) are limitless.[32]

This critical approach—which Adrian Martin has dubbed "film criticism's expressive complex" for the way in which it reads all filmic elements in author-expressive terms[33]—often resulted in rich and suggestive readings of films and scenes, but the above example reveals the limitation of this hermeneutic approach. For here, the image of the sea is addressed only to the extent that it can be translated into some non-visual meaning. Indeed, effects that such images may have on the viewer seem to be limited in this mode of criticism to effects of "meaning."

Gestures—the stuff of which cinephiliac moments are so often made—are similarly read by the *Movie* critics, or else they are ignored. In his essay on Preminger's *Advise and Consent,* for example, Robin Wood writes,

We are kept aware, in the interests of clarity, of acting *as* acting—the meaningful gesture or expression is given just sufficient emphasis for the significance to be taken. The burden falls squarely, then, on the actors: camera-movement, camera-angle, editing are all subordinated to the demand for the utmost clarity, precision and conciseness in the playing. It is this that makes the film peculiarly difficult to write about, for what is essential is a gesture, a movement, an intonation which words cannot convey.[34]

As an example, Wood cites the moment when longtime senate member Seab Cooley (Charles Laughton) passes a young, redbaiting colleague "with bowed head and a contemptuous, if Churchillian, wave of the hand."[35] Though Wood has a fine eye for such details of performance—and this above-cited bit takes place at the extreme left side of the frame, when our eyes are more clearly being drawn elsewhere—these details are, for him, notable only insofar as they fill out and focus character or clarify relationships.[36] If they cannot be "read," they go unacknowledged.

The *Movie* critics' emphasis on "meaningful" filmic elements is due in part, no doubt, to the cultural and historical context from which they emerged. The journal's founders—Cameron, Perkins, and Shivas—had all written film criticism in the late 1950s and early 1960s for their university magazine, *Oxford Opinion.* As Pam Cook explains, this was a time and place of intense debate over the long-standing opposition between high art and mass culture. For most critics and scholars, high art "was capable of providing moral insights for the perceptive reader, while [popular culture], because it was mass produced for the entertainment of a passive audience, could do no more than reproduce the status quo."[37] More carefully and systematically than their *Cahiers* influences, the *Movie* critics sought to justify the work of certain commercial directors on terms that had been applied exclusively to high art. These terms were not limited to issues of authorship and self-expression but, more importantly, extended to moral edification. Indeed, Wood began his review of *Advise and Consent* by proclaiming Preminger "one of the cinema's great moralists."[38]

Unlike other film publications of the time, whose criticism so often jumped past any consideration of visuals straight to a consideration of a film's theme (for example, *Sight and Sound*), the *Movie* critics, like their influences at *Cahiers,* argued that *mise-en-scène* was the vehicle by which themes were expressed; thus, they paid it careful attention. But the tradition of British literary criticism in which they were schooled led them to a method of careful analysis and explication of visuals only to the extent that those visuals could be interpreted as meaningful, and thus as enriching the viewer's experience of the film in question. Absent from this writing is any celebration of gestures for their own sake. John Caughie notes that, compared to the "excited, frequently over-heated subjectivism which typifies *Cahiers,*" *Movie* criticism was a "more controlled, academic writing."[39]

Writing in the United States at roughly the same time as the *Movie* critics, Andrew Sarris also took up the auteur/*mise-en-scène* issue, and it is perhaps his name above all that one associates with auteurism. Professionally and culturally, Sarris occupied a middle position between the academics of *Movie* and the journalists (and future filmmakers) of *Cahiers.* Sarris began his career as a critic, writing reviews for *Film Culture* and later as the regular film critic for *The Village Voice.* As his reputation grew, he began teaching film appreciation at a number of schools, including a long-term stint at Columbia University in New York. Nevertheless, his academic role was secondary, and he did not have the same commitment to (or bear the same weight of) a literary critical tradition in the way that *Movie* did. As a result, his approach to *mise-en-scène* analysis was somewhat less rigid than that of his British counterparts. Indeed, Sarris was quick to acknowledge that there was something else at work in *mise-en-scène* other than that which was translatable into meaning. In a 1965 *Film Comment* article on Preminger, Sarris wrote,

What's art to Preminger or Preminger to art? Preminger's champions on *Movie* and *Cahiers du Cinéma* would retort that Preminger's art is of the highest order. I find myself in a dangerous middle position that I would like to explain in some detail. To do so, I must begin with a very personal definition of *mise-en-scène*.

For me, *mise-en-scène* is not merely the gap between what we see and feel on the screen and what we can express in words, but it is also the gap between the intention of the director and his effect upon the spectator. [. . .] [T]o read all sorts of poignant profundities in Preminger's inscrutable urbanity would seem to be the last word in idiocy, and yet there are moments in his films when the evidence on the screen is inconsistent with one's deepest instincts about the director as a man. It is during these moments that one feels the magical powers of *mise-en-scène* to get more out of a picture than is put in by a director.[40]

Sarris is willing to acknowledge that there are elements even in the films of an acknowledged auteur that escape auteurism's theory of authorship. He again noted this quality in Preminger's cinema in his review of *Bunny Lake Is Missing*. Though he concedes that "the plot collapses" and that "there are really no characters to consider," Sarris proclaims, "Preminger's *mise-en-scène* is the most brilliant I have seen all year." He goes on:

To watch his camera prowling around a girl's school, an unoccupied house, a pervert's lair, a lackluster pub, from room to room, up- and downstairs, in and out of doors, with the sustained frenzy of a director concerned with integral space is to realize the majesty of *mise-en-scène*. There is one sequence when Olivier walks up the steps to the school with a fixed focus on the revolving police light in the foreground. Preminger virtually tosses the effect away, and this is only one of many such visual coups that make his movies so hard to evaluate.[41]

So hard to evaluate, indeed—at least according to the assumptions of an auteurist/*mise-en-scène* practice that had begun to simplify and secure itself as a critical approach. Though he's clearly onto something, Sarris seems conflicted about what he finds. He readily acknowledges a "gap between what we see and feel on the screen and what we can express in words," thus demonstrating that what he sees is outside the realm of language or meaning, but he is unsure what to do with this excess. The attacks heaped on Sarris after the publication of "Notes on the Auteur Theory in 1962" branded him the flag-bearer of auteurism, even though his primary influence—by his own, ready acknowledgment—was André Bazin.[42] Indeed, it might be said that the "gap" referred to above resulted from Sarris's uneasy attempt to synthesize both of *Cahiers*'s critical positions: Bazinian realism and Young Turk auteurism. Though I have insisted on the importance of Bazin's influence on the younger *Cahiers* critics, it should be remembered that, just as Bazin was not an auteurist to the extent that his protégés were, the young critics' position on film's ontology led them to less rigid conclusions about film language and formal techniques than those of their mentor.

In effect, the synthesis that Sarris sought had already been achieved by the young *Cahiers* critics themselves. In spite of their ongoing struggle to secure the acceptance of cinematic authorship, they were well aware that "something more" was operating in cinematic writing than could be explained by a notion of authorship that was understood or applied in the same way that it was in other of the arts. Adrian Martin has noted that Jacques Rivette's critical writings of the 1950s mark a crucial moment in the history of the term *mise-en-scène,* and in his 1954 review of Preminger's *Angel Face,* Rivette suggested what this something more might be.[43] Rivette began his review by acknowledging the inadequacy of the critical approach that interprets a film's formal properties as determined by its content. He avoids the trap of this method, remarking, "I can see very well that this would be the right moment for a predictable elaboration of the themes or the characters [. . .] but the devil is whispering in my ear, 'Is it really important; is that false and criminal purity not the very sight of convention and artifice?' "[44] While he readily acknowledges a preference for "the possibly more naive conception of the old school, of Hawks, Hitchcock or Lang, who first believe in their themes and then build the strength of their art upon this conviction," Rivette sees something in Preminger's approach that demands his attention.[45]

Rivette argues that Preminger's work balances the traditional approach of analysis carried out in advance of production with an unplanned method designed to facilitate an encounter, a discovery. While there can be no question that Preminger prepared his films to some extent in the traditional way, Rivette argued that "there is more to Preminger than the mere ability to get the best out of skillful scripts, excellent actors and the technical resources of a well-equipped studio."[46] Rivette further specified this extra quality: "unpredictability attracts him, the chance discoveries that mean things cannot go according to plan, on-the-spot improvisation that is born of a fortunate moment and dedicated to the fleeting essence of a place or person."[47] Thus, Rivette focuses on what he identifies as "the *raison d'être* of [Preminger's] film, and its real subject": not plot or characters, but "particular gestures, attitudes and reflexes."[48]

Rivette's emphasis on such details, less composed than captured, was influenced not just generally by Bazin's writings, but more specifically by his essay on Renoir, discussed in my previous chapter. Indeed, the title of Rivette's essay suggests "the fleeting essence of a place or person," giving the "particular gestures, attitudes, and reflexes" the same name that Bazin gave them: "the essential." Recall Bazin's claim that, "for Renoir, what is important is not the dramatic value of a scene. Drama, action—in the theatrical or novelistic sense of the terms—are for him only pretexts for the essential, and the essential is everywhere in what is visible, everywhere in the very substance of cinema."[49] Perhaps especially in the grass into which Boudu steps and in the dust he stirs up. In a beautiful musical analogy, Rivette writes that what interests Preminger is

the rendering audible of particular chords unheard and rare, in which the inexplicable beauty of the modulation suddenly justifies the ensemble of the phrase. This is probably the definition of some kind of preciosity . . . its enigma—the door to something beyond intellect, opening out onto the unknown. [. . .] Such are the contingencies of *mise-en-scène*.[50]

Importantly, what Rivette describes here is not simply the mechanics of a particular style, but something much more complex: a generalizable concept of the cinema. For as Rivette noted, in the cinema, "talent is first and foremost the function of a specific *idea* of the cinema."[51] This idea of the cinema is intimately linked to "an interest outside that of the plot" that "continually rivets our attention on the gestures of characters" in spite of the fact that these gestures are not in any way linked to depth or meaning.[52] Rivette continues, "In the midst of a dramatic space created by human encounters [Preminger] would instead exploit to its limit the cinema's ability to capture the fortuitous (but a fortuity that is willed), to record the accidental (but the accidental that is created) through the closeness and sharpness of the look."[53]

This closing phrase squares with the explanation of *mise-en-scène* and auteurism given by William Routt. As Routt argues, *la politique des auteurs* was based not simply on a belief that certain directors expressed a consistent worldview through the visual and thematic particulars of their films (that is, through their cinematic "writing"), but on something more subtle and complex.[54] What distinguished directors as different as Hawks, Hitchcock, and Rossellini, and what brought them together, was that each had a specific "way of looking." Though this term may be understood figuratively, as an attitude or manner of considering things, it should best be taken literally, as designating a manner of seeing. Routt reminds us, "In French film criticism *mise en scene* has always involved a way of seeing as well as a way of disposing objects and people."[55] If the latter activity refers to self-expression through activity, the former refers to the revelation of a distinct personality through its habits, manner, and style of observation.

In contrast to the commonly voiced criticism that aligns auteurism with Romantic ideas of self-expression, Routt notes that the "auteurs chosen as exemplars seem the antithesis of artists anxious to express themselves."[56] Indeed, *le style evident* employed by the *Cahiers* critics' favorite directors—that classical approach marked by "clarity and conspicuousness, . . . no decoration and no waste"[57]—is a style that "effaces the usual markers of directorial personality."[58] That is, while these directors use the dominant language, they naturally inflect it with their own voice; but perhaps paradoxically, this voice is never distracting or intrusive. Here again we see in the younger *Cahiers* critics the vestiges of Bazinian thought, for their privileged filmmakers were as much observers as they were composers or orchestrators. *Mise-en-scène* might then best be defined as a particular director's particular way of looking.

The task of the auteur critic, then, was to adopt the director's way of looking in order to validate it as such. "*Cahiers* auteurism is not merely director oriented criticism, it is criticism oriented through a director's way of seeing," Routt writes. The auteur is ultimately "not so much a personality as an activity," and engaging in the auteur's way of looking demands "an active relation with films"—one the great auteurs seemed to invite. This activity, however, is a challenging one. "Close observation is required, and an 'open' looking that endeavors to 'see everything,' but also a way of looking that maintains the sensibility of director and spectator simultaneously."[59] Routt argues that only if we understand auteurism and *mise-en-scène* in this way can we then make sense of critical practices like "the search for directorial 'touches' or identifying marks appearing . . . as material evidence of authority."[60]

One of the most important and most often overlooked aspects of auteurism was its elevation of the status and autonomy of the critic. One the one hand, Routt explains, the experiencing of an auteur's "look" meant the "subordination of one's self . . . to a field of vision, a world, present in the film."[61] On the other hand, the task of distinguishing an authentic "way of looking" from a superficially stylish application of cinema's dominant formal grammar could only be carried out by those with special abilities. Auteurism implicitly argued for "the value of [the auteurist/cinephile's] *regard* over and above that of other viewers."[62] The auteur critic—functioning as a kind of translator, mediating between work and viewer—enjoyed self-designation as a viewer who had special knowledge or skill, one who could see and show to others. Thus,

Routt explains, the practice of "elevating the power of the individual artists to supremacy in film making, paradoxically raised the viewer to a position of creative power."[63]

This explanation can further help us to see how critics committed to a notion of film authorship could also value and celebrate that which exceeded a notion of authorship—what we have been calling "cinephiliac moments." For the practice of close observation typical of the cinephile—"an 'open' looking that endeavors to 'see everything'"—was not limited to the identification of "auteurprints"; indeed, such a manner of looking, learned from the directors whose works they admired, led the cinephile to privilege his or her own moments of revelatory encounter. When Jacques Rivette writes that Preminger is "the one who invents Jean Simmons's uncertain footfall, her huddled figure in the armchair,"[64] he suggests that Preminger is the one who has created the opportunity that enabled him to see it. Through the auteurist's way of looking, one may find in the deceptively simple works of great auteurs a certain depth and complexity that comes not simply from them, but through the cinematic apparatus itself, from us: "True complexity is what calls to us from simple things, mundane details: a gesture, a face, a glance."[65]

This emphasis on a way of looking over and above theme—style over substance—suggests a certain dandyism at work in the auteurist enterprise. Indeed, when *Cahiers* critic André Labarthe was challenged with the remark that "dandyism is an attitude which has profoundly marked the history of *Cahiers*," he replied, "Dandyism? Perhaps, but dandyism without a mirror."[66] The emphasis was on the appreciation of a subtlety of style, one that does not call attention to itself. This definition is consistent with the origins of dandyism in that tendency's most famous figure, Beau Brummel. As Ackbar Abbas notes, Brummel sought "to be fashionable without being seen to be fashionable. In other words, fashion had to be invisible."[67] It was Brummel's belief that if the average person in the street notices your attire, then you are not well dressed. But if both a fashionable appearance and its invisibility are the goal, who is to appreciate the achievement? As Ackbar explains, this invisibility existed only for the average man; it was readily apparent to devotees of the dandy's code. The *Cahiers* auteurists were precisely these devotees, and they could see what the average viewer could not: the meticulous, distinctive stylishness in the work of an apparently conventional filmmaker.

Defining auteurs in terms of a "way of looking," and designating the auteurist critic as a privileged viewer, evokes a similar set of issues and conflicts from France of the 1920s. Film theory and criticism of this era had a catchword as mysterious, provocative, and controversial as *mise-en-scène*. The word was "*photogénie*." Armed with it, Jean Epstein—whom Jean Mitry identified as "the first real theoretician of the cinema"[68]—attempted to construct

a theory of the cinema out of what we have been calling by another name: "cinephiliac moments."

Photogénie and *Mise-en-Scène*

De Baecque and Frémaux identify France in the 1920s as a period of "proto-cinephilia," for it saw a burgeoning film culture movement that was a kind of preview of things to come, but not for several more decades. During these years, a group of cinema enthusiasts, many of them artists, embraced cinema as the great art medium of and for a mechanized, modernized world. Louis Delluc, Jean Epstein, Germaine Dulac, Ricciotto Canudo, and Léon Moussinac formed the core of this group that came to be known as the "Impressionists." Together, they arranged screenings, set up film societies, and wrote criticism. And like the *Cahiers* critics, some would eventually become filmmakers in their own right.[69]

In one of the earliest examples of film theory—that is, in one of the first attempts to identify the characteristic that differentiated cinema from the other arts—the Impressionists designated *photogénie* as "the law of cinema." In his analysis of the theories of the Impressionists, David Bordwell summarized the meaning of the term.

The concept of *photogénie* grows out of an attempt to account for the mysteriously alienating quality of cinema's relation to reality. According to the impressionists, on viewing an image, even an image of a familiar object or locale, we experience a certain otherness about the content; the image's material seems to be revealed in a fresh way.[70]

The smallest unit of cinema, they maintained, was not the photo*graph,* but rather the photo*gene.* With this statement, Delluc, Epstein, and others acknowledged that this defining characteristic was to be encountered not so much in individual images as in image fragments, which often appeared in movement over a succession of individual still frames. This definition should clearly echo some of what I have been arguing about cinephiliac moments; indeed, Paul Willemen draws an explicit link between cinephiliac moments and *photogénie.*[71] Nevertheless, in spite of a general agreement that the term designated what was uniquely and ineffably cinematic, the Impressionists were not always in agreement as to how *photogénie* was achieved or what specific instances of cinema qualified for such designation.

Louis Delluc is generally (though perhaps incorrectly) credited with coining the term "*photogénie,*"[72] and for him it referred primarily to an activity of cinematic composition; that is, he used the term to designate what was orchestrated by the filmmaker and could be understood as an expression of his imagination. Jean Epstein, however, understood it as not the filmmaker's, but the camera's extraordinary ability to reanimate and make mysterious the most common objects and occurrences of our everyday lives. Sounding like many other critics and observers (Bazin, Benjamin, etc.), Epstein wrote that the camera lens "is an eye endowed with inhuman analytical properties . . . an eye without prejudice, without morality, free of influences, and it sees in the human face and gestures traits that we, burdened with sympathies and antipathies, habits and inhibitions, no longer know how to see."[73]

Epstein specified two requirements for the achievement of *photogénie.* First was the essential quality of motion: "only mobile aspects of the world . . . may see their moral value increased by filmic reproduction," he wrote.[74] Ordinary filmic motion was raised to the photogenic by the fact that it urgently signaled the continuity of space and time that the cinematic apparatus offered in representation. Even close-ups, which Epstein regarded as "the soul of cinema," needed motion. "The close-up, the keystone of cinema, is the maximum expression of the *photogénie* of movement. When static, it verges on contradiction. The face alone doesn't unravel its expressions but the head and lens moving together or apart."[75] Furthermore, the motion that achieved *photogénie* was not the continuous motion the cinema presented, but bits of movement, here and there.

If it is too long, I don't find continuous pleasure in it. Intermittent paroxysms affect me the way needles do. Until now, I have never seen an entire minute of pure *photogénie*. Therefore, one must admit that the photogenic is like a spark that appears in fits and starts. [. . .] Even more beautiful than a laugh is the face preparing for it. I must interrupt. I love the mouth which is about to speak and holds back, the gesture which hesitates between right and left, the recoil before the leap, and the moment before landing, the becoming, the hesitation, the taut spring.[76]

Second, *photogénie* revealed the personality or personal aspect of the thing reproduced—that is, its specificity. "Personality is the spirit visible in things and people, their heredity made evident, their past become unforgettable, their future already present. Every aspect of the world, elected to life by the cinema, is so elected only on condition that it has a personality of its own."[77] Rather than being slaves to the narrative in which they are caged, photogenic objects spring forth, declaring their existence as things in their own right. "An eye in close-up is no longer the eye, it is AN eye."[78] This specificity disrupts and challenges, but also pleases and is both the source and product of cinema's own specificity. Like Bazin, Epstein saw the cinema's ability to bestow a special kind of life on things as having an effect akin to primitive mimetic practices. By "summoning objects out of the shadows of indifference into the light of dramatic concern," he wrote, the lives cinema creates "are like the life in charms and amulets, the ominous tattooed objects of certain primitive religions."[79]

One of the most commonly cited specific instances of *photogénie* identified or encountered by Epstein came in this passage celebrating the silent-era actor Sessue Hayakawa.

The Honor of His House [1918] is an improbable yarn: adultery and surgery. Hayakawa, the tranced tragedian, sweeps the scenario aside. A few instants offer the magnificent sight of his harmony in movement. He crosses a room quite naturally, his torso held at a slight angle. He hands his gloves to a servant. Opens a door. Then, having gone out, closes it. *Photogénie,* pure *photogénie,* cadenced movement.[80]

This example is not only instructive about the specific quality of *photogénie,* it also reminds us of the similarity to cinephiliac moments. First, Epstein's example shows the extent to which *photogénie,* like the cinephiliac moment, is indifferent to traditional categories of aesthetic evaluation, for it is as likely to make itself visible in a second-rate potboiler as it is to appear in the works of an acknowledged film artist. Also of note is the fact that it was Hayakawa's natural movements, captured disinterestedly by the camera, that were occasions of *photogénie* and not any stylized or affected movements. As with the cinephiliac moment, *photogénie* results not from what has been aestheticized, but from the real shining through deliberate aestheticization.

The above passage further alerts us to the fact that the body in motion was one of the most common sites for *photogénie*, and this in turn leads us to Malcolm Turvey's point that the encounter with the photogenic provoked in Epstein a bodily reaction, much like that provoked by cinephiliac moments. Throughout Epstein's writings are references to physical sensations experienced while viewing films: needles in skin, vertigo, centrifugal motion, bodily cravings. At one point he defines *photogénie* as "the taste of things."[81] Turvey emphasizes that "the strong, overwhelmingly physical nature of the sensations . . . is a central component of [Epstein's] . . . perceptual experience of the cinema."[82] Thus, Turvey argues, Epstein's theories challenge what Martin Jay has described as the "Cartesian scopic regime," in which the eye, aligned as it is with knowledge, offers transcendence from the physical.[83] By emphasizing film's "sensuous proximity to the world," Epstein envisaged "a cinema of *immanence*."[84] For him cinema was not simply a visual experience, but one that began with the visual and extended to the bodily.

Though Epstein acknowledged that initial encounters with *photogénie* were encounters with the aleatory, the accidental as captured by the camera against the intentions of its operator, he soon realized that certain filmmakers had, to use William Routt's phrase, a "way of looking" that facilitated the appearance of *photogénie*.

Mechanically speaking, the lens alone can sometimes succeed in revealing the inner nature of things in this way. This is how, by chance in the first instance, the *photogénie* of character was discovered. But the proper sensibility, by which I mean a personal one, can direct the lens towards increasingly valuable discoveries. This is the role of an author of film, commonly called a film director. Of course a landscape filmed by one of the forty of four hundred directors devoid of personality whom God sent to plague the cinema as He once sent the locusts into Egypt looks exactly like this same landscape filmed by any of those other locust filmmakers. But this landscape or this fragment of drama staged by someone like Gance will look nothing like what would be seen through the eyes and heart of a Griffith or L'Herbier. And so the personality, the soul, the poetry of certain men invaded the cinema.[85]

For Epstein, a filmmaker with true "personality" is not so much preoccupied with expressing himself as with revealing the personality of things and beings. Or rather, it is in what and how he reveals that his own personality becomes apparent. Further, he or she helps the viewer to see on his or her own, and to develop in turn a genuine personality of looking (or a personality through looking). For as with cinephiliac moments, encounters with *photogénie* were inevitably subjective. Indeed, Paul Willemen argues that *photogénie* "clearly sets in place a viewer's aesthetic."[86] As Epstein's Hayakawa example suggests, Willemen notes that the "founding aspect of cinematic quality . . . is located not in the recognition of an artistic sensibility or intentionality beyond the screen as it were, but in the particular relationship supported or constituted by the spectatorial look, between projected image and viewer."[87]

Furthermore, as with Routt's account of auteurism and *mise-en-scène*, Willemen argues that *photogénie* was "a term mobilised to demarcate one set of viewers—those able to 'see'—from others."[88] Epstein himself acknowledged this: "Just as there are people insensitive to music, there are those—in even greater number—insensitive to *photogénie*. [. . .] For the moment, at least."[89] But while Epstein seemed to be in favor of cultivating a widespread sensitivity to *photogénie,* just as often in his writings there seemed to be an elitist desire to protect the purity of *photogénie* by keeping its meaning elusive. It remained a kind of free-floating signifier, usable only to those insiders sensitive and dis- criminating enough to understand it. In much the same way, the *Cahiers* crit- ics, by managing to never concretely define *mise-en-scène,* kept it as a kind of secret password that had true meaning and usefulness only to members. The ability to use these terms—proof that one was able to truly "see"—also drew the line between true cinephiles and mere film enthusiasts. At stake, then, was a social distinction between viewers, "restricting the right to speak and write about cinema to those who are able to perceive, to see what others cannot."[90] How exactly one came to possess this ability, Epstein never said; and so it re- mained that the way in which one became schooled into this sensitivity was as mysterious as the object of its appreciation.

If Delluc and Epstein, with their differing conceptions of *photogénie,* respectively represent the writing and recording functions of cinema, the *Cahiers* critics found a way to reunite those functions with the term *mise-en- scène.* Recording—that is, what one looked at and how one looked at it—was itself an act of writing. This definition further alerts us to the complicated, sometimes contradictory position that virtually all the *Cahiers* critics felt about the cinema's relationship to writing. On the one hand, the auteur theory was based on an explicit analogy between cinema and writing; and as we have seen, the cornerstone of this argument was laid by Alexander Astruc in his highly influential 1948 essay, "The Birth of a New Avant-Garde: *La Caméra-stylo.*"[91]

But in spite of the importance Astruc's essay held for the *Cahiers* critics, François Truffaut's auteurist manifesto, "A Certain Tendency of the French Cinema," published in 1954, presents another view. This essay, whose issue was literary adaptation, exemplifies the contempt the *Cahiers* critics held for those filmmakers who regarded cinema as the poor relation of literature. In general, Truffaut attacked the French cinema's "Tradition of Quality," a cinema he maintained was controlled by writers, specifically scenarists Jean Aurenche and Pierre Bost, authors of numerous literary adaptations. "When [Aurenche and Bost] hand in their scenario," Truffaut wrote, "the film is done; the *metteur-en-scène*, in their eyes, is the gentleman who adds the pictures to it and it's true, alas!"[92] As an alternative, Truffaut calls for a cinema of *auteurs*, directors who participate in the conception and writing of the scripts they will film. In addition, he calls for a method which supplements foregone analysis with an embracing of the contingencies of on-the-spot discovery. Criticizing the tradition of quality, he writes that, dependent as it is on literary formulas, "This school which aspires to realism destroys it at the moment of finally grabbing it, so careful is the school to lock these beings in a closed world, barricaded by formulas, plays on words, maxims, instead of letting us see them for ourselves, with our own eyes."[93] This criticism extended to the "closed world" method of filming, in which no unplanned, contingent, or natural occurrence was allowed to enter the frame. Truffaut admonished these filmmakers in Bazinian style: "The artist cannot always dominate his work."[94] Rather, when working within the cinema, a technology that writes even in the absence of an author, the artist must sometimes give himself up to what the machine offers and be guided by it.

Astruc would later write a kind of corrective to his earlier *caméra-stylo* essay, balancing his initial insistence on writing with an insistence on something more cinema-specific. "What is *mise en scène*?" he asked. "Watching how people act? . . . Not exactly. It could more aptly be described as presenting them, watching how they act and at the same time what makes them act."[95] He continued, "What is caught by the lens is the movement of the body—an immediate revelation, like all that is physical: the dance, a woman's look, the change of rhythm in a walk, beauty, truth, etc."[96] This summary confirms Routt's contention that, for these critics, *mise-en-scène* was both a way of looking and a way of disposing people and objects. Furthermore, what was revealed thanks to the preferred director's way of looking was the mysterious quality of ordinary things. Serge Daney once remarked that what continued to preoccupy the *Cahiers* critics, even well after the changes wrought by May '68, was "a cinema haunted by writing."[97] It was not only the scripting by directors, or the filmic writing of auteurs, but also the *excess* of writing beyond what was being actively written. Moments of *photogénie*. Cinephiliac moments.

Simulating Transitional Cinema

It was precisely this excess of writing that Jacques Rivette saw in the films of Otto Preminger (as well as others). In effect, what Rivette saw and responded to in *Angel Face* was a strange mixture of the characteristics of open and closed forms, extremes he had celebrated in his reviews of Roberto Rossellini's *Voyage to Italy* and Fritz Lang's *Beyond a Reasonable Doubt*.

In his review of the noirish *Beyond a Reasonable Doubt*, Rivette compared Lang's film to science fiction, for here (as in other of his films) Lang had created "a *totally closed* world."[98] Rivette wrote, "No concession is made here to the everyday, to detail: no remarks about the weather, the cut of a dress, the graciousness of a gesture; if one does become aware of a brand of make-up, it is for purposes of plot. We are plunged into a world of necessity. . . ."[99] Every element has its place, and if it has no place then it has been excised. The characters played by Dana Andrews and Joan Fontaine have neither depth nor texture: they "have lost all individual quality, are no more than human concepts."[100] This is a narrative cinema stripped to the bare minimum. "The film is purely negative," Rivette concludes, "and so effective in its destructive aspects that it ends ultimately by destroying itself."[101]

Rossellini's *Voyage to Italy* was the flip side of the coin for Rivette: a fiercely positive film, one not removed from the external modern world, but rooted firmly within it, opening out to embrace and consider it, in both its material and spiritual aspects. Rossellini's style—or rather, his "eye, his look"[102]—is one of "unremitting freedom."[103] In contrast to the controlling professionalism of Lang's work, Rivette exclaims that "Rossellini's films have more and more obviously become *amateur* films; home movies."[104] Whereas Lang is interested only in abstractions, Rossellini is filming not "just his ideas, . . . but the most everyday details of his life."[105] Documentary and fiction intermingle in the same image, in the same figure. Beyond the characters we see not ideas, but the flesh and blood of real people: Ingrid Bergman and George Sanders at a particular time in their lives, on particular days in their lives. If Lang's film was an analysis or an "*experiment*,"[106] Rossellini's is a "quest" of discovery;[107] he "does not demonstrate, he shows."[108]

If Rivette's claim that Preminger's style marks the conflation of these two extremes seems an exaggeration, one might consider Jean-André Fieschi's point: "It has been no secret since at least as far back as Epstein that the films described by film-makers are the films of their dreams."[109] This seems clearly to be the case for Rivette. Indeed, his description of what he sees in Preminger sounds more like the experience of what Rivette's own films would aspire to: a radical mixture of the characteristics of open and closed forms. Near the end of his review of *Voyage to Italy*, written in 1955, Rivette boldly remarked, "Here is our cinema, those of us who in our turn are preparing to make films (did I tell you, it may be soon),"[110] but this commitment did not mean a complete abandonment of the "possibly more naive conception of the old school, of Hawks, Hitchcock or Lang."[111] Indeed, from Lang he would draw the conspiratorial plots, the setting up of an "experiment," while from Rossellini he would borrow the "amateur" style and the interest in modern life. Jonathan Rosenbaum, Rivette's most astute American admirer, has written, "Every Rivette film has its Eisenstein/Lang/Hitchcock side—an impulse to design and plot, dominate and control—and its Renoir/Hawks/Rossellini side: an impulse to 'let things go,' open one's self up to the play and power of other personalities, and watch what happens."[112] But for Rivette, this radical mix could be achieved only through a radical method of production. Rivette described it thus:

> Time was, in a so-called classical tradition of cinema, when the preparation of a film meant first of all finding a good story, developing it, scripting it and writing dialogue; with that done, you found actors who suited the characters and then you shot it. This is something I've done twice, with *Paris Nous Appartient* and *La Religieuse,* and I find the method totally unsatisfying, if only because it involves such boredom. What I have tried since—after many others, following the precedents of Rouch, Godard and so on—is to attempt to find, alone or in company . . . , a generating principle which will then, as though on its own (I stress the "as though"), develop in an autonomous manner and engender a filmic product from which, afterwards, a film destined for screening to audiences can be cut, or rather "produced."[113]

After these films, Rivette embarked on a strategy of radical collaboration. This process began with *L'Amour fou* (1968), a film that focuses on a theater director (Jean-Pierre Kalfon) mounting a production of Racine's *Andromache,* the rehearsals of which are being filmed by a documentary film unit. The play is to feature his wife (Bulle Ogier), but when the pressures of being constantly filmed force her to withdraw, the director replaces her with his former mistress. Rivette scripted portions of the film, but these were sometimes altered during filming in collaboration with the actors; in addition, other scenes were totally improvised. But in the most dramatic departure from dominant film practice, Rivette asked Jean-Pierre Kalfon to actually cast and direct the production of *Andromache* according to his own conception (not Rivette's); and the documentary unit (shooting in 16 mm, while the rest was shot in 35 mm) was to film these rehearsals as it saw fit. From this wealth of material—some planned, much spontaneous—Rivette cut together a film that ran four hours and fifteen minutes.

If *L'Amour fou* was dominated by the Rossellinian impulse, Rivette's next two features brought the Langian side back into play, at least at the level of narrative. *Out One* (1971), running over twelve hours, and *Out One: Spectre* (1972), a shorter (over four hours) reworking of the same material, again focus on theatrical troupes and feature lengthy documentary sequences of the performers in rehearsal. Rivette himself remarked that, "in the long version almost nothing happens for the first three or four hours."[114] But into this extreme of openness there was introduced a Langian *complot:* thirteen individuals form a secret alliance in a somewhat vague attempt to attain power. These films, too, were produced using Rivette's method of radical collaboration, which is not limited to collaboration among individuals, but also, in an unorthodox way, among the different phases of production. Jean-André Fieschi has written of this method, "the filming is no longer a transfer from the script, or the montage a transfer of the filming. On the contrary, a dialectic is set up between planning, filming and editing in which each phase, each stage, is a criticism (a critical transcending) of the previous one."[115]

With his next film, *Céline and Julie Go Boating (Céline et Julie vont en bateau,* 1974), Rivette struck the clearest balance between the two opposing stylistic influences. This is not to say that the film is "smooth" in the commercial sense, but rather that there are roughly equal parts of each, sometimes mixing harmoniously, sometimes not. With this film there was no script, only a general scenario, developed by Rivette, his main actors, and writer Eduardo de Gregorio in collaboration. Gilbert Adair has provided a clear summary of this film, one that is easy to understand on viewing, but most difficult to summarize.

It is not the least charming aspect of *Céline et Julie vont en bateau* that its "plot" is almost impossible to relate. [. . .] Anyhow, here goes: Juliet (Dominique Labourier) is a librarian living in Montmartre, whose existence is upset one day by the intrusion of Céline (Juliet Berto), a lady musician who performs in a cheap nightclub. After a brief flirtation (in a sense as sexual as you please to make it) the two girls move in together and the film properly begins. Céline has a story to tell—but is she making it up?—about a house in which she plays nurse to a little girl, around whose life glides a strange trio, consisting of two languid young ladies (Bulle Ogier and Marie-France Pisier) and a no less "phantom" gentleman (Barbet Schroeder, also the film's producer).

Next morning, as a title helpfully informs us, Julie sets off and is ushered in turn into the mysterious house, from which she emerges, dazed and with a piece of candy in her mouth, to be whisked off in a waiting taxi, like the Rolls-Royce of the Princesse of *Orphée.* By sucking on the sweets which they never fail to discover on their tongues after a visit to the house, Céline and Julie are able, in a kind of bizarre "private screening," to re-view the drama, solve the mystery and, in a sequence both hilarious and disturbing, exorcise the demons therein.[116]

Thomas Elsaesser has described Rivette's cinema as a fascinating and perplexing admixture of the Bazinian "image of the world" (Rossellini) and the modernist "world of the image" (Lang).[117] But there is, perhaps, another way of describing this mixture: as an attempt at simulating transitional cinema and its effects on spectatorial activity. In order to clarify and explore this claim, we might begin by recalling the chronology offered by Rivette himself of the stages in the evolution of film language.

So one might, very schematically, distinguish four moments: the invention of montage (Griffith, Eisenstein), its deviation (Pudovkin–Hollywood: elaboration of the techniques of propaganda cinema), the rejection of propaganda (a rejection loosely or closely allied to long takes, direct sound, amateur or auxiliary actors, non-linear narrative, heterogeneity of genres, elements or techniques, etc.), and finally, . . . the attempt to "salvage," to reinject into contemporary methods the spirit and the theory of the first period, though without rejecting the contribution made by the third, but rather trying to cultivate one through the other, to dialectize them and, in a sense, to *edit* them.[118]

In this chronology, however, Rivette has skipped two steps: early cinema and transitional cinema. The first of these stages has been described by Tom Gunning in his influential essay, "The Cinema of Attractions." From its origins until about 1907, Gunning argues, cinema based itself not in its ability to tell a story, but from "its ability to *show* something," be it a dancing girl, the electrocution of an elephant, or a skeleton-suited man magically appearing and disappearing on the screen.[119] As such, the cinema of attractions constructed a different relationship with its spectator than dominant cinema later would. Marked by "exhibitionist confrontation rather than diegetic absorption,"[120] the cinema of attractions "aggressively subjected the spectator to 'sensual or psychological impact.'"[121]

With this concept, Gunning challenged not only the belief that early cinema was merely a "primitive" version of narrative cinema but also the long-standing opposition of documentary/Lumière and fiction/Méliès modes.[122] In fact, he argued, the films of both those pioneers can be united in "a conception of cinema that sees cinema less as a way of telling stories than as a way of presenting a series of views to an audience, fascinating because of their illusory power," regardless of whether that illusion is realistic, as with Lumière, or magical, as with Méliès. Furthermore, it alerts us to the fact that "attractions" may include not only moments of performed spectacle (a dance or a chase) but also captured reality: the wind in the tress.

Transitional cinema, then, was the evolutionary period in which cinema began to adopt narrative as its primary mode and devoted itself to developing a visual grammar of continuity and invisibility.[123] Gunning summarizes: "The transformation of filmic discourse that D. W. Griffith typifies [during these transitional years] bound cinematic signifiers to the narration of stories and the creation of a self-enclosed diegetic universe."[124] But this evolutionary process was not complete until the late 1910s, and so the films of this period—for example, Griffith's Biograph shorts and the first true features—are an uneasy mixture of the characteristics of early cinema and classical cinema. Classical cinema would, of course, find a way to retain elements of the cinema of attractions—in the form of chases and musical numbers—but these moments were subordinated to the interests of the plot, so narrative was never completely forsaken for the thrill of an attraction. During the transitional years, however, this formula was still in development, and the films—both in their grammar and their plots—seem to veer back and forth, first toward the complexities of classical cinema, then back to the simplicities of early cinema. Thus, transitional films pulled their viewers between two different, somewhat conflicting spectatorial positions: one organized around absorption in a narrative, the other in stimulation by a spectacle. My suggestion is that if certain parallels can be drawn between avant-garde cinema and early cinema (indeed, Gunning's "Cinema of Attractions" essay makes just this point), then perhaps the narrative avant-garde practice of Rivette, Godard, and others—what Peter Wollen has dubbed a "second avant-garde"[125]—might be seen as parallel to transitional cinema. More precisely, because of the way in which they, too, are an uneasy mixture of narrative and attraction, Rivette's films position their spectators in the same divided way that transitional cinema did.

Gilbert Adair's synopsis of *Céline and Julie* gives a clear sense of the film's narrative, and its presentation is carried out in a rough accordance with traditional film grammar (shot/reverse shots, eyeline matches, etc.). But the film is equally marked by the characteristics of early cinema in both its narrative and formal aspects, and it is those that I want to focus on here. For while it can be clearly understood that the film's plot and visual grammar encourage the absorption of the classical spectator, the ways in which the film employs aspects of early cinema to encourage a different spectatorial activity need to be clarified. The opening sequence perfectly situates the film in relation to transitional cinema, for it presents its own version of what Gunning identifies as the first linking of narrative and attractions in the history of cinema: the chase.[126] The film begins with Julie sitting on a park bench, reading; Céline rushes past and, unaware, drops her glasses. Julie picks them up and goes after her to return them. Soon, however, this pursuit gives way to a playful game of cat-and-mouse. It becomes clear that Céline is aware of Julie's attempts to catch her, but rather than stopping to find out why, she hurries along faster. She then encourages the pursuit by dropping her scarf. Julie takes the cue and begins to behave less like she intends to return the dropped items and more like a detective shadowing a suspect. Julie follows Céline to a hotel, then returns the next morning to find her at the adjacent café, where she finally returns the possessions.

Unlike classical cinema, in which attractions such as chase sequences are always subordinated to plot and character, this opening sequence offers none of the typical narrative grounding. The characters have not been introduced; indeed, we know nothing about them other than what we might (rather questionably) infer from their clothing and physical demeanor. Here, the chase is completely abstracted from any narrative context. Other attraction-like scenes are introduced throughout the film, such as the scenes in which Céline and Julie perform their respective magic and singing routines, or the one in which Céline, presenting herself in a curly wig as Julie, stages an improvised dance with Grégoire/Guilou, Julie's childhood beau, before a group of onlookers at a park gazebo. It is, as Jonathan Rosenbaum has remarked, "Rouch spiced with a dash of Minnelli."[127]

Duration is also a key factor in this film. Though the length of Rivette's films has been much remarked on, it should be noted that it's not just the films as a whole that are long; individual scenes and sequences are long as well. Indeed, the opening chase sequence runs for nearly fifteen minutes! A roughly analogous chase scene opening a mainstream film might run four or five minutes at most, and only then after having established certain particulars of plot and character for context. Furthermore, the individual shots that comprise this opening and other scenes are often quite long, unnecessarily so according to the rules of dominant cinema, for nothing of particular relevance is occurring. For example, the film opens with a medium close-up of Julie sitting on a park bench, holding her book open, but looking down at something on the ground. The second shot shows a medium close-up of her legs as she traces a design in the sand with the heel of one shoe. As she finishes, the camera tilts up and she returns her attention to the book. But rather than cutting to another shot or introducing another action, the shot continues for another fifteen seconds. We wait expectantly for something else to happen, but it doesn't—at least, not right away. Rivette then alternates between shots of Julie reading or looking around with loose point-of-view shots of the park (the wind in the trees, a cat stalking a bird). Finally, after another couple of minutes, Céline makes her appearance.

Also notable is the rough, "amateurish" quality of the camerawork and editing. The scene has a decidedly documentary quality about it deriving largely from the natural lighting, uncontrolled setting, and direct sound recording. The pans and tilts are often awkwardly executed (in the manner of Renoir), and only some of the cuts follow strict adherence to continuity rules. Before Céline appears, for example, we are treated to ten or so shots of Julie and of the park, but while some shots of the park are motivated by Julie's look, others clearly are not. The cut to the third shot—a panning shot of the park—seems to be motivated by the shouts of some children, but when the cut comes, there are no children to be seen. We return to the shot of Julie, and when she looks up, we get a clear point-of-view shot of the trees. Then, the next shot of her turning her head from left to right is followed by a panning shot moving from right to left. While many scenes and shots in *Céline and Julie* are presented in accordance with dominant cinema's demand for continuity and efficiency, just as many are not, and it is the imbalance and unpredictability—from shot to shot and scene to scene—that creates "a mood of pregnant pause and magical suspension in which anything at all might happen."[128]

All of this serves to provoke in the viewer what Noël Burch has dubbed a "topographical" reading. In his essays on early cinema, Burch suggests that the spectators of this period possessed a visual acuity that enabled them to "gather signs from all corners of the screen in their quasi-simultaneity, often without very clear or distinctive indices immediately appearing to hierarchise them."[129] This is quite similar to the perceptual mode I have been calling "panoramic"—the visual habit of scanning the image to register all its details. Burch argues that while some cinemagoers were trained in this practice by lecturers at the movie houses, others developed it naturally by viewing other entertainment forms geared for the proletariat class—the circus, the music hall, the variety show—for these, like the cinema, regularly featured broad, panoramic tableaux in which multiple events of interest were occurring simultaneously. Well into the period Gunning designates as transitional cinema, the means of harnessing the spectator's gaze had not yet been completely realized. Burch notes that "it is striking how many tableaux and even whole films were shot in all the major producing countries up to 1914 (think of scenes from *Fantômas* or *Judith of Bethulia*) which demanded a topographical reading by the spectator." [130]

While the shots in Rivette's film are never as cluttered or uncentered as those typically found in the earliest films, the effect contemporary viewers experience in watching those earlier films is introduced into a modern narrative feature. Because shots are so often held well past any narrative necessity, and because links between shots are often not clearly made, we are constantly on alert, both cognitively and visually. As a result, often times, when the narratively important element of a shot has concluded, but the shot continues, our gaze becomes unhooked and we begin looking at the image more panoramically or topographically. Rivette is not the only one of the New Wave directors whose films could be considered attempts at simulating transitional cinema. The other obvious choice is Jean-Luc Godard, who was specific about his efforts on *Breathless:* "What I wanted was to take a conventional story and remake, but differently, everything the cinema had done. I also wanted to give the feeling that the techniques of film-making had just been discovered or experienced for the first time."[131] The opening sequence of *Céline and Julie* functions in a similar way and cues us to its strategy, alerting us that our gaze will have to be more sharp and active, but that it is also allowed to be more free, to encounter what it will.

Burch's reference above to Louis Feuillade's *Fantômas* offers another connection between Rivette and transitional cinema, for numerous critics have remarked on the similarity between Rivette's films and Feuillade's film serials—*Judex* (1913), *Les Vampires* (1915), *Fantômas* (1916), and *Tih Minh* (1918). Richard Roud described *Out One: Spectre* as "not unlike the films of Feuillade or the paintings of Magritte: melodrama in a realistic setting, anguish on the boulevards, anxiety in cafés, terror in the repeated shot of the peripheral ringroad."[132] (Indeed, the long version of *Out One* had been planned as a serial for French television.) Gilbert Adair made a similar connection between *Céline and Julie*'s "fantasy in the open air" and the style of *Les Vampires* and *Judex*.[133] *Céline and Julie*'s intertitles interspersed throughout the film—for example, "But, the next morning . . . "—cannot but evoke silent narrative cinema. Rivette acknowledged the Feuillade influence explicitly in the film's subtitle, "Phantom Ladies over Paris," and in at least one scene: when Céline and Julie stage a break-in to the library where Julie works, the two are dressed in tightly fitting black suits in the manner of Feuillade's infamous villainess, Irma Vep.

In addition to the mixture of closed narrative in an open setting, it is likely that Feuillade's serials had an impact on Rivette's ideas about duration. As Dominique Païni noted, Rivette and the other *Cahiers* critics would have seen Feuillade's serials not at their local cinemas in weekly installments, as they were originally programmed, but rather many years later at the Cinémathèque, and all at one go, over a six- or eight-hour period. "Rivette based his experiments with urban temporality on a Feuillade who in fact never existed, a museum Feuillade," Païni wrote.[134] Though Feuillade's films had been enormously popular with the public on their initial release, they soon disappeared from sight—indeed, from cinema history—until Henri Langlois organized a revival of *Fantômas* in 1944.[135] Richard Roud writes, "It is no accident, I think, that the Feuillade revival of the mid-40s coincided both with the rediscovery of location shooting in the Italian neo-realist cinema and also with the new interest—sparked off by the European release of Orson Welles' first two films—in composition in depth, and the concomitant critical downgrading of montage."[136] Of course, Feuillade was an exact contemporary of Griffith, so one can see Rivette's films as exemplifying not only that fourth phase of cinema's evolution that he described—the attempt to synthesize and dialectize the first phase's montage approach with the third phase's realist tendency—

but also the two tendencies of transitional cinema: the tension generated by the pull backward toward the tableaux of early cinema (Feuillade) and the pull forward toward a more complex cinema language (Griffith).

As I have tried to show, Rivette's films simulate the experience of transitional cinema by employing strategies typical of both, and by placing the spectator in a divided position, one that is simultaneously absorbed and distracted, visually anchored as well as unmoored. Indeed, we should recall Dominique Païni's claim that it was precisely in viewing the films of the transitional years that he found himself in this divided spectatorial position I have been describing, one "between lassitude and perception . . . a sort of oscillation between the fluidity of a dream and the dynamism of waking, between appearances— the norm—and apparitions—the exception."[137]

5 Film and the Limits of History

In the previous chapters, I have joined in the project of a history of cinephilia by focusing on one element of cinephilia: the fetishizing of details in the motion picture image. I showed the ways in which some of the most important critics of historical cinephilia, as well as some of the cinephiles of proto-cinephilia, accounted for the appearance of cinephiliac moments in their theoretical positions. Further, I discussed certain stylistic approaches that facilitated or were related to the appearance of cinephiliac moments. Central to my discussion of cinephiliac moments was my consideration of them in relationship to the general conditions of modernity: it is my contention that the encounter with cinephiliac moments is facilitated by the cinephile's habit of what I have been calling, after Schivelbusch, "panoramic perception." Though primarily given over to absorption in the cinematic experience, the cinephile is a divided spectator who supplements the absorbed gaze of dominant cinema's viewer with the distracted glance of the early-era cinemagoer, attempting to increase the possibility of experiencing cinephiliac moments. When encountered, these cinephiliac moments register for the spectator not just visually, but also in a more broadly sensuous manner. As I explained, this experience can be understood as a recovery of sensuous experience via the very technologies that otherwise subordinate all bodily experience to the visual.

But while this recovery of sensuous experience via the machines of modernity is in itself a valuable thing, there is something more at stake here. In summarizing Walter Benjamin's account of the conditions and effects of modernity, Susan Buck-Morss explains that the individual inhabiting the modern world lives behind a stimulus shield—in a perpetual state of distraction in which ordinary sense experience is cut off from cognition. But this individual is also cut off from memory. She elaborates this point: "Under extreme stress," the synaesthetic system—that apparatus where "external sense-perceptions come together with images of memory and anticipation"—breaks apart. "The ego employs consciousness as a buffer, blocking the openness of the synaesthetic system, thereby isolating present consciousness from past memory. Without the depth of memory, experience is impoverished"[1]—and without sensuous experience's connection to cognition, memory is out of reach. In Benjaminian terms, cinephiliac moments, experienced as an eruption of the sensuous, the haptical, or the tactile in the domain of the visual, reconnect sense experience with cognition, and thus with memory. But Benjamin, along with his colleague Siegfried Kracauer, saw both the machines of modernity—especially film—and the vagaries of memory as being deeply implicated in the writing of history and in its potential transformation. In chapter 2, I argued that, marking as they do the *mise-en-abyme* of the cinephile's passionate relationship with cinema, cinephiliac moments occupy a privileged place in the history of cinephilia. I would further argue that such moments mark the *mise-en-abyme* of history itself, for cinephiliac moments are both the point of history's disappearance and the point of its potential recovery. Out of this potential, Benjamin constructed an alternative theory of history, taking the first steps toward an alternative practice of the writing of history.

Photographic History

Though Walter Benjamin may be the figure most readily associated with a "photographic" or "filmic" concept of history,[2] his theoretical writings were strongly influenced by his Weimar-era colleague, Siegfried Kracauer. For many years, Kracauer was best known in film studies as the theorist who played second fiddle to André Bazin on the issue of realism; in more recent years, he has occupied a similar secondary position behind Benjamin on issues of moder-

nity. But recent scholarship on Kracauer has shown him to be the originator of many of the ideas that Benjamin would later take up—but put to decidedly more radical ends.[3] Kracauer's work is divided into two acts, as it were: first, during the 1920s and 30s in Germany, where he worked as a journalist and cultural critic and wrote a number of essays on culture and modernity that were collected in *The Mass Ornament;* and second, in the United States, from 1941 through to his death in 1966, when he wrote his two most famous books, *From Caligari to Hitler* (1947) and *Theory of Film* (1960). Arguments have been made both for and against the continuity of his theories from the 1920s through 1960, but it seems clear that certain preoccupations remain: photography, its relationship to both physical reality (nature) and modern culture, the cinema as extension of photography's mission, and the relationship of these to history and memory.

In *Theory of Film,* whose subtitle is "The Redemption of Physical Reality," Kracauer clearly stated his belief about film's mission. In his introduction, he wrote that "film is essentially an extension of photography and therefore shares with this medium a marked affinity for the visible world around us. Films come into their own when they record and reveal physical reality."[4] This position clearly places him in league with Bazin, and from here, a number of further similarities—as well as striking differences—between the two theorists may be discerned. In spite of those differences (or perhaps because of them), Kracauer's work remains useful for my consideration of cinephiliac moments for a number of reasons. Most generally—and in contrast to Bazin—Kracauer placed his consideration of film within the context of a theory of modernity and its effects on the individual. Also, again somewhat unlike Bazin, Kracauer's work is less an overall theory of film than it is, as Miriam Hansen suggests, "a theory of a particular type of film experience."[5] I would like to note several other aspects of Kracauer's theory and its relationship to my own project.

First of all, Kracauer not only saw it as cinema's task to reveal physical reality, he repeatedly emphasized the ways and manner in which film carries out this revelatory process. In the section of *Theory of Film* entitled "Inherent Affinites," Kracauer argued that it is film's tendency to reveal, in particular, "the unstaged," "the fortuitous," "the indeterminate," and "the flow of life." That is, "notwithstanding its ability to reproduce, indiscriminately, all kinds of visible data," film, he argued, "gravitates toward unstaged reality."[6] While he regarded the kind of staging associated with dominant fictional narrative cinema to be wholly legitimate, he believed that a motion picture must acknowledge and embrace this basic property of the medium. Kracauer wrote that "films conform to the cinematic approach only if they acknowledge the realistic tendency by concentrating on actual physical existence—'the beauty of moving wind in the trees,' as D. W. Griffith expressed it in a 1947 interview."[7] In what Gertrud Koch notes is an echo of Heidegger, Kracauer suggests that it is at these moments and in these details that film gives us a glimpse of "a 'thing-in-itself,' prior to any semiotic properties it may have."[8] Though some films are able to present this quality of things immediately, many others reveal it to us only after much time has passed. We are often less engaged by an old film's narrative or general aesthetic properties than we are charmed by it as a record of a particular moment. Kracauer describes the transformative power of these old films:

In a flash the camera exposes the paraphernalia of our former existence, stripping them of the significance which originally transfigured them so that they changed from things in their own right into invisible conduits.

Unlike paintings, film images encourage such a decomposition because of their emphatic concern with raw material not yet consumed. The thrill of these old films is that they bring us face to face with the inchoate, cocoon-like world whence we come—all the objects, or rather sediments of objects, that were our companions in a pupa state.[9]

Second, although he saw film's mission as the revealing of nature (i.e., the world, physical reality), Kracauer was less committed than Bazin to the belief that certain techniques facilitated revelation more than others. Indeed,

Kracauer was quick to point out that the revelatory experience offered by film is inevitably a subjective experience, one requiring a "requisite perceptual capacity."[10] The subject with this perceptual capacity might be the filmmaker—recall Jean Epstein's claim about those filmmakers who produce *photogénie* versus those who don't—but it may also be the spectator. As Heide Schlüpmann has described it, for Kracauer, "reception in a profound sense [is] the real act of production. Even the work of the filmmaker is in the end conceived in terms of reception."[11] Kracauer devotes an entire section of his book to "The Spectator," and in one subsection he describes the perceptual capacities and activities of one type of spectator, "the film addict," a figure who, he writes,

recalls the nineteenth century *flâneur* (with whom he has otherwise little in common) in his susceptibility to the transient real-life phenomena that crowd the screen. According to the testimony available, it is their flux which affects him most strongly. Along with the fragmentary happenings incidental to them, these phenomena—taxi cabs, buildings, passers-by, inanimate objects, faces—presumably stimulate his senses and provide him with the stuff for dreaming. [. . .] Evidently, these loosely connected images, which he may of course interweave in many ways, are so profoundly satisfactory to the dreamer because they offer him routes of escape into the mirage-like world of concrete objects, striking sensations, and unusual opportunities. To quote Chaperot, "sometimes right in the middle of a film whose intrigue we know and whose lamentable threads we even anticipate, do we not suddenly have the feeling that the image rises to a superior plane and that the 'story' is not more than of secondary importance."[12]

This tendency of Kracauer's "film addict" to look beyond those parts of the image that are strictly related to the drama, and to see instead—and be mesmerized by—fantastic images of the concrete world is, of course, my argument about the cinephile, panoramic perception, and cinephiliac moments. Here, too, the idea of distraction as a disengagement from the narrative's pull toward absorption is presented not negatively, but as a posture that leads to revelatory experiences of the image. Kracauer cites Michel Dard as locating the birth of this spectator in the 1920s, during France's first wave of cinephilia.

Does the spectator ever succeed in exhausting the object he contemplates? There is no end to his wanderings. Sometimes, though, it may seem to him that, after having probed a thousand possibilities, he is listening with all his senses strained, to a confused murmur. Images begin to sound, and the sounds are again images. When this indeterminate murmur—the murmur of existence—reaches him, he may be nearest to the unattainable goal.[13]

It must be noted that, in both the above passages, Kracauer's description evokes not only the image I am presenting of the cinephile, but comes close to sounding like something written by Jean Epstein, or to an account of the viewing habits and experiences of the Surrealists.[14]

Third, it was Kracauer's contention that the spectator's primary experience of film—especially those films that were, according to his definition, truly "cinematic"—was sensual or somatic, one that affected not just her vision, but her entire body. Gertrud Koch describes Kracauer as offering, in part, "a sensualist theory of filmic perception."[15] In contrast to other art forms, which engage their spectators intellectually, Kracauer argued that film images "affect primarily the spectator's senses, engaging him physiologically before he is in a position to respond intellectually."[16] Recalling the argument I made in chapter 3 about copy and contact, the contention here is that film engages not only the material reality of what it records but also the material reality of the spectator—"with skin and hair."[17] Kracauer summarized, "The material elements that present themselves in film directly stimulate the *material layers* of the human being: his nerves, his senses, his entire *physiological substance*."[18]

Lastly, Kracauer specified that

film not only records physical reality but reveals otherwise hidden provinces of it. . . . The salient point here is that these discoveries (which have been exhaustively treated in earlier contexts) mean an increased demand on the spectator's physiological make-up. The unknown shapes he encounters involve not so much his power of reasoning as his visceral faculties. Arousing his innate curiosity, they lure him into dimensions where sense impressions are all-important.[19]

Two related points need to be made here. First, Kracauer's belief that the sensual experience of film registers most powerfully at those points where cinema is most true to its basic properties—the revealing of the physical world, especially the marginalized, overlooked ephemera of everyday life—corresponds to my own claim about cinephiliac moments and their relationship to film's ontology. Second, Kracauer's assertion that film makes "an increased demand on the spectator's physiological make-up" resonates with my own argument that the cinephile, as the most highly skilled, efficient spectator, can experience these "discoveries" more regularly and with less effort than can the ordinary spectator.

Kracauer's interest in the power of filmic details was, like his interest in other ephemera of everyday life, an interest in those marginal cultural phenomena that "eluded the optics of dominant bourgeois culture"; and his goal in considering these contingencies was to engage them in all their "material density and multiplicity, to read them as indexes of history in the making."[20]

Kracauer had begun a consideration of the link between film, its inherent properties, and the question of history several decades prior to *Theory of Film*. In his 1927 essay "Photography," Kracauer developed a complex analogy between the photographer and the historian, and the ways in which memory complicates what each produces. He began by comparing the photographic image to the picture of history offered by historicism, that dominant historiographic practice that believes it "can grasp historical reality by reconstructing the course of events in their temporal succession without any gaps."[21] He wrote that, in effect, historicism offers temporal continuity in the same way that photographs offer spatial continuity. In contrast to these continuities, memory "encompasses neither the entire spatial appearance of a state of affairs nor its entire temporal course. Compared to photography, memory's records are full of gaps."[22] With memory, we have only fragments—memory images—that are retained only insofar as they have significance for us. But photography also has its limitations, for while memory images possess the structures by which we can attribute significance to something, photography does not, or at least not in any fixed way. That is, once a photograph records a moment of history, it simultaneously begins to strip that moment of the structuring context that allows us to make sense of it and see meaning in it. Though a photograph may initially possess this structuring context, it eventually loses it over time and through recontextualization (which is part of the mysterious charm of old films and old photos).

But there is also a distinction to be made between the continuity offered by history and that offered by photography. While historicism *constructs* a (temporal) continuity, including some facts or details and leaving others out, a photograph *copies* an existing (spatial) continuity, registering all its elements indiscriminately. Unlike photography, history does not recognize anything in nature that it cannot subordinate to its own ends; it represses what it regards as marginal or contingent to its story. Thus, the details in photographs are signifiers of the contingency that historicism cannot contain; they reveal "the *provisional* status of all given configurations."[23] Kracauer wrote, "The disorder of the detritus reflected in photography cannot be elucidated more clearly than through the suspension of every habitual relationship among the elements of nature. The capacity to stir up the elements of nature is one of the possibilities of film."[24] Though Kracauer located the implications of photography for historiographic practice in these marginal details, he identified the potential power of those details, perhaps paradoxically, as coming not from the fact that they are full of meaning or significance, but that they are empty of it. For in them we get a glimpse of nature stripped of false or superimposed significance. Through photographs, then, we see nature's elements not as symbols, but as residues of a theretofore unseen, undeveloped history. Kracauer summarized the implications for historiography: "to couch it in the language of film: the aesthetics of film can be assigned to an epoch in which the 'long-shot' perspective, which believed that it in some way focused on the absolute, is replaced by a 'close-up' perspective, which instead sheds light on the meaning of individuated things, of the fragment."[25]

Walter Benjamin extended Kracauer's ideas about the relationship between photographs, memory, and history, complicating the analogies in suggestive ways.

First, in his 1931 essay, "Little History of Photography," Benjamin similarly emphasized that marginal details—indifferently recorded, suddenly illuminated—are the points where photography's intimate link to reality and its challenge to traditional aesthetic values are most clearly located. He explained:

The most precise technology can give its products a magical value, such as a painted picture can never again have for us. No matter how artful the photographer, no matter how carefully posed his subject, the beholder feels an irresistible urge to search such a picture for the tiny spark of contingency, of the here and now, with which reality has (so to speak) seared the subject, to find the inconspicuous spot where in the immediacy of that long-forgotten moment the future nests so eloquently that we, looking back, may rediscover it.[26]

The indexical power of photographic imagery is made clear here (reality has "seared" the subject), as is the fact that that power is clearest not in the ostensible subject of a photo, but in its "tiny spark[s] of contingency." Elsewhere in the same essay, Benjamin offered an example, emphasizing the way in which he was struck, in a photograph of the philosopher Schelling, by creases in the coat the old man is wearing. Benjamin suggests the link of such contingencies to history by noting that the coat "will surely pass into immortality along with him."[27]

Then, in further describing the effects of photography, Benjamin made one of his most provocative analogies: "For it is another nature which speaks to the camera rather than to the eye: 'other' above all in the sense that a space informed by human consciousness gives way to a space informed by the unconscious."[28] This last phrase leads to Benjamin's famous designation of photography as the technology that reveals an "optical unconscious."[29] Several years later, in his most famous essay, "The Work of Art in the Age of Mechanical Reproduction," Benjamin developed the analogy between photography and psychoanalysis more extensively.

The film has enriched our field of perception with methods which can be illustrated by those of Freudian theory. Fifty years ago, a slip of the tongue passed more or less unnoticed. [. . .] Since the *Psychopathology of Everyday Life*, things have changed. This book isolated and made analyzable things which had hereto-fore floated along unnoticed in the broad stream of perception. For the entire spectrum of optical . . . perception the film has brought a similar deepening of apperception. [. . .] by focusing on hidden details of familiar objects, . . . [film] reveals entirely new structural formations of the subject. [. . .] The camera introduces us to unconscious optics as does psychoanalysis to unconscious impulses.[30]

Though Benjamin argued that film focuses us on previously ignored details in images in the way that psychoanalysis focuses us on previously ignored experiences like slips of the tongue and forgetting, he does not explicitly draw the conclusion that photographic details—like parapraxes—are reservoirs of meaning or significance. Nevertheless, the choice of analogy seems to suggests this conclusion, or rather that photographic details are reservoirs of *potential* meaning and significance. How that meaning might be uncovered—or composed—is not addressed until his later works, most explicitly in his theorizing about historiography and his experiments with historiographic form—issues I will return to later.

In the meantime, I want to extend Benjamin's analogy, emphasizing not only the ways in which, in both domains, details become crucial, but also the perceptual posture required to bring these details into focus. As I have argued, in the cinematic experience, the details that provoke cinephiliac moments are revealed most readily via the spectatorial practice I have called panoramic perception. Freud's psychoanalytic method depended on an analogous perceptual posture. We must first recall that Freud's theory of the unconscious contended that both dreams and the banal recollections fixed in our minds like snapshots are, in fact, emotionally laden memories which contain, in a form radically reorganized by condensation and displacement, all a patient's crucial psychical information. Unlocking these dreams or "screen memories" (as Freud called them) could only be carried out through the patient's free association/stream of consciousness monologue. Freud gave this advice to his patients: "You will be tempted to say to yourself: 'This or that has no connection here, or it is quite unimportant, or it is nonsensical, so it cannot be necessary to mention it.' Never give in to these objections, but mention it even if you feel a disinclination against it, or indeed just because of this."[31] Freud further provided a metaphor to help the patient adopt the desired approach: "Say whatever goes through your mind. Act as though, for instance, you were a traveler sitting next to the window of a railway carriage and describing to someone inside the carriage the changing views you see outside."[32]

Freud was thus encouraging his patient to adopt a "panoramic" approach to his or her past—like the passenger on the railway or the cinephile in the movie theater—productively distracted, selecting the discrete indiscriminately. Or at least *apparently* indiscriminately. For Freud, of course, what had generally been regarded as marginal or irrelevant—slips of the tongue, forgetting—was crucial to the development of knowledge, understanding, insight. These details were the key to a history different from the one Freud's patients would give while in an attentive frame of mind. In effect, Freud was telling his patients: If you talk to me in a rational, absorbed state, you will recount one story about yourself; but if you adopt a posture of seemingly irrational distraction, you will become attentive to other things, and from them we can construct an alternative history of your life. The key to composing this other history was in regarding the marginalia of psychical life in the same way that details in photographs—paving stones, scattered leaves, the shape of a branch—were regarded by their early viewers.

Such photographic details were, for Benjamin, evidence of the way in which modern technologies of reproduction served not simply to undermine, but also to offer a site for the redemption of, auratic experience—a concept whose definition varies from place to place and over time in Benjamin's writing. The earliest definition he offered was in the 1931 essay on photography.

> What is aura, actually? A strange weave of space and time: the unique appearance or semblance of distance, no matter how close it may be. While at rest on a summer's noon, to trace a range of mountains on the horizon, or a branch that throws its shadow on the observer, until the moment or the hour become part of their appearance—this is what it means to breathe the aura of the mountains, that branch.[33]

As Miriam Hansen notes, crucial to this part of the definition is Benjamin's emphasis not just on space (proximity/distance) as a component of aura, but also on temporality, on "the momentary, epiphanic character of auratic experience."[34] Benjamin continued his definition: "Experience of the aura thus rests on the transposition of a response common in human relationships to the relationship between the inanimate or natural object and man. The person we look at . . . looks at us in turn. To perceive the aura of an object we look at means to invest it with the ability to look at us in return."[35] In the photography essay, Benjamin quoted the photographer Dauthendey to just this end: "We didn't trust ourselves . . . to look long at the first pictures [Daguerre] developed. We were abashed by the distinctness of these human images, and believed that the little tiny faces in the picture could see *us*, so powerfully was everyone affected by the unaccustomed clarity and the unaccustomed fidelity to nature of the first daguerreotypes."[36] This phenomenon, Hansen notes, which extended from images of people to images of things, is clearly related to the sphere of Freud's uncanny in its potentially unsettling aspects. The redeemed aura is based not on uniqueness, but on its opposite: doubling and repetition; it marks "the fleeting moment in which the trace of an unconscious, 'prehistoric' past"—one leading to a different present than the one that has come to pass—"is actualized in a cognitive image."[37] In the end, Benjamin concluded, all of this experience—the marginal detail experienced as revelatory, the uncanny effect—"corresponds to the data of the *memoire involuntaire.*"[38]

With these words, Benjamin invoked Proust's theory of memory (which he also acknowledged as linked to Freud's) with its two registers: recollection and remembrance. The former are those memories or memory-images that obey the call of consciousness and can be summoned up at will and at any time. They possess the structuring significance that gives them meaning, and are thus allied with historicism in that they "fixate the image of memory in an already interpreted narrative event."[39] The latter memories—what Proust called *memoires involuntaires*—are beyond "the promptings of memory which obey the call of attentiveness," and are thus not implicated in or exhausted by any preexisting discourse.[40] For Proust, these most powerful of memories—images we have never seen before we remember them—are a signal that "the past is 'somewhere beyond the reach of the intellect, and unmistakably present in some material object (or in the sensation which such an object arouses in us), though we have no idea which one it is' [in advance of encountering it]."[41] Most often, these involuntary memories were prompted by haptic, bodily encounters: the feel and taste of the *madeleine,* or the sensation of awkward footing on uneven walkway stones.[42]

As I suggested in chapter 2, there is a complex relationship between cinephiliac moments and memory. Lesley Stern's essay on the uncanny exemplifies the way in which, at the simplest level, we remember cinephiliac moments vividly and anticipate them with excitement on subsequent viewings. But her account of the way in which the moment from *Blade Runner* "always surprises her"—even though she has been anticipating it—brings the processes of remembering and forgetting into intimate proximity. This closeness appears also in the cinephile's first encounter with a cinephiliac moment, for it has the quality of an involuntary memory—something that we seem to remember, even though we are seeing it for the first time. Edward Casey has argued that this experience describes the general experience of film viewing itself. In watching a film, he suggests, "we are in a strange no-man's land in which past and present are not clearly distinguished—opening up a new space in which we can quasi-remember. It is very much as if we were remembering what is being presented to us in images: as if it were familiar enough to be genuinely recognized by us."[43] Some moments register more powerfully as quasi-memories than others, and in these moments, the sense of uncanny recognition is felt most forcefully.

Given their concern with the place of the present in relationship to events and experiences of the past, both Kracauer and Benjamin regarded filmic details—indexes of a past, but one without any structuring context—as hints of an alternative, nonlinear temporal order for the conception and representation of history. These details are "sediments of an experience that are no longer or not yet claimed by social and economic rationality, making them readable as emblems of a 'forgotten future.'"[44] In "Theses on the Philosophy of History," Benjamin further articulated his position, distinguishing between two practices of historiography: historicism and historical materialism. As Kracauer had done in his essay on photography, Benjamin defined historicism as offering an image of the past as a linear continuity marked by a clear cause-and-effect order; furthermore, although the picture of history given by historicism leads inexorably to the present, the role of the present in the construction of that history is denied. Historical materialism contrasts both these aspects: first, it seeks to "blast open the continuum of history"[45] and replace it with a nonlinear historical temporality; furthermore, it foregrounds the role (or even the desire) of the historicizing subject in the present and its attempt to engage in a dialogue with experiences and events of the past. "Historicism gives the 'eternal image' of the past; historical materialism supplies a unique experience with the past," Benjamin summarized.[46] All elements of the past, no matter how marginal or apparently insignificant, are sites for this experience. "A chronicler who recites events without distinguishing between major and minor ones acts in accordance with the following truth: nothing that has ever happened should be regarded as lost for history."[47] Most often, Benjamin claimed, these lost experiences appear not as stories, but as images: "The true picture of the past flits by. The past can be seized only as an image which flashes up at the instant when it can be recognized and is never seen again. [. . .] To articulate the past historically . . . means to seize hold of a memory as it flashes up at a moment of danger."[48] This flash, appearing to the historian who acts as medium, is the first exchange in a potential dialogue between past and present, illuminating what has been previously unseen in both moments. Developing this history can only be carried out in pieces because it is subject to the gaps and omissions typical of memory, and any contrary claim falls into the trap of mastery that historicism falsely claims to achieve. We should, of course, keep in mind the historical context in which Benjamin's essays on historiography were written—namely, Europe poised between the threat of fascist totalitarianism on one hand, and full-blown class revolution on the other. The failure of the latter, however, should not prompt us to treat

these writings as dead objects of study, or to dismiss the relevance for the consideration and writing of history they might have for other times, places, and situations. Indeed, Benjamin saw a kind of proto-materialist historiography being practiced in other ways, at other times, and by others than those who are traditionally thought of as historians.

The Collector of Moments

For Benjamin, one of the key models for the historian seeking to work in the materialist mode was, of course, the *flâneur:* the city stroller given over to looking beyond what was explicitly on offer for observation to something "more" in "the minute and the inconspicuous, the 'scent of a particular threshold or the touch of a particular tile.'"[49] In a sense, these physical encounters resulted from wandering in a diegesis (a city, its things, its history) and locating points where that diegesis might be suddenly expanded to include what has been repressed. These points in the cityscape, Miriam Hansen explains, "become spatial allegories of temporal crossing or historical change," a change or crossing that "harbors a density of meanings, at once habitual and disjunctive, intersecting past and future, history and myth, loss and desire, individual recollection and collective unconscious."[50] Each site becomes a *mise-en-abyme* of history itself, a black hole drawing together what we know and what we don't, what we've experienced as individuals and what we've forgotten as cultures.

Though the *flâneur's* panoramic scanning of the city might at first be construed as a supreme form of scopic mastery, he challenged that very mastery by orienting his eye ultimately toward that which refused to submit to the powers of his gaze. With this point, we can extend our comparison of the *flâneur* and the cinephile that was begun in chapter 2. First, rather than maintaining the prescribed and "proper" distance from what is being observed, the *flâneur,* like the cinephile, positions himself both too close and too far away. With the perceptual distancing afforded by the distracted state, the *flâneur* can spot those striking, evocative points and then move into intimate proximity with them. Miriam Hansen has drawn a connection between this latter posture and certain marginalized forms of cinematic spectatorship, notably the "excessive" mode of reception engaged in by female spectators of classical-era cinema. The extreme sensitivity of female spectators (in contrast to male spectators) to "synaesthetic and kinetic aspects of film," their overidentification with certain characters or situations, their tendency to recall individual images and emotions over plot or even title, and their general "failure to maintain a narratively stabilized distance" mark these female spectators as participating in a "different economy of distance and proximity."[51] We might extend this comparison to include the cinephile. Think, for example of Truffaut's celebration of the CinemaScope screen as enabling the viewer to "get closer"; or recall his own claim that, as a young cinephile, "I felt a tremendous need to enter *into* the films. I sat closer and closer to the screen so I could shut out the theater. I passed up period films, war movies and Westerns because they were more difficult to identify with."[52] He also noted that the best training he had for being a screenwriter was working as a critic and having to provide each film's synopsis; prior to that, he claimed, he couldn't recount plot because he was so drunk on images. Though we might not think of cinephiles as marginalized, it should nevertheless be clear that theirs is not the dominant spectatorial experience. In contrast to the above-described female spectators, cinephiles understand cinema's dominant economy of distance and proximity, but they develop the ability to supplement the dominant economy with another system. Or perhaps it is the other way around: the cinephile quickly learns the dominant economy of distancing, but refuses to abandon the less proper economy of proximity that marks his or her initial experience of the movies. Jonathan Rosenbaum has offered a vivid account of this initial experience of "inappropriate" proximity to a film, one that he, as a professional film critic, clearly still experiences alongside his more appropriate posture.

The principal moment I'm left with [from *I Married a Witch* (1942)] is a shot of two smoky essences in bottles, the sound of dry autumn leaves rustling through a chill night wind, and the voices of Cecil Kellaway and Veronica Lake, father and daughter, conversing from their adjacent bottles. Most of this has to do with Veronica Lake's deep, husky voice: a smoky spirit whose name and form collectively conjured up a feminine aura of water, vapour, air, smoke and flesh at the same time; a floating dreamboat that any boy of six would be proud to be married to.[53]

For Benjamin, another important model of the materialist historian appears with the positional shift that takes place when marginalized sites are encountered by the *flâneur*. Tom Gunning, summarizing Benjamin, writes that the *flâneur*'s "leisurely observation," undertaken with a certain "epistemological confidence," is disrupted when he encounters something or someone that he cannot read because it does not "conform to any established typology."[54] This provocative illegibility, Walter Benjamin argues, pushes the *flâneur* into one of two alternative positions: either he loses his detached individuality and is swallowed by the crowd, becoming a *badaud* (gawker), one of the city's unthinking horde, dumb before the spectacle;[55] or else he actively investigates what he cannot read so as to render it legible like everything else in his gaze, and he thus becomes an amateur detective, a role that puts his gaze back on the road to absorption.[56] For the cinephile, however, such encounters provoke not anxiety, but rather intense pleasure, and instead of being either paralyzed into passive illiteracy (suggesting sudden incompetence as a visual reader) or active hermeneutic investigation (suggesting an intended "meaning" behind what is seen), the cinephile suddenly becomes another important Benjaminian figure: the collector. Paul Willemen confirms, "the notion of collecting is not a bad analogy" for cinephiliac moments in that "you are talking about discrete objects, moments, which are being serialised in your mind into collections, which is how Walter Benjamin talked about it. In the end, perhaps, the moment of cinephilia has to do with the serialisation of moments of revelation."[57] Though he makes this link, Willemen does not explore what is, for this study, the more important implication—the collector's status as alternative historian.

According to Benjamin, there are two aspects to the collector's activity. First of all, in the same way that the *flâneur* resisted the utilitarian layout of the city, the collector rejects dominant definitions of both the use and exchange value of commodities. Indeed, he or she is drawn precisely to what has been put out of circulation or has been marginalized as meaningless. Like the cinephile, who fetishizes discrete moments outside of their function in any system of narrative, character, or style (or especially those moments which have no such function), the true collector, Benjamin writes, "detaches the object from its functional relations"; he liberates "things from the drudgery of being useful."[58] After the collector rescues objects from the cultural trap in which they are caught, and which circumscribes their uses and meanings, he then brings them into another web of meanings, associations, and values. In doing so, the collector carries out an act of historical destruction and reconstruction. Like the process initiated by the photographer with the click of the camera shutter, the collector wrenches an object from the context that gives it meaning. He then initiates a process of historical (re)construction by placing it into a new, partly developed context—one consisting of values and meaning unrecognized by dominant functional relations. This insertion into a new order, Benjamin explained, "is a grand attempt to overcome the wholly irrational character of the object's mere presence at hand through its integration into a new, expressly devised historical system: the collection."[59]

Benjamin elaborated the relationship between the collector and the historian in his complex 1937 essay on Edward Fuchs, who was a collector, significantly, of images (caricatures and erotica).[60] The activity of collecting, Benjamin believed, is a proto-historical materialist act because of the ways in which it challenges historicism's claim to objectivity and control, to being the arbiter of value and meaning of events and experiences of the past. For beyond historicism's order, the collector (like the historical materialist, or Klee's *Angelus Novus*) sees disorder: "Perhaps the most deeply hidden motive of the person who collects can be described this way: he takes up the struggle against dispersion. Right from the start, the great collector is struck by the confusion, by the scatter, in which things of the world are found."[61] Benjamin compares the canon into which the collector organizes her treasured objects to that of the *mémoire involuntaire* in that both represent a kind of "productive disorder."[62] Furthermore, Benjamin identified collecting as another activity that refuses the dominant economy of proximity and distance regarding commodities. "Collecting is a form of practical memory," Benjamin wrote, "and of all the profane manifestations of 'nearness' it is the most binding."[63]

An analogous description may be applied to the cinephile open to cinephiliac moments: like the *flâneur*, ignoring norms of distance and proximity, she scans panoramically beyond what has been ordered and organized for viewing and locates instead the unorganized—the contingent, aleatory, ephemeral element, or what Malraux called the highlight in the chaos. Certain of these elements register with a peculiar force, like that of an involuntary memory, suggesting a clear but uncertain significance. Most often, these encounters register in a sensuous way, and Benjamin notes this shift in his descriptions: "Possession and having are allied with the tactile, and stand in a certain opposition to the optical. Collectors are beings with tactile instincts. Moreover, with the recent turn away from naturalism, the primacy of the optical that was determinate for the previous [i.e., nineteenth] century has come to an end. The flâneur optical, the collector tactile."[64] Of course, the cinephile collects not tangible objects that can literally be held in one's hand (coins, buttons, salt and pepper shakers, etc.), but rather he collects something intangible: memories of image moments. As Jean-Louis Leutrat has summarized it: "The cinephile joins together the spirit of the collector and the competence of the connoisseur, but a connoisseur who would collect only in his memory."[65] But even these intangible image-moments were encountered through a spectatorial activity that shares some of the same features of the trawling activity of the collector. Recall Roger Cardinal's remarks, quoted in chapter 2, that the viewer alert to such contingencies engages in a mode of viewing that "roams over the frame, sensitive to its textures and surfaces—to its ground. This mode may be associated with non-literacy and with habits of looking which are akin to touching. The mobile eye which darts from point to point will tend to clutch at fortuitous details or to collect empathetic impressions of touch sensations."[66]

The cinephile's practice of collecting moments involves aspects of two of the three primary types of collecting activity identified by Susan Pearce and later clarified by John Windsor. The first, Pearce explains, is systematic collecting, wherein "an ostensibly intellectual rationale is followed, and the intention is to collect complete sets which will demonstrate understanding achieved";[67] here, as Windsor clarifies it, systematics is "the construction of a collection of objects in order to represent an ideology."[68] The second is fetish collecting, in which "the objects are dominant" and there is an "obsessive gathering [of] as many items as possible . . . to create the self";[69] in contrast to systematics, fetishism is marked by "the removal of an object from its historical and cultural context and its redefinition in terms of the collector."[70] Thirdly there is souvenir collecting, in which "the individual creates a romantic life-history by selecting and arranging personal memorial material to create what . . . might be called an object autobiography, where the objects are at the service of the autobiographer";[71] in souvenir collecting, Windsor clarifies, "the object is prized for its power to carry the past into the future."[72]

A cinephile's collection of cinephiliac moments shares similarities with the second and third of these types. I have already noted the fetishistic aspect of the cinephile's activity, as well as the point, emphasized by Roger Cardinal, that any cinephile's list of such moments constitutes a self-portrait, a "mirror-image." [73] Further, in contrast to the systematic approach—that would seek to articulate the historically and culturally specific situation from which a collection (or a collected item) emerged in order to illuminate its relationship to a given ideology—the fetishistic approach at least partly detaches the collected object from its originating context. Or rather, when encountered, the fetish item appears as already partly detached from that context, its meaning and function only partly secured by it. This is certainly the case with cinephiliac moments: the cinephile encounters them as part of a larger context in which they are contained (a given film or film scene), but experiences them as coming unmoored from the security of that context. Rather than seeking to re-secure these image-moments in their originating context via some critical activity that would recover the ideology from which they emerged, the cinephile wants to maintain their detachment from the larger context, or even move them partly into other contexts, for this is the surest way to maintain the pleasure of the original encounter.

In addition, cinephiliac moments function also as souvenirs because they reside in the memory of the cinephile. As an image-moment that is encounterable by any viewer, cinephiliac moments exist of course in their film of origin; but as part of a cinephile's collection, they exist only in the memory of that particular film lover. Outside of that context, these moments exist, but without the intensity and not as part of any collection. Furthermore, cinephiliac moments possess the souvenir's power "to carry the past into the future." This sense of the collected item as a nodal point of interaction between past and present echoes Walter Benjamin's claim that historical materialism "supplies a unique experience with the past"—one mobilized by the desire of the collector in the present engaging with specifics (items, images) from the past.

The cinephile's collection, then, like all collections, functions as a kind of archive out of which one might construct a new history—just as the collection of films at Henri Langlois's Cinémathèque Française functioned as the archive out of which the *Cahiers* critics conceived a new history of cinema, one based on individual filmmakers. The question then becomes: Precisely how does one go about constructing a history out of a collection of cinephiliac moments? Indeed, for the most part, the collector has been regarded, at best, as a kind of primitive historian. For example, in their study, *Film History: Theory and Practice,* Robert C. Allen and Douglas Gomery make a clear distinction between the activities of the collector and those of the historian. "What is a historian?" they ask.

At the most elementary level it is someone who studies the past. Obviously this definition is too broad, since not everyone who studies the past is a historian. For example, collectors often possess extraordinarily detailed knowledge about objects from the past . . . , but the collector's possession of and knowledge about historical objects do not in themselves make him or her a historian. [. . .] The historian's study of the past seeks to explain why a particular set of historical circumstances came about and with what consequences.[74]

What the collector confuses, it would seem, is the distinction that historians must make between *a fact of the past* and *a historical fact*. Allen and Gomery elaborate the difference:

Everything that has ever happened is a fact of the past, and thus is potentially, at least, a source of historical data. However, history could not possibly consist of all the facts of the past, even those facts of which traces have survived. They would be so numerous as to be meaningless. A fact of the past becomes an historical fact when a historian decided to use that fact in constructing a historical analysis.[75]

   To a certain extent, of course, Allen and Gomery are correct. But it is precisely these facts of the past (or, as Keith Jenkins has termed them more provocatively, *traces of the past*),[76] ones that seem never to rise to the level of historical facts, that are overlooked, dismissed, or taken for granted, and that the materialist historian is drawn to. If no discourse is developed out of facts of the past, or if no discourse can make use of any of them, then they fail to become historical facts. But ultimately, it is the discourse by which such facts will be employed that determines whether they can make this transition from fact of the past to historical fact. For Allen and Gomery, one historical discourse is clearly privileged above others: Realism—a discourse that "consists of describing . . . the observable layer of reality, [and] also the workings of the *generative mechanisms* that produced the observable event."[77] This history "insists that historical explanations can and should be tested by reference to both historical evidence and to other, competing explanations."[78] The emphasis, here again, is on scientist processes of explanation and interpretation: while the realist theory of history acknowledges that events are massively overdetermined, and while it seeks to investigate as many of these determinants as is reasonably possible, the focus is still on constructing a cause-and-effect sequence of narrative events, emphasizing certain figures and forces as of greater or lesser significance.[79] In some variant or another, this realist historiographic practice as defined by Allen and Gomery largely dominates film studies.
   One way of imagining an alternative to this realist practice can be achieved if we shift the terms slightly. Virtually all histories written in the field of film studies are rational histories; what I am imagining, via Kracauer and Benjamin, might best be described as an *irrational* history—a historical practice that focuses on discarded or ignored facts of the past and, in investigating them, employs research methods and representational strategies that are anathema to rational historiography. In his critique of the dominant historiographic method, Hayden White has similarly proposed engaging with experimental forms. White characterizes dominant historical methods as archaic, explaining that, while historians routinely describe their discipline as "a combination of science and art, they generally mean that it is a combination of late-nineteenth-century social science and mid-nineteenth-century art"[80]—that is, "a combination of *romantic* art on the one hand and of *positivistic* science on

the other."[81] For the past century or more, due in part to "the outmoded conceptions of objectivity" that characterize their methods,[82] historians have been "locked into conceptions of art and science which both artists and scientists [of the nineteenth century] had progressively to abandon if they were to understand the changing world of internal and external perceptions offered to them by the historical process itself."[83] Though White acknowledges some interest on the part of historians in developments in the social sciences, he sees no such interest in developments in the arts; rather, there has been the resolute commitment to realism. "There have been no significant attempts at surrealistic, expressionistic, or existentialist historiography in this [i.e., the twentieth] century (except by novelists and poets themselves)"[84]—no engagement, that is, with those representational methods that embrace the irrational as well as the rational. The cinephiliac moment demands such an experimental historical approach, for it is where rational historical methods come up short, and where film's "irrational power," to use Bazin's phrase, is felt most powerfully.

But if we take Benjamin's and Kracauer's claim that filmic details disrupt realist historiographic practice, and further that they provide the doorway to an alternative practice, we cannot escape the irony that film history, committed as it has been to realism, has refused to acknowledge (much less embrace) the implications of what its own object of study offers. A cinephiliac history, on the other hand, embraces the implications of Benjamin's and Kracauer's insight, and uses it to imagine and to put into practice another way of writing cinema history.

The project proposed by Antoine de Baecque and Thierry Frémaux gives some indication of what a cinephiliac history might be. The goal of this history, de Baecque and Frémaux explain, is far-reaching:

> to hold together, within the same analysis, the film and the life organized around it. In methodological terms, this cultural history of cinema requires that the view of the film be anchored in all the diversity of its possible sources. The film is placed in a situation of being seen in the context of the texts which receive it; of the ceremonial gestures which guide the watching of it; of the political and intellectual events which direct our comprehension of it; of the social upheavals which alter its meaning; and of some many long-neglected historical registers, neglected not in their specificity but in their dialogue with the film itself.[85]

This project stands for de Baecque and Frémaux as a kind of corrective to so much that has passed for film history in recent years. Beginning in the early 1970s, they argue, film history was taken away from cinephiles. First, the work of scholars like Marco Ferro and Pierre Sorlin shifted away from the concept of history *of* cinema to the concept of history *and* cinema, their goal being to show how the values of a given culture or society were mirrored in its films.

In spite of what was learned from these studies, de Baecque and Frémaux complain, "The deformations of such reflections served to construct a discipline which risked the absence of cinema itself."[86] More recently, even with the return to a concern with the history of cinema, focus has often fallen on members of different cultural identity positions and the ways in which they read or make sense of the films they encounter. But too often in these studies, cinema is just one more cultural product in a sociological analysis, its unique and specific characteristics ignored. "What is needed today," de Baecque and Frémaux write, "is to reintroduce cinema into historical discipline, to recover the materiality of the source, even the pleasure of the gaze."[87] Their call, then, is not simply for a history of cinephilia, but a history of cinema emerging from and modeled on the cinephile's own relationship to the object of his love.

Such a history, they write, would by definition be a "reflexive" history, for rather than effectively repressing one's cinephilic identity in the way that Metz deemed necessary, and thus restricting oneself to addressing the social, generalizable elements of cinephilia, the cinephile historian would mobilize *all* the spectatorial experiences of the film worshiper in his temple: the collective and the individual, the public and the private, the shared and the secret, the intellectual and the emotional. For de Baecque and Frémaux, the model is the collector/connoisseur eulogized by Benjamin, one whose position "falls halfway between the passionate practitioner and the intellectual," one who holds both "the proximity proper to the desire to tell a story, and the distance necessary to write a history."[88] Starting from the combination of public and private, the result would further be an intertextual history, one drawing freely from and mixing various voices and discourses, mirroring as it does the concatenation of forces that produced cinephilia, as well as the cinema itself. De Baecque and Frémaux argue, "The historian must be literary critic, anthropologist, sociologist, political historian, and a cinephile him- or herself." These shifting roles, as well as the variety of sources drawn from and combined, leads inevitably to "very different ways of writing history."[89]

The world of the film is not closed. It welcomes, it aspires to, alterity. Often the film is nothing more than an impure mediation, the necessary element, bubbling with culture, which leads from one source to another. This dialogue is important, because this is how the materiality of this history takes shape, which we could call the dense or compacted source. Even if it entails provocation, we must contend that while all sources are not born free and equal, nevertheless they all have the right to the same consideration, to being dissolved into a continuous but heterogenous whole.[90]

6 A Cinephiliac History

In the course of reminding us that the cinema's origins and its history are "quite clearly a function of how we define what actually constitutes cinema," Thomas Elsaesser has encouraged the exploration of what he calls "counterfactual" histories—that is, histories that would mine undeveloped or unconsidered points of entry into the cinema as object of study.[1] He argues that, in starting this project, the historian is wise to keep in mind the signs that appear at railroad crossings in rural France: "Un tren peut en cacher un autre" ("One Train May Be Hiding Another"). In other words, Elsaesser suggests, the historian can easily become so focused on the historical discourse in front of him that he fails to see the other discourse of history that is passing immediately behind, showing through only intermittently, in flashes. Elsaesser explains:

Such a counter-factual conception of history is not the opposite of a "real" history, but a view prepared to think into history all those histories that might have been, or might still be. . . . Film history is, strictly speaking, inconceivable if we cannot find in it the appropriate space that recognizes the cinema's place in our dreams as well as in our industries, but also its role in giving substance to all kinds of other possible universes and alternative histories which human beings have imagined and tried to make real.[2]

It could be argued that the history of film historiography has been an ongoing project of locating these alternate points of entry, nearly all of which began with some individual's experience of the movies, often in which that person watches differently, notices something, and becomes curious about what he or she sees. Thus begins the construction of a "counter-factual" history that may ultimately become part of the "real" history.

Cinephiliac moments are more points of entry, clues perhaps to another history flashing through the cracks of those histories we already know. A cinephiliac history—a history developed out of these cinephiliac moments—would then be another "counter-factual history," one that might eventually be folded into our overall conception of the forces and effects that constitute the entirety of the history of cinema. This is the question that must be addressed: How might one "develop" (I use the filmic term deliberately) one of these moments so that the resulting discourse maintains and even extends the initial experience, and at the same time constitutes part of a history in that it imparts information, knowledge, and insight? This question was posed more generally by Roland Barthes nearly fifty years ago, in the closing paragraphs of *Mythologies,* where he described "two equally extreme" critical methods:

either to posit a reality which is entirely permeable to history, and ideologize; or, conversely, to posit a reality which is *ultimately* impenetrable, irreducible, and, in this case, poeticize. . . . We constantly drift between the object and its demystification, powerless to render its wholeness. For if we penetrate the object, we liberate it but we destroy it; and if we acknowledge its full weight, we respect it, but we restore it to a state which is still mystified.[3]

At present, scholarship in the discipline of film studies is dominated by the former critical method, one in which the scholar produces knowledge about the object of study; more importantly, film scholars are suspicious of the latter method, refusing to proceed from or even to acknowledge their own experiences of the thing in question. The period of grand theory, which saw film studies secure its position as an academic discipline, was marked by a cinephobia that resulted in film academics seeing as their responsibility the systematic undermining and exposure of virtually all of the most basic cine-

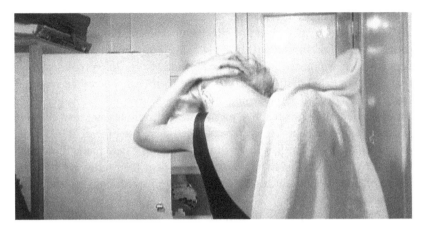

matic pleasures—this in spite of the fact that the majority of these academics were devout cinephiles. Films were "decoded" such that all pleasures could be explained away and the film experience could be captured and contained. With these critical moves, academic cinephiles gained a world (or a discipline they could call their own), but they lost their cinephiliac souls.

On the other hand, film studies is haunted by the latter method, which manifested itself most explicitly in *photogénie*, a concept and critical writing approach that did a wonderful job of emphasizing the mysterious, the impenetrable in the cinema. But this critical method fell short in the sense that it did not produce knowledge about its object, only registered its effects (and primarily on particular viewers).[4] Traces of this method are to be found in Bazin's writings on realism and, even more powerfully, the *Cahiers* critics on *mise-en-scène*. This critical method must be recovered but, importantly, it must not simply take the place of the former: rather, the two methods must be reconciled so that the resulting discourse simultaneously achieves the goals of both approaches: the production of knowledge along with (or via) an extending of the registering of effect.

Counter Histories

Imagining a way to construct a history out of cinephiliac moments, we find a productive model in another example of counter-factual history: new historicism. In their collection of essays, *Practicing New Historicism*, Catherine Gallagher and Stephen Greenblatt describe the goals, impulses, and desires of new historicism, a practice they describe as a counterhistory: one that "opposes itself not only to dominant narratives, but also to prevailing modes of historical

thought and methods of research."[5] The primary motive behind these scholars' shift was an urgent desire to reignite their passion for the authors and texts
to whom they had committed themselves, for those canonical authors "had
begun to seem exhausted"[6]—at least for the kind of close interpretive readings
that had dominated first New Criticism and then High Theory. In reality, it
was not the canonical authors and texts that were worn out, but rather it was
the dominant critical approach—"pick a passage from a literary text, examine
it closely, and show how an entire representational system is disclosed in its
narrow compass"—that had lost its force.[7] Finding a new method of study
seemed the best way for these scholars to reorient themselves vis-á-vis the
works of literature in which they had so much invested, both professionally
and personally.

In addition, after years of dominance by Theory, these scholars felt the
impulse to again read literary texts against and through the historical contexts
of their production—to see these texts not just as exceptional, but also as typical of the cultural/historical place and time from which they emerged. Following Clifford Geertz's model of treating culture in its broadest sense as a text
to be read, the new historicists begin their process—of aesthetic reinvigoration
through historical investigation —not through the literary texts themselves,
but through "ordinary," nonliterary texts from the same historical period.
These documents alert them to previously unknown contextual forces, and
they then return to the literary texts and examine them through this new
historical frame. Most often, they explain, their approach is to mine counter-
histories "that make apparent the slippages, cracks, fault lines, and surprising
absences in the monumental structures that dominated a more traditional historicism."[8]

New historicism's representative point of entry—the one most commonly
offered by these nonliterary historical texts—is the anecdote: a quintessentially
counterhistorical form, one that can be "counterpoised against more ambi-
tiously comprehensive historical narratives."[9] As the scholar goes about her
research in the historical archives, she encounters some anecdote—some brief
historical account—that registers in an intense way as particularly enigmatic,
mysterious, puzzling. Its "meaning" is unclear—that is, the event described
is only partly legible—and this is part of its mysterious appeal. But just as
important is the fact that the anecdote is suggestive of some meaning, one
that some absent historical context, hovering just out of view, might restore.
Gallagher and Greenblatt cite as an important precursor for this experience
Michel Foucault's "Lives of Infamous Men," a book consisting of brief, odd
anecdotes about nonfamous individuals, all culled from historical records. For
example:

Mathurin Milan, placed in the hospital of Charenton, 31 August 1707: "His mad-
ness was always to hide from his family, to lead an obscure life in the country, to
have actions at law, to lend usuriously and without security, to lead his feeble
mind down unknown paths, and to believe himself capable of the greatest em-
ployments." [10]

The selection of each anecdote, Foucault explained, "was guided by nothing
more substantial than my taste, my pleasure, an emotion, laughter, surprise, a
certain dread, or some other feeling whose intensity I might have trouble justifying." [11] Initially, Foucault's instinct was to subject these anecdotes to analysis, but "the primary intensities" of his initial encounter were sapped by such
analysis, and he was left unsatisfied. Since it was the intensity that fascinated
him and that he wanted to preserve, he concluded that it was best to leave the
anecdotes in the very form in which he had discovered them. Thus, what his
book consists of is a collection of these anecdotes, drawn together as the raw
material of some as-yet-undeveloped alternative historical discourse.

For the new historicist critics, too, the historical anecdote is a new source
of aesthetic experience. Indeed, what the enigmatic qualities of these historical anecdotes may be said to produce is an effect of literariness in a nonliterary
text (at the level of narration, not necessarily of language)—and this effect is
one of intense pleasure. But where the new historicists depart from Foucault's
impulse is that they set it as their task to recover the missing historical context
that will make their anecdotes fully legible, and with that information they
return to some literary text of the same period and locate evidence of that
context operating there as well. [12] But here, their project stalls: aesthetic experience is again set aside in favor of ideology, and the result is cultural studies
as usual. It seems that the unconscious hope of these scholars is that some of
the aesthetic effect produced by the prompting anecdote will trail along into
the analysis of the literary text, but what is most often highlighted instead is
the absence of that effect. The anecdote, which teeters on the verge of full
meaning without falling into it, is a kind of mystery, one resembling in its
effect a moment like the one in the short story "Silver Blaze," where Sherlock
Holmes refers to "the curious incident of the dog in the nighttime." When his
host replies, "But the dog did nothing in the nighttime," Holmes answers,
"That is the curious incident." If a moment such as this produces a flush of
intense pleasure, its explanation is always a bit of a disappointment, for it inevitably deflates the number of imagined potential meanings, settling comfortably and unambiguously on just one.

So with regards to new historicism, what I am interested in is not its critics' application of newfound historical information to texts; but rather I am

interested in the anecdote as a form and these critics' experience of it, for both are relevant to my consideration of cinephiliac moments.

1. *Revelatory Experience.* The new historicists describe their experience of the anecdotes as epiphanic in much the same way that cinephiles describe their encounters with their privileged moments, and furthermore, the new historicists also regularly describe their experiences in filmic or cinematic terms. As David Simpson has described it, new historicism "emphasize[s] the cinematic bringing to life of the past—avowedly 'representational' but giving the effect of the real. . . . Like a slice of movie footage, the new historicist past was wholly there and yet not there, and not implicated in any pattern beyond that of its own telling, except by loose association with something in the teller's own place and time that was itself resistant to full knowledge."[13] Citing Ezra Pound, Gallagher and Greenblatt designate theirs as "'the method of the Luminous Detail,' whereby we attempt to isolate significant or 'interpreting detail' from the mass of traces that have survived in the archive."[14] This labeling of these anecdotes as "luminous details"—details of light—is significant in its relation to the cinephiliac moment.

2. *The Real.* Gallagher and Greenblatt emphasize that they are most often taken by those anecdotes that possess "what William Carlos Williams terms 'the strange phosphorus of the life.'"[15] That is, these anecdotes provide a unique experience of access to the real. Out of an enormous archive of documents, one strikes the scholar with a particular urgency as the representation of a prior reality; the close relationship between the anecdote and the real it refers to is suddenly and unexpectedly *felt.* As Joel Fineman further explains, the anecdote

is the literary form or genre that uniquely refers to the real. This is not as trivial an observation as might first appear. It reminds us, on the one hand, that the anecdote has something literary about it. . . . On the other hand, it reminds us also that there is something about the anecdote that exceeds its literary status, and this excess is precisely that which gives the anecdote its pointed, referential access to the real.[16]

I have discussed at length, after Bazin, the ways in which film's unique and privileged relationship to the reality it represents affects viewers, and Willemen describes the cinephiliac moment in precisely these terms: "that dimension of the real which shines through" the cinematic structure that contains it.[17] The filmic quality of the new historicist anecdote, and its links to the reality it so forcefully represents, may be summed up in one phrase by Gallagher and Greenblatt: "The frisson of the anecdotal rupture, the flash of the undiscernible real. . . . "[18]

3. *The Way of Looking.* The reading process by which the new historicist

locates these provocative anecdotes is remarkably similar to the panoramic perception mode of film viewing employed by the cinephile. Rather than being focused in advance on some particular bit of information she is looking for, the new historicist trolls, *flâneur*-like, through the archive, on alert for whatever curiosity might pique her interest. As the most adept of historical readers, these scholars, like the *flâneur,* are on alert for that which cannot be easily read, that which appears as puzzling, enigmatic, suggestive. Robert Darnton has described the pleasure and potential of this method:

There is no better way, I believe, than to wander through the archives. One can hardly read a letter from the Old Regime without coming up against surprises. . . . What was proverbial wisdom to our ancestors is completely opaque to us. Open any eighteenth-century book of proverbs and you will find entries such as: "He who is snotty, let him blow his nose." When we cannot get a proverb, or a joke, or a poem, we know we are on to something. By picking at the document where it is most opaque, we may be able to unravel an alien system of meaning. The thread might even lead to a strange and wonderful world view.[19]

The cinephile engaged in a panoramic mode of perception is on alert for moments, details, gestures that excite his imagination in similar ways. These encounters, as Paul Willemen has summarized it, fix on what "escapes existing networks of critical discourse and theoretical frameworks."[20] These points of resistance may also be the doorway into some "alien system of meaning."

4. *The Challenge to History.* The anecdote disrupts traditional discourses of history and criticism in the same manner as the cinephiliac moment or the filmic detail as described by Benjamin and Kracauer. The anecdote is not quite a historical episode, but more like a historical aside. It may be connected to any number of larger events and historical narratives, but it cannot comfortably be contained by any one of them. As Gallagher and Greenblatt explain, "the miniature completeness of the anecdote necessarily interrupts the continuous flow of larger histories; . . . [it is] an interruption that lets one sense that there is something—the 'real'—outside of the historical narrative. The anecdote thereby exposes history."[21] That is, it exposes historicism—i.e., realist historiography—as the selective construction of the past. In contrast to the historiography that constructs history but effaces the process of its construction, partly by offering a closed and complete discourse, Fineman writes,

the anecdote is the literary form that *lets history happen* by virtue of the way it introduces an opening into the teleological, and therefore timeless, narration of beginning, middle, and end. The anecdote produces the effect of the real, the occurrence of the contingency, by establishing an event as an event within and yet without the framing context of historical successivity.[22]

That the anecdote "lets history happen" resonates with the claim that the cinephiliac moment is less that which has been orchestrated than that which has been captured and recorded; the presence of this contingency produces an effect of the real, and in doing so disrupts realist narrative's closed, controlling discourse—be it cinematic or historical. Gallagher and Greenblatt explain the historiographic implications of their interest in the anecdote: "Approached sideways, through the eccentric anecdote, 'history' would cease to be a way of stabilizing texts; it would instead become part of their enigmatic being."[23]

What I want to make clear here is that the new historicist anecdote is the precise verbal-discursive equivalent of a cinephiliac moment. It thus offers itself to us as a form for how to use cinephiliac moments to write a counter-factual history. I am not suggesting that we recover anecdotes from the past in the same way that the new historicists do; rather, I am suggesting that we com-pose our own anecdotes—cinephiliac anecdotes. These anecdotes would begin with the cinephiliac moment and expand outward into a variety of related contexts—personal, historical, critical. By composing our own cinephiliac an-ecdotes, we may find a way to extend the experience of the cinephiliac moment (far enough, but perhaps not too far), while at the same time engaging with history via a form that, like the filmic detail itself, challenges the dominant discourses of historicism. This is, of course, just one possible strategy for writ-ing with cinephiliac moments.

Paul Willemen has said of cinephiliac moments, "These are moments which, when encountered in a film, spark something which then produces the energy and the desire to write, to find formulations to convey something about the intensity of that spark."[24] For this reason, film magazines that have fea-tured such cinephiliac discourse have been perhaps less important for those who read them than for those who write in them. "It is as if cinephilia de-mands a gestural outlet in writing: if not in magazines then on index cards or in list making. The excess experienced needs an extra, physical ritual, a gesture, in addition to watching and talking."[25] My goal here is to imagine how the "fanzine" aspects of this writing might be incorporated into, or united with, scholarly writing. The goal, to paraphrase Roland Barthes, is to "subject the objects of knowledge and discussion—as in any art—no longer [just] to an instance of truth, but [also] to a consideration of *effects*."[26]

The Cinephiliac Anecdote

But write *what* exactly—or rather, write *how*? Several strategies suggest them-selves as methods by which such anecdotes might be generated. As I enumerate these strategies, I will have occasion to refer to other writers about cinema who have employed similar strategies—some wittingly, some perhaps unwittingly.

1. *Metonymy.* Because they are narratives, anecdotes operate via metonymy; in addition, filmic details have been described as possessing a metonymic potential.

Like Willemen, Fredric Jameson has described the impulse to write, and also suggested some methods of how. Roland Barthes, Jameson explains, "thought certain kinds of writing—perhaps we should say, certain kinds of *sentences*—to be *scriptible,* because they made you wish to write further yourself; they stimulated imitation, and promised a pleasure in combining language that had little enough to do with the notation of new ideas." But even more than writing, Jameson claims, "what is scriptible indeed is the visual. . . . "; and what is scriptible in the visual is that which is "call[ed] into being by suggestion and by a kind of contamination. We don't write about these things, it is not a metaphorical representation that the sensory pretext summons but rather something related by affinity, that prolongs the content of the object in another, more tenuous form, as though to prolong a last touch with the very fingertips." [27]

In these lines, Jameson emphasizes again the sensory aspect of such visual moments, especially the tactile aspect of the way they are located and experienced, and he also suggests a way that we might begin writing. "We don't write *about* these things," Jameson says; instead, we write with them or from them. We are not searching in our writing for "a metaphorical representation"—not *meaning* in any traditional sense—but rather a way to extend the experience itself, to mimic it or simulate it, or rather, to tell a story about it or with it, but in another form. The first move in writing from such a moment, then, is not metaphoric, but metonymic. With this claim, Jameson echoes another statement by Roland Barthes. In an essay on Proust, *"Longtemps, je me suis couché de bonne heure . . . ,"* Barthes explained,

Metaphor sustains any discourse which asks: "What is it? What does it mean?"—the real question of any essay. Metonymy, on the contrary, asks another question: "What can follow what I say? What can be engendered by the episode I am telling?" this is the Novel's question. . . . [Each] incident in life can give rise either to a commentary (an interpretation) or to an affabulation which imagines the narrative *before* and *after:* to interpret is to take the Critical path, to argue theory . . . to think incidents and impressions, to describe their development, is on the contrary to weave a narrative, however loosely, however gradually.[28]

The anecdote, being a narrative form, naturally employs metonymy. But the goal is not simply to trade metaphor for metonymy, but to engage with both. What Barthes himself imagined was a "third form," one that refused to settle decisively on just one of these approaches, but instead sought to combine aspects of the two methods in the same way that he sought to combine the critical acts of ideologizing and poeticizing. Academic film studies, as I have stressed, has consisted almost exclusively of the former method, and film scholars are hard-pressed to imagine a way to proceed critically from any filmic moment or detail other than to interpret it.[29] But cinephiliac moments resist such conventional interpretation.

In *Camera Lucida*, his book on photography, Barthes described the *punctum* as possessing a "power of expansion. This power is often metonymic."[30] Roger Cardinal has echoed this point, describing Barthes's manner of reflecting on third meanings and *puncta* as a mode of reading that implies a "tactile-metonymic dimension as much as a visual-metaphoric one."[31] So, it is perhaps what Barthes called *puncta* or "third meanings" that, more than anything else, demand this "third form" of writing; but to avoid falling directly into the trap of metaphor (hermeneutics), one must postpone interpretation and begin instead with metonymy. Let me offer two examples of this method in action.

In the essay on one of her privileged moments—the scene from *Blade Runner* in which Pris suddenly somersaults toward the camera (described in chapter 2, pp. 32–33)—Lesley Stern makes precisely this metonymic move: Stern acts as an advanced collector of cinephiliac moments, allowing the first moment to associatively trigger "a cascade of somersaulting images,"[32] from the woman acrobat flipping across the courtroom in *Adam's Rib*, to Gena Rowlands's back-flip off the swimming pool diving board in *Love Streams*. These moments are linked to one another not by metaphor—that is, not by any similarity at the level of the signified—but by metonymy: their similarity at the level of the signifier. Once grouped, this mini-collection then leads Stern to a consideration of the way in which the somersault "embodies a certain cinematic potentiality, that it may be a conduit through which we can begin to think about . . . the cinema as a medium of motion with the capacity to embody time, to temporalize bodies."[33] Metonymy leads to new metaphor, a new way of understanding the "meaning" of the moment of Pris's somersault and its relationship to cinema in general.

Further, Stern's writing is an extension of the cinephile's spectatorial habits, for not only does she watch a film panoramically, waiting for a cinephiliac moment; but when she encounters one and starts to write, she maintains the multifaceted posture of the cinephile before the screen. In considering her subjective moment and developing it through writing into the realm of knowledge, she not only opts for proper critical distance and contemplation—the absorbed state appropriate for the writing of critical essays—but also scans panoramically beyond these limitations or proprieties, embracing also distracted association and sensuous proximity. With this essay, Stern is, in effect, extending a viewing practice into a writing practice.

We can thus begin to establish a set of oppositions:

Ideologize—Poeticize
Metaphor—Metonymy
Signified—Signifier
Abstract—Concrete
Hermeneutics—Heuretics

The critical move of ideologizing is linked with metaphor because both approaches involve uncovering and articulating a text's meaning, its signified. Poeticizing, on the other hand, means extending the effect of the text (or moment) via association, a move that involves sliding at the level of the signifier (of language or image). In contrast to the abstraction of metaphor, poetic metonymy works via the concrete (in the example above, a somersault) in a process whose goal is not hermeneutics (the interpretation or decoding of that which has been encoded), but its antonym, heuretics—which is not *re*covery, but rather a process of *dis*covery ("Eureka! I have found it!").[34]

Another example of metonymic association at work in the service of heuretics can be found in Robert B. Ray's *The Avant-Garde Finds Andy Hardy*. Ray proposes using the vanguard arts as models for creating an avant-garde critical writing practice, one that engages specifically with the film viewing experiences ignored or repressed by dominant scholarly practice. In one chapter, entitled "Roland Barthes: Fetishism as Research Strategy," Ray describes an assignment in which students are to take Barthes's essay on the third meaning as "a new kind of research derived from photographic logic." His instructions:

Select a detail from a movie. The detail you choose should resemble those discussed in "The Third Meaning": it should not be obviously symbolic, and the purpose to which you put it should not be the filmmaker's obvious intention. Follow this detail wherever it leads and report your findings. Your goal is to propose a new way of understanding the movie you discuss.[35]

One student begins with the bowler hats that are ubiquitous in Fritz Lang's *M*, but explores the bowler's other meaning: "*The Encyclopedia Brittanica* reveals that while bowling has existed in almost every culture, bowling *at pins* originated in Germany, specifically as a religious rite: placed at one end of a runway, the pins represented the Heide (the "heathen"); knocking them down purged the community of evil and sin."[36] Beginning with a filmic detail, and sliding metonymically at the level of language, at the level of the signifier, the student is brought to a new metaphorical reading of the film. "In *M*, Schranker's men chase Peter Lorre down the *alleys* of the city where he (one of the *Heide*) must *hide*. M portrays a city cleansing itself of its greatest sin. The entire society, both outlaw and official, combines to topple Lorre, thereby driving from its midst one of what the movie's original title called *The Murderers among Us*."[37] Here, the student has postponed metaphor until he has given himself over to metonymic exploration, which takes him in directions that metaphor alone cannot.

If the cinephiliac moment is the starting point, and this starting point has a variety of features, how can one know in what direction to proceed? One cannot know for sure in advance what direction will be fruitful, so the best answer might be this: intuition. If this seems too unsystematic or "unreasonable" an answer, we might remember what Stanley Cavell has said about intuition. Contrasting intuition with hypothesis (and all the scientist processes implied by that term), Cavell explains that he begins with some intuition about a text (e.g., a film, a Shakespeare play), and then he explores it unsystematically, engaging with his feelings as well as his processes of thought in order to learn something. While hypothesis asks us to predict in advance what the outcome of our investigation will be, intuition asks nothing more than that we have a feeling that some direction, some line of inquiry, will yield some payoff in the form of knowledge about the text we are examining. As for the results, "Both intuitions and hypotheses require what may be called confirmation, but differently," Cavell explains. While a hypothesis requires evidence, and "must say what constitutes its evidence," an intuition, "does not require or tolerate evidence, but rather, let us say, understanding of a particular sort."[38] Intuition does come with a demand, however; namely, that we make our intuition intelligible, to ourselves and to others. We can do that only by following our intuition to the point of tuition—to the point where our intuition teaches us something. The goal of the cinephile is, similarly, to bring our interest in (or our intuition about) a particular filmic moment to the point where we can learn from it, or with it. It is also relevant that the term "intuition" implies proceeding by a "feeling": not separating off emotion from reason, but rather extending experience and bringing it into contact with a thought process that is not completely systematized.

Film historian Pierre Sorlin has made a similar point about the value of intuition. When we know too little, it is perfectly acceptable to rely on intuition as a way to get started, but when we know too much, intuition becomes discredited as not rigorous enough, not systematized.[39] As an academically sanctioned discipline, film studies "knows enough" that intuition seems no longer acceptable; yet the discipline's major discourses have not yet found an acceptable way of thinking and writing about phenomena like cinephiliac moments, so an intuitive approach seems not only acceptable, but absolutely necessary. Sorlin is not calling for the return of intuition in the sense of "psychological impressionism in criticism or to a certain kind of idealism of aesthetic discourse, but as a method, a method which functioned when it was impossible to have access to everything."[40] The model, once again, is based on the young *Cahiers* critics, sitting in the dark at the Cinémathèque Française, working with what they had access to. If we cannot truly designate auteurism as a theory or even a hypothesis (it wasn't rigorous enough), we can surely designate it as a powerful intuition those critics had about certain filmmakers—an intuition that paid off.

2. *Personal Memory.* Anecdotes are commonly the recounting of a memory of some personal experience; and cinephiliac moments have been described as possessing the quality of a memory.

Because cinephiliac moments are themselves intensely subjective, bound up perhaps with a personal value of some unrecoverable meaning, writing about such moments will often mobilize personal information. Particularly relevant here is the issue of memory. As Lesley Chow has insisted, our memory of "the specific way things seemed and felt" is "an essential condition of the movies" and the cinephile's relationship with them.[41] In the previous chapter I discussed the complex relationship between memory and the experience of cinephiliac moments, and there are two points to emphasize here. Not only do these encounters exist as quasi-memories, but oftentimes, cinephiliac moments are not identified except upon reflection. Roland Barthes remarked that, most often, the *punctum* does not make itself felt in him until he no longer has the photo in front of him, and for cinephiles, the experience is a similar one. The film critic Gilbert Adair's book *Myths and Memories* makes use of the memory of marginalia—both of moviegoing specifically, and of his life in general—in an interesting and illuminating way. In the second half of the book, Adair offers a collection of 400 memories from his life, "slivers of memory, actually."[42] Though many of these are shared cultural memories, many are strictly personal memories, and all are recounted in a sentence or two (e.g., "I remember owning a gyroscope whose support was a miniature Eiffel Tower"). Here are a few of Adair's memories that are of films or are film-related:

I remember Pierre Clémenti's gold teeth in Buñuel's *Belle de Jour*.

I remember that the poster for *How to Marry a Millionaire* depicted the film's trio of leading actresses (Marilyn Monroe, Betty Grable and Lauren Bacall) vivaciously striding toward us, arm in arm.

I remember the bizarrely curdled appearance of the Red Sea when "divided" by Moses (or Charlton Heston) in Cecil B. DeMille's *The Ten Commandments*.

I remember, in *Lacombe Lucien,* the pungent Southern accent of Pierre Blaise when, asked whether he was pleased with his new plus-fours, he replied, "Pas telle-ment." I also remember that Blaise bought a motorcycle with his fee from the film and was killed soon after when it crashed.

I remember that Graham Greene, uncredited, played a tiny role in Truffaut's *La Nuit américaine.*

Though Adair does not restrict himself to moments from films, but extends himself to memories related to films and film culture, the similarity between his collection of memories and the cinephile's collection of cinephiliac moments —such as those cited in chapter 2—should be obvious. Indeed, these are true screen memories. That is, they are not only about cinema, but they resemble the screen memories Freud's patients reported—striking and memorable, but apparently insignificant. Furthermore, Adair's model is useful for locating cinephiliac moments. One of the easiest ways to locate such encounters is on recollection, scanning panoramically beyond anything linked to plot or theme, and saying to one's self, "I remember _____." For example, I remember how Florence Darel slices a tomato in Eric Rohmer's *A Tale of Springtime*.

These memories recall a list of a dozen or so personal memories offered by Roland Barthes in the entry in his autobiography titled "Pause: Anamnesis." Here are two:

A bat came into the bedroom. Fearing it would get caught in her hair, his mother hoisted him up on her shoulders, they wrapped themselves in a bedsheet, and chased the bat with fire tongs.[43]

Very distinguished, M. Grandsaignes d'Hautervie, the fourth-form teacher, wielded a tortoiseshell lorgnette and smelled of pepper; he divided the class into "camps" and "rows," each one with its "leader." All for contests about Greek aorists. (Why are old teachers such good "conductors" of memory?)[44]

Barthes goes on to explain, "I call *anamnesis* the action—a mixture of pleasure and effort—performed by the subject in order to recover, *without magnifying it or sentimentalizing it,* a tenuity of memory: it is the haiku itself." In an echo of Foucault's "Lives of Infamous Men," Barthes does not analyze or interpret these memories, merely collects them. Furthermore, Barthes insists, his memories are not interpretable: "These few anamneses are more or less *matte,* (insignificant: exempt of meaning)."[45] This exemption from meaning, for Barthes, was of especial significance, and he further explained this quality in another of the autobiography's entries: "it is not a question of recovering a pre-meaning, an origin of the world, of life, of facts, anterior to meaning, but rather to imagine a post-meaning: one must traverse, as though the length of an initiatic way, the whole meaning, in order to be able to extenuate it, to exempt it."[46] As I explained in chapters 2 and 4, cinephiles operate in a similar fashion, allowing moments devoid of meaning to linger in their memories. The most skilled of film viewers and "readers," the cinephile allows these moments to persist even after the critical activities of interpretation and analysis have been exhausted.

Though he almost certainly knew of Barthes's list, Adair's memory book was specifically modeled on one by Georges Perec, *Je me souviens,* which had itself been modeled on the American Joe Brainard's book *I Remember,* originally published in 1975.[47] By way of explanation for his own list, Adair cites Perec's introduction as noting that the memories offered are

little fragments of the everyday, things which, in such and such a year, everyone more or less the same age has seen, or lived, or shared, and which have subsequently disappeared or been forgotten; they were not worthy of being memorized, they did not merit inclusion in History, or in the memoires of statesmen, mountaineers and movie stars. They might well re-emerge, nevertheless, several years later, intact and minuscule, by chance or because they have been sought out, one evening, among friends: it might be something that one had learned at school, the name of a sports champion, a crooner or an up-and-coming starlet, a song which had once been on everyone's lips, a hold-up or a catastrophe which had made headline news, a bestseller, a scandal, a slogan, a custom, an expression, an article of clothing or the way it had been worn, a gesture, or something even humbler, even more trifling, something completely banal, miraculously retrieved from its insignificance, fleetingly reclaimed, to produce, for no more than a few seconds, an impalpable little nostalgic *frisson.*[48]

In addition to being an "explanation," this passage clearly suggests that the collection of memories can be conceived of as signifiers of an alternative history, one that clearly contrasts with the official "History" of significant events and people that one is supposed to remember. The link to Benjamin's project is made explicit in Perec's phrase, "a song which had once been on everyone's lips," which strikingly echoes Benjamin's query, "What form do you suppose a life would take that was determined at a decisive moment by the street song last on everyone's lips?"[49] This provocative question appears in his essay on Surrealism—which, as Max Pensky notes, is another of Benjamin's key essays on memory[50]—in a passage where Benjamin is considering the way that André Breton's aesthetic is a model for an alternative historical method. Breton, Benjamin wrote, "was the first to perceive the revolutionary energies that appear in the 'outmoded,' in the first iron constructions, the first factory buildings, the earliest photos, the objects that have begun to be extinct, grand pianos, the dresses of five years ago, fashionable restaurants when the vogue has begun to ebb from them."[51] Kracauer had commented on the way in which, so often, the marginal details that catch a viewer's eye in a given film are those things that, with the passage of time, have begun to date, or that are linked to a specific moment in time. For the materialist historian, the outmoded is often precisely that which is about to be lost from history. As the signifier of an alternative history, it appears first a concrete object in the world of things evoking not a narrative, but more powerfully, as Benjamin suggested, an *atmosphere*.[52] "In the fields with which we are concerned, knowledge comes only in lightning flashes," Benjamin wrote; "The text is the long roll of thunder that follows."[53] Insisting that the image-moment be graphic or concrete, Benjamin wrote that in this new history (recall here his remarks about Schelling's coat), "The eternal would be the ruffles on a dress rather than an idea."[54] From these "smallest and most precisely cut components," the materialist historian "assemble[s] large scale constructions."[55] The collection of memories of Adair, Perec, and Brainard are the equivalents of these revolutionary ruffles, these small components of history.

Though the difference between these three authors' subjective recollections and Benjamin's materialist historian might at first seem dramatic, it turns out not to be so. For even Benjamin's alternative historical method—which would find expression in his own *Arcades Project*—depended greatly on the vagaries of subjectivity, and on the bringing of memory to bear on the question of writing history. As Max Pensky explains, the essays on Proust and Surrealism, which Benjamin identified as "prolegomena" for the Arcades Project, constitute "explorations and critiques of tactics of remembrance, critical models for the way that *subjective memory* [italics mine], directed onto a collection of cultural artifacts, might serve to disrupt a hegemonic historical continuity, thereby rescuing images from the past of an individual life or of an entire historical epoch."[56] The issue we are left with, Pensky notes, is that neither Benjamin's own model, nor his theoretical speculations, offer "methodological clues as to how dialectical images are to be distilled" from the chaos of the past as he has distilled them from the nineteenth century Arcades.[57] The further issue becomes the ways in which these images, once encountered, might be developed into some form of a discourse that produces knowledge. Pensky poses these questions explicitly:

> Would the historiographic imagination Benjamin had in mind have been the ability to "read" the mass of objects, so that the "meaning" of these piles of junk, shops, signs, and boarded-up storefronts would leap out? Or would historiography rather consist in the skill for constructing a critical text, one that might rely on these objects for its alphabet but resist the temptation to venture too deeply into the enchanted regions they inhabit? Does the memory of the critic provide a medium for the representation of a historical truth already encoded within things, or is memory itself creative, relying, in a platonic sense, on objects only as souvenirs, as reminders of Ideas?[58]

It would seem that, for Benjamin, the answers are the latter: memory itself is creative, and it has a crucial role to play in the materialist historian's construction of a critical text. The fact that Proust was a model for Benjamin testifies to this fact. Proust understood the rhythmic interruptions of everyday experience in *mémoires involuntaires* in terms of a theory of aesthetic creativity. The aesthetic enterprise that followed from these experiences involved "the transformation of this rhythmic interruption into an artwork; transforming the life, the self, into an *arranged pattern* of involuntary memories held fast in writing."[59] This enterprise—the developing of the encounter with the lightning flash into a discourse of thunder—is a tricky proposition for the materialist historian, and it is no less for the cinephile writing a counterhistory of cinema out of cinephiliac moments. Though the flash must be developed at least partially in order to have a generalizable knowledge effect, it must remain a fragment in order to retain its initial illuminatory power, and also in order to resist co-optation into yet another historicist-style narrative. Proust's first move was to "confront the involuntary memory with a voluntary memory, one that is in service of the intellect," one that would enable him to begin thinking about his involuntary memory.[60] The cinephile can do the same: counter the experience of the cinephiliac moment as involuntary memory, and follow it with a voluntary memory or association.

But for the cinephiliac anecdote to have an effect of knowledge about a given film, the chain of metonymic association cannot simply come to rest on some personal memory linked to the moment in question. Rather, the anecdote must always return to the text, for that above all is what is seeking to be illuminated. In *S/Z*, Barthes offered a useful distinction between two kinds of metonymic elaborations: "We must not confuse connotation with association of ideas: the latter refers to the system of the subject; connotation is a correlation immanent in the text, in the texts; or again, one may say that it is an association made by the text-as-subject within its own system."[61] While the cinephiliac anecdote may productively engage with the viewer's personal memory—"the system of the subject"—it must put these associations ultimately in the service of the film-text under investigation.

3. *The Uncanny.* Anecdotes regularly trade on the uncanny, and the effect of cinephiliac moments has been described as that of the uncanny.

The term "uncanny" should be remembered by both its definitions: as a feeling, an odd sensation of unease or pleasure; and as a coincidence, a repetition where one does not expect it. This concept has perhaps a closer affinity with the cinema than with any other art form, as Michael Arnzen has explained.

One "new and strange" way of experiencing life in the 20th century has been through that relatively young medium, the "motion picture." Literally embodying the uncanny in the manner in which its technology animates a series of inanimate still pictures, the cinematic eye has become a metaphor for subjectivity—from "mindscreens" to the "male gaze"—and we haven't "looked" at the world in the same way since its emergence.[62]

As I explained in chapters 2 and 3, the cinephiliac moment evokes the feeling of the uncanny in a specific way, partly due to the fact that the filmic event is perceived as a remarkable copy of another instance, the pro-filmic event: the perception of an unanticipated doubling provokes the sensation of the uncanny.

In everyday life, the experience of the uncanny is oftentimes shared through a particular narrative form: the anecdote. The story of an individual encounter with a coincidence prompts the feeling of the uncanny—a somewhat unsettling, oftentimes delightful sensation—as well as the desire to share the experience by telling about it. As novelist Paul Auster has described it, anecdotes are stories about events that defy our expectations of the world, stories that focus on and reveal "the mysterious and unknowable forces at work in our lives, in our family histories, in our minds and bodies, in our souls."[63] In other words, anecdotes are stories that do not fit neatly with the larger narratives we construct for ourselves about our lives, for those narratives so commonly follow the realist model, privileging devices such as cause and effect, distinction between significant and insignificant events, and so on. In response to the marginalization of these narratives, Auster has collected his coincidences in writing, in a slim volume called *The Red Notebook*.[64] As with Breton's accounts of objective chance, or the accounts collected by Foucault in "Lives of Infamous Men," Auster does not analyze or interpret these incidents, but he simply recounts them so that their force may be acknowledged and shared.

Another film scholar who has employed anecdotal methods in writing about cinema is Peter Wollen. Several of the entries in his essay, "An Alphabet of Cinema," engaging with the intimate link between cinema and the uncanny, turn on striking coincidences.

Bambi was the first film I ever saw and it left, no doubt, a deep mark on me, even a traumatic one. After seeing it, I repressed it, I put it out of my mind—until one day, on the outskirts of Santa Barbara, California, I was driving down the road with friends, sitting in the back of an open car, when I looked up and suddenly had a vision of my terrifying childhood memory, right there: the forest fire in *Bambi*. At first I couldn't grasp what I had seen but, as I recovered from the shock, I realized there was a huge drive-in movie screen right across the road and we happened to drive past it precisely at the traumatic moment.[65]

Here, an extraordinary coincidence prompts the series of metonymic associations —some personal, some historical. Wollen realizes that the "horror and pity" that he associated with the film, and this scene in particular, "were not simply explicable in terms of the little Disney deer. There was something else at stake. *Bambi* was made during [World War II] and, in a hidden sense, it was a war film. In fact, it was released in August 1942, at the onset of the Battle of Stalingrad."[66] The metonymic slide thus leads him to a new metaphor: Wollen now considers the film as an allegory about the war, an interpretation that is especially suggestive, given that the critic first saw the film as a child, in the north of England, during the time of the Blitz. In other entries, the order is reversed: metonymic development and personal memory intersect, giving rise to striking coincidences.

The links between the cinema, personal memory, the anecdote (metonymy), and the uncanny are strong—indeed, uncanny. With the cinephiliac anecdote, the cinephile tells a story about—or a story that embodies—his or her relationship with the cinema, a story that has the effect of knowledge in the generalizable sense about its object, as well as in some personal sense. From the specific moment, the cinephile moves metonymically, partly into personal recollection, partly into public information and history, until the snap of the uncanny is encountered. This experience of the uncanny, prompted by coincidence in the anecdote itself, doubles the experience of the uncanny in the initial encounter with the cinephiliac moment; this doubling, then, is a discursive echo, a simulation through research and writing of the initial filmic experience.

Walter Benjamin has explained, "The true method of making things present is to represent them in our space (not to represent ourselves in their space). The collector does just this, and so does the anecdote. Thus represented, the things allow no mediating construction from out of 'large contexts.' . . . We don't displace our being into theirs, they step into our life."[67] Much film theory and history of the past twenty-five years has been preoccupied with articulating and exposing the means by which dominant narrative cinema creates a world of drama, adventure, and enchantment that we can step into and lose ourselves in. The cinephiliac anecdote, by contrast, seeks to illuminate the ways in which movies—especially moments from movies—displace themselves out of their original contexts and step into our lives.

7 Five Cinephiliac Anecdotes

For this final chapter, I have composed (or co-composed) five cinephiliac anecdotes according to the principles described in the previous chapter. They vary somewhat in length and tone as a way to indicate something of the range of kinds of writing that might qualify as a cinephiliac anecdote.

* * *

Light on His Feet

At the climax of John Ford's *The Searchers,* as the cavalry raids the compound of the Comanche chief Scar, Ethan Edwards (John Wayne) charges his horse through the scurrying Indians to find his niece, Debbie, kidnapped five years earlier. Martin Pawley (Jeffrey Hunter), convinced that Ethan intends not to rescue Debbie, but to kill her, chases after Ethan in an attempt to stop him. "No, Ethan!" he screams. Shirtless and on foot, Martin tries in vain to slow Ethan or pull him out of his saddle. As Ethan turns and gallops away, Martin makes a final, desperate leap up onto the rump of Ethan's horse.

This is the moment I wait for every time I watch the film. As the dust kicked up by Ethan's horse swirls around him, Martin's leap seems to transform his motion; and in contrast to the jerking and pulling of the horse, Martin's body seems to float. While the rest of the action remains at regular speed, Martin seems momentarily to slow down, his right leg bending gracefully at the knee. These movements seem to transform the dramatic meaning of the action from conflict to coordination, from fighting to dancing. This moment—this action—is for me the most beautiful in the entire film.

Interestingly, Martin's movement here is not exceptional. In many ways, it recalls his first appearance in the film. Framed through the doorway of the Edwardses' home, Martin gallops up on a horse, and as he is riding bareback, he dismounts by simply slinging his right leg over the horse's neck and sliding off, landing on the ground with a short, smooth hop. The horse never breaks stride. It's all continuous motion: the galloping of the horse, Martin's cavalier dismount. Here, that term—"cavalier"—is doubly appropriate, for it refers not only to the casual, free and easy demeanor of Martin's dismount, but also to the term's other definition—"horseman."

My college's library has a copy of the script for *The Searchers*—not a published screenplay, but a mimeograph of Frank Nugent's "Revised Final Script." The script differs from the finished film in some significant and interesting ways, but the scene in which my cinephiliac moment occurs is described more or less accurately.

EXT. OPEN COUNTRY—MED. CLOSE SHOT—MARTIN AND DEBBIE
Martin hears Ethan's horse riding down at them; he turns, and Debbie pulls free and starts to run away.

MARTIN
No, Ethan! No!

He goes running into the path of Ethan's horse.
EXT. OPEN COUNTRY—MOVING SHOT—ETHAN
As Martin runs and grabs hold of his stirrup, trying to fight the horse to a stop. Ethan swings on him—once, twice—and Martin is knocked sprawling. Ethan rides on relentlessly.

There is, however, an additional notation. In the margin of the script, with an arrow pointing to this above-described section, the script's original owner—someone involved in the film's production—has scribbled the word "retake."

This notation clearly indicates that there was some need to re-shoot this part of the sequence, either because of some technical problem or because director John Ford wasn't happy with it in some indefinable way. It is this latter possibility that I am most interested in. Directors often request additional takes of a scene, and not just because of technical problems. Often, retakes are shot simply because something isn't quite "right." In some cases, of course, the retake may be prompted by a failure in an actor's performance—that is, by an unsatisfactory line reading or expression—but even this might be classified as a technical problem. If it is the actor's job to register fear, surprise, affection, worry, or any other emotion in a particular scene, any failure to do so is in many ways no different from a panning shot that moves awkwardly or a crane shot that misses its cue. But beyond what is planned and intentional—both the formal and dramatic elements of a scene—there is always the accidental, the unintentional, no matter how minute or how momentary, that gives a scene a certain exceptional quality, a certain life. Sometimes it is nothing more than the absence of this ineffable quality that prompts a director to request a re-take of a scene or shot. It is not only something *seen,* but something *felt.* It is not what is planned or calculated, but what is natural, in other words, *cavalier.*

We generally think that retake means re-shoot or re-do (which it does); but if it is the attentive director who evaluates if a scene is acceptable, retake also means an opportunity to re-view, re-watch. This directorial act (of re-watching) is doubled by the cinephile, whose experience of the cinephiliac moment prompts something like a "double take." With the double take, a person reacts to something in one way (often in a manner inappropriate to the situation); then, on momentary reflection, realizing more fully what has been seen, the person's reaction changes. This is one way of describing the experience of the cinephiliac moment. The cinephile sees something on screen (or feels it), and though his gaze never falters, the film moves on, and he searches in vain as if looking hard enough might make it appear again. Re-watching, re-viewing, is the way to complete the double take.

This moment of Martin trying to pull Ethan from his horse is the first, true cinephiliac moment that I can recall having, and my pleasure of it was radically enhanced by the technology of the VCR. I first saw *The Searchers,* on videotape, when I was a college freshman in 1981, and I remember replaying this moment over and over for several of my close friends, who didn't exactly see what I saw, but understood the experience I was having. Raymond Bellour anticipated this kind of casual use of a film in his essay "The Unattainable Text," which was written in 1975, only a few years before the video boom began: "One can imagine, if still only hypothetically, that one day, at the price of a few changes, the film will find . . . a status analogous to that of the phonograph record with respect to the concert."[1] Indeed, with the VCR, my friends and I started watching movies—and above all, parts of movies—the way we listened to records or read books: in parts, selecting a particular song off an LP for repeated listening, or reading a favorite passage of literature (anything from chapter IX of *A Coffin for Dimitrios* to an excerpt from *The Catalog of Cool*).

Bellour further speculated about the implications for film studies of being able to own a movie the way one owns books or records: "If film studies are still done then, they will undoubtedly be more numerous, more imaginative, more accurate, and above all more enjoyable than the ones we carry out in fear and trembling, threatened continually with the dispossession of the object."[2] The first step in this more imaginative, more enjoyable film study involves being able to re-watch movies, and re-watch them differently. The appearance of the VCR and now the DVD player have radically enhanced the possibility of panoramic perception because they permit re-watching films according to aberrant strategies not unlike those used by the Surrealists: in slow-motion or fast-forward, in selected parts, or out of order. And the loosening of narrative power that results from this contrary method of watching encourages the viewer's eye to wander around in the image for marginal points that are of interest. That first VCR of mine was the aptly named RCA "Selectavision."

While we are aware of how home video formats have transformed both the conditions by which we see films and the structure of the film industry, we have been less alert to the ways in which these changes—and the change in how we *watch* films—serve to transform the object (the film) itself. Because films are more mobile than ever before, they are brought into contact with infinitely more contexts—with other parts of our lives and with the lives of other films. These new contexts call our attention to the fact that, in addition to their obvious unity, films possess a remarkable heterogeneity. As films move into new contexts, their heterogeneous elements are highlighted.[3]

The video boom of the early 1980s meant an explosion in the potential for the kind of cross-referencing of films for which the *Cahiers* critics had been noted. Studios opened their vaults and released hundreds of old films onto videotape, but in contrast to their original historical releases (planned and chronological), films were now released in a manner that appeared unsystematic (illogical), capricious, arbitrary, *cavalier*. One result was that the new contexts of re-release had a profound impact on the films themselves, linking them to other films and other parts of our lives in powerful and mysterious ways.

For example, one film that is for me forever linked to *The Searchers* is *Singin' in the Rain*. Both were Hollywood classics that I had read about for years but had never seen, and importantly, both turned up (for the first time) on the 1982 *Sight and Sound* Top Ten poll. However, and this was something of a novelty for me in that time, *Singin' in the Rain* was a film I first saw not on video, but in a 16 mm print during my sophomore year of college (1982–83). In this film, Don Lockwood (Gene Kelly) gets his big break in the movies as a cowboy light on his feet. Don and his friend Cosmo Brown (Donald O'Connor) start out providing musical accompaniment to silent films in production, but when a cowboy stuntman in one of the films gets knocked out during a gag, Don steps in. When he gets hit, he reacts accordingly: he goes flying up in the air and over a saloon bar. The director loves it.

Don becomes a big star at Monumental Studios thanks to a string of hit films with Lina Lamont (Jean Hagen). When sound comes in with *The Jazz Singer*, the studio boss thinks nothing of it; but when the film unexpectedly becomes a huge success, he does a double take. Thinking on their (light) feet, Don and Cosmo transform Don and Lina's current film from a silent costumer to a musical, and the title of the picture changes: from *The Duelling Cavalier* to *The Dancing Cavalier*.

* * *

A Shot in the Arm

Bonnie and Clyde, Buck and Blanche, and C. W. Moss are holed up in a motor hotel in Platte City, Iowa. They are ambushed by "the laws," and a horrible, violent, exhausting shootout ensues. Eventually, they escape and find refuge and rest in a field, but it's only a momentary respite; when the sun comes up, the shooting starts again. The gang members struggle back into their car and attempt an escape, but they can only buzz in circles, randomly, as the posse fires at will.

There is a medium close-up looking in the driver's side window: Clyde is at the wheel, the car hurtling screen left. Suddenly, a shotgun blast tears into Clyde's shoulder, jolting him back into the car, away from us. But he does not let go of the wheel. There are two powerful motions: the car racing forward, Clyde being thrown perpendicularly away.

This moment is, of course, typical of the film's historically infamous presentation of violence and death, one that established "a new threshold for screen violence."[4] It was this graphic violence that prompted so many outraged critics to attack the film, and so many others—most famously, Pauline Kael—to defend it. "Nobody in the movie gets pleasure from the violence," she pointed out.[5] Quite the opposite. As Lester Friedman has explained, director Arthur Penn's goal was to make the audience "feel the physical pain and suffer the mental anguish that inevitably accompanies death. His goal for the audience was a deeply visceral, rather than intellectual or even emotional, apprehension of death in *Bonnie and Clyde*."[6] What seems to have upset so many people, Kael concludes, is that rather than presenting its scenes of violence and death discreetly and tastefully, *Bonnie and Clyde* throws it full in our face—it has "put the sting back into death."[7]

My first viewing of *Bonnie and Clyde* was on the film's re-release in the early 1970s. I was probably about nine years old—much too young to be seeing it. I had been taken to the film—along with four older siblings, all in their early teens—by my college-aged brother, Tim, and his friend, Cathy Reed. I had heard all about the film's final massacre scene, and with the above-described shootout functioning as a preview, I was getting anxious. During the shootout, Cathy noticed my discomfort and offered to wait with me in the lobby until the film was over. Relieved, I accepted. It was for things like her extraordinary kindness and empathy that Cathy was a favorite of ours. We were always excited to see her driving down the street toward our house, and hers was an easy car to spot. The front license plate ironically sported her initials: CAR. This screening of *Bonnie and Clyde* was the last time any of us would ever see Cathy. Two weeks later, she was dead from meningitis.

I did not see *Bonnie and Clyde* again for several years—until I was a teenager and could watch the film on video. When I did see it, it was the moment of Clyde being hit by the shotgun blast that provoked a *frisson* of involuntary recognition. Since that second viewing, every time that I have seen the film, I have waited for this moment with anticipation, and with dread.

But when I saw the film that second time, was I really *remembering* the moment of Clyde hit by the shotgun blast from the first screening when I was nine? It was about this point in the film that Cathy took me out to the lobby. Was that image of Clyde the final one I saw; was it the last memorable image I had from the film? The only mental image I can recall from after that moment is one of Cathy sitting on a bench in the theater lobby: long, straight brown hair, gold-rimmed aviator-style glasses, tan overcoat. Hers is the death that stings.

It is remarkable, and often forgotten, that André Bazin—that theoretician who, more perhaps than anyone, celebrated film's force of realism, its life force—wrote just as much about film's relation to death. The "Ontology" essay begins with a consideration of the ways in which the plastic arts have been, historically, an act of "embalming the dead," and that at their origins lay evidence of a "mummy complex."[8] But it was in his essay "Death Every Afternoon" that Bazin offered his clearest statement about film's relationship to death. "Death is surely one of those rare events that justifies the term, so beloved of Claude Mauriac, *cinematic specificity.* Art of time, cinema has the exorbitant privilege of repeating it, a privilege common to all mechanical arts, but one that it can use with infinitely greater potential." For while the other time arts are bound by aesthetic time, "the cinema only attains and constructs its aesthetic time based on lived time, Bergsonian '*durée*,' which is in essence irreversible and qualitative." He continues:

I cannot repeat a single moment of my life, but cinema can repeat any one of these moments indefinitely before my eyes. If it is true that for consciousness no moment is equal to any other, there is one on which this fundamental difference converges, and that is the moment of death. [. . .] The qualitative time of life is retroactively defined in relation to it. It marks the frontier between the duration of consciousness and the objective time of things. Death is nothing but one moment after another, but it is the last."[9]

Cinema's intimate link to the inexorability of real time, and its uncanny ability to subvert it, are present for me in this moment from *Bonnie and Clyde*. Every time I watch the moment of Clyde getting shot in the arm, I feel Cathy is still alive—just as this violence reminds me of her death.

The first person to achieve this paradoxical "image of time" was the person who first invented a motion picture camera: Etienne-Jules Marey. Unlike his contemporary, Eadweard Muybridge, who photographed the movement of a horse using twelve different cameras in twelve different spots, Marey was the first to examine motion by photographing it with a single camera from a single fixed point. This study of motion Marey called "ballistics"—a term we now associate almost exclusively, thanks to countless movies and TV shows, with an examination of bullets, the guns they are fired from, and the objects or people they strike. It is appropriate then that Marey's first camera—the first true motion picture camera—was fashioned in the shape of a gun. With his *fusil photographique* (or chronophotographic gun), perfected by 1882, Marey produced extraordinary images that are marked by simultaneous motion and stasis, both the free movement of life and the capture or cessation of life. These images are the first true examples of what Bazin said the cinema offered: "change mummified."[10] Marey's goal with his motion studies was neither simply to break movement into parts (like Muybridge) or simply to reconstitute it (as the Lumière Brothers would); rather, he sought to chart and quantify a body's movement as it occurs across space, to register a single image that would present the path of movement at all its points. He was prompted first of all in this endeavor by his interest in registering the physical motions of birds in flight, and he wrote excitedly to his mother of his success with his new instrument: "I have a photographic gun that has nothing murderous about it and that takes a picture of a flying bird . . . in less than 1/500 of a second. I don't know if you can picture such speed, but it is something astonishing."[11]

Bonnie and Clyde makes explicit the link between cameras and guns. The gang's fame, after all, comes as much from shooting photos—like the infamous one of Bonnie kissing Texas Ranger Frank Hamer—as from shooting people.

And the sound of the clicking camera shutter that is heard over and over in the film's credit sequence is indistinguishable from the sound of a shotgun shell being pumped into the barrel. And in the film's final, bloody scene—the scene I was too anxious to sit through on my first viewing—just before the posse, in hiding behind a thick cluster of bushes, empties its machine guns into the couple in an action filmed at a variety of different speeds, a flock of birds leaps startled from the shrubs and takes for the heavens.

* * *

The Boy on the Corner

In *Shadow of a Doubt,* there is a scene in which Uncle Charlie and his niece, young Charlie, walk into downtown Santa Rosa, California. At one busy inter-section, where a policeman stands directing auto and pedestrian traffic, the pair waits their turn to the cross the street surrounded by an unusually large crowd of other townspeople. Just behind Uncle Charlie, over his left shoulder, we see a teenaged girl and boy standing unnaturally close together, the boy with a curiously severe expression on his face.

The unsettling quality of the boy's presence in the street corner shot is underscored when, two shots later, he has vanished—only to reappear two shots after that, now on the other side of the intersection, and wearing differ-ent clothes. The boy's appearances (and disappearances) in this brief sequence can be summarized as follows:

1. Low-angle medium shot of traffic cop.
2. Medium-wide shot of young Charlie and Uncle Charlie stopping at the in-tersection. Two of young Charlie's high-school girlfriends step up on either side of them. "Good morning, Charlie." *Boy and girl are not present.*
3. Medium shot of Uncle Charlie and one of the girlfriends. *Boy and girl are present behind them. The boy wears a V-neck sweater over a collared shirt, with the sleeves rolled up.*
4. Medium shot of young Charlie and the other girlfriend.
5. Same as shot 2. Uncle Charlie and young Charlie, flanked by the two girl-friends, respond to the traffic cop's whistle and move to cross the street. *Girl is present, but boy is suddenly and inexplicably absent.*
6. Wide panning shot of young Charlie and Uncle Charlie crossing the busy downtown street.
7. Medium-wide shot of young Charlie and Uncle Charlie on the other side-walk, walking toward us. *Boy is present again (though he clearly was not in the previous shot). He is seen, as before, just over Uncle Charlie's left shoulder,*

but he now wears a T-shirt. As the two Charlies turn and enter a bank building, the boy overtakes them and exits screen left.

Though the boy's sudden appearance in shots 3 and 7 could be explained if
there were a temporal ellipse between those and their respective previous
shots, this is not the case. We are cued to a brief temporal ellipse (no more
than a few seconds) between shots 5 and 6, but there is no indication of any
ellipse between shots 2 and 3 or between shots 6 and 7.

There is, of course, a rational explanation for the boy's appearance, disappearance, and reappearance: it is simply a continuity error. Such errors inevitably remind us that the filming of a single, brief scene takes place over a
much longer span of time—sometimes several days—and the changes in camera setups and staged action increase the possibility of inconsistencies such as
this. But why does this continuity error pique my attention when so many others register as just simple mistakes? Why does this boy, who appears superficially to be completely ordinary, unsettle me so? Perhaps if I push past the
rational explanation of a continuity error (a rationalization that stops me from
thinking about him), and instead see these inconsistencies as part of the film's
design—or rather, part of its *system*—I might discover things that the rational
explanation keeps out of our sight, outside the frame, off-screen.

A deliberate continuity error—starting the camera, stopping it and changing the scene, and then starting again—can be an effective way to produce a
spectacular effect, as can be seen in the disappearing and reappearing phan-
toms in the early trick films of Georges Méliès. Indeed, the boy's ability to
appear and disappear at will reminds us of these and other disturbing movie
characters who possess such supernatural traits: ghosts, demons, vampires. As
several critics have noted, Uncle Charlie himself is clearly something of a vam-
piric character, stalking unsuspecting wealthy widows, charming them into
marriage, and then killing them. And it is possible to locate other references
to vampirism in *Shadow of a Doubt*. In one case, the reference is direct, when
Detective Graham says to young Charlie's little sister, "Come on, Anne. Tell
Catherine the story of Dracula." But mostly, this theme relates indirectly to
the character of Uncle Charlie. There is his refusal to be photographed, his
dark telepathic powers, and especially his ability to appear and disappear at
will, as in the film's opening sequences, when he impossibly eludes the two
detectives pursuing him. But in the moment I am interested in, it is not Uncle
Charlie who seems creepy, menacing, uncanny; rather, it is the boy standing
behind him, peering over his shoulder.

There is more that is odd about the boy's first appearance. About halfway
through this six-second shot, the boy suddenly breaks into a smile. It seems as
if, looking ahead, into the off-screen space behind the camera, he has been

prompted to smile by someone or something he has seen. What is the boy looking at, what does he see in the space behind the camera? (Himself, on the other side of the street, in another dimension of reality, dressed in different clothes?) Noël Burch notes that, of the six zones of off-screen space, it is the one behind the camera—the direction in which the boy on the corner is looking—that is most distinct, most troubling perhaps because it alerts us to that most unseeable of spaces: behind us, over our shoulder.[12] In horror films, of course, this is the direction from which threat most often comes to victims—when Dracula sneaks up from behind and goes for the throat.

The fact that what the boy sees in the off-screen space behind the camera goes unrevealed is not typical of Hitchcock's style. Though he sometimes used off-screen space in suggestive ways, Hitchcock rarely left it unshown. Influenced as he admittedly was by Kuleshovian montage, Hitch was most likely to follow the basic three-shot sequence: a character is shown looking (usually at something off-screen); we are shown what he sees; we see the character's response. In this schema, off-screen space goes unseen only momentarily; otherwise, unless it is motivated by a character's glance, off-screen space goes unacknowledged by both characters and filmmaker.

So, the boy's reaction to something off-screen that remains unseen underscores the unsettling effect: "appearing/disappearing" extends to "seeing/not seeing." The emphasis here on the boy's reaction follows James Naremore's point that the camera's "ability to 'give' the focus of the screen to any player at any moment, also means that films tend to favor *reactions*. [. . .] As a result, some of the most memorable Hollywood performances have consisted largely of players isolated in close-up, responding nonverbally to offscreen events."[13] Though the boy in the above-described shot is not isolated in a close-up, Naremore's description fits, and it also confirms something about the strangeness of the moment. Because what the boy is reacting to is not revealed to us—that is, because dominant cinema's rules about the distinction between on-screen and off-screen spaces have not been respected here—the boy's reaction registers as unreadable and, thus, strangely disturbing.

The importance of respecting the continuity rules regarding on-screen and off-screen space, of making sure that relevant visual information is carefully presented or concealed, is crucial for narrative clarity and spectator comfort and attention. Hume Cronyn has recalled how he learned this lesson while filming a scene from *Shadow of a Doubt*.

During the meal, I said something upsetting to the character played by Teresa Wright. She turned to me with unexpected violence. I stood up in embarrassment and surprise and automatically took a step backward. However, at the point of the rise, the camera moved in to hold us in a close two-shot, and to accommodate this—that is, to stay in the frame—it became necessary for me to change that instinctive movement so that when I got up from the chair, I took a step toward the person from who I was retreating. . . . I was convinced that the action would look idiotic on the screen, but I was wrong.[14]

In addition to alerting us to some of the peculiarities of acting for the screen, this anecdote makes clear that, by stepping back, Cronyn would have moved into off-screen space, which would have conflicted with Hitchcock's usual manner of treating that unseen realm.

Off-screen space is treated differently in films of different styles. While realist or "open" film styles often signal us to the richness of reality extending beyond the confines of the frame (as in a Renoir film, for example), in more expressionistic or "closed" film styles, off-screen space may represent the world of an unseen danger or threat—as in a horror film for example, when the monster suddenly appears out of the darkness, looming over the shoulder of an unsuspecting victim.

Forgoing the rational explanation for the boy's extraordinary supernatural acts allows us to ask—indeed, draws us urgently to—the compelling question: Who is this mysterious boy? No doubt the actor was one of the many residents of Santa Rosa, California, who were recruited to appear as extras when Hitchcock came to town to shoot exteriors for the film. And we might credit the awkwardness of his sudden smile to his not being a professional actor. (Another native Santa Rosan, Estelle Jewel, who appears here in her only film role in the supporting part of young Charlie's girlfriend, Catherine, gives a similarly awkward performance. Catherine is the one who hears the story of Dracula from the young sister, Anne—though the recounting of the story takes place after the two have stepped out of the frame, off-screen.)

But beyond this, is there anything to be known about this boy? Is it possible that he is Robert Quarry? The Internet Web site www.imdb.com lists this actor as appearing in *Shadow of a Doubt* in an uncredited bit part. Born in Santa Rosa, California, in 1925, Quarry would have been in his mid-teens at the time of filming—about right for the boy in the downtown sequence. Apparently, young Robert decided to become a film actor, and this scene was thus not only something of a screen test, it foreshadowed his career. It took a few years for Quarry's career to get going. In 1955, twelve years after *Shadow of a Doubt,* he appeared uncredited in two films: Edward Dmytryk's *Soldier of Fortune,* with Clark Gable and Susan Hayward, and Sam Fuller's *House of Bamboo,* with Robert Ryan. That same year, he acted in Henry Koster's *Good Morning, Miss Dove,* with Jennifer Jones and Robert Stack, but his scenes were deleted from the finished film (appearing/disappearing).

When he finally got a big part, it was in the title role of a 1970 film, as a character he would play again and who would subsequently enjoy a kind of cult stardom—*Count Yorga, Vampire.*

* * *

For the cinephiliac anecdote to be an effective addition to dominant historiographic methods in cinema studies, it must demonstrate its pedagogical usefulness. The form must be teachable, and individual examples must be sharable, for the purposes of knowledge about the movies and our relationship to them throughout history. Here are two more cinephiliac anecdotes. The first one was originally written by Eliza Mitchell, a student in my Senior Seminar in Film Theory at Middlebury College. I have revised it somewhat, but the basic discoveries remain hers. I wrote the second in collaboration with Alison LaTendresse.

* * *

The Swing of the Key

In Otto Preminger's *Laura* (1944), police detective Mark McPherson (Dana Andrews) is assigned to investigate the murder of the young, talented, and beautiful Laura Hunt (Gene Tierney). McPherson quickly focuses his suspicions on the two men closest to Laura: her fiancé, Shelby Carpenter (Vincent Price), and her mentor, newspaper columnist Waldo Lydecker (Clifton Webb) —both of whom have been smitten by the sweet and glamorous young woman. Early in the film, there is a scene in which McPherson, accompanied by Lydecker and Carpenter, visits Laura's apartment for the first time. McPherson unlocks the door of the apartment and allows it to swing open. The light from the hallway casts a beam into the darkened room. McPherson pauses at the door, and then takes three steps into the room. He pauses again to survey the scene, turns around, and then walks back to the doorway where Waldo and Shelby are still standing.

What has kept me thinking about this scene, these few brief seconds devoid of dialogue and presenting little action? The answer lies in this minute detail: in his right hand, McPherson holds the key to Laura's apartment, and as he examines the crime scene, he holds the key at his side and swings it back and forth—subtly, freely, nonchalantly. It is the repetitive and varying motion of the key swinging in his hand that I find so mesmerizing.

More specifically, in this film that so often feels carefully worked out, calculated in all its aspects, this swinging of the key feels like an action that might have been improvised. With this in mind, I turned to Stephen Nachmanovitch's *Free Play: Improvisation in Art and Life.* The key concept presented in

Nachmanovitch's book is that an artist needs to recognize and accept that im-provisation exists in everything, both art and life. One's everyday activities are a form of improvisation, "as we know what *might* happen in the next day or minute, but we cannot know what *will* happen."[15] He goes on to say:

The unexpected awaits us at every turn and every breath. The future is a vast, perpetually regenerated mystery, and the more we live and know, the greater the mystery. When we drop the blinder of our preconceptions, we are virtually pro-pelled by every circumstance into the present time and the present mind: the moment, the whole moment, and nothing but the moment. This is the state of mind taught and strengthened by improvisation, a state of mind in which the here and now is not some trendy idea but a matter of life and death.[16]

This matter of life and death is exactly what presents itself when Laura, who was thought to be dead, suddenly shows up at her apartment alive and in full radiance—something neither McPherson nor the audience would ever have expected.

That Otto Preminger became the director of *Laura* is something that was almost as equally unexpected. In the early 1940s, Preminger was under con-tract to 20th Century Fox, where he initially found favor with studio boss Darryl Zanuck. But when he refused the assignment of directing a film version of Robert Louis Stevenson's *Kidnapped*, which Zanuck regarded as a prestige job, the studio boss turned on him. Zanuck swore that Preminger would never again direct a feature while at Fox: "To produce, yes. To direct, never!" Because all the studio heads closed ranks in unison against anyone who fell into disfa-vor with one of them, Preminger could not find directing work at any other studios either. By 1944, Preminger as Hollywood director was a dead man. Zanuck put him to work producing B movies, the first of which was *Laura*. However, when the assigned director, Rouben Mamoulian, delivered work that both Preminger and Zanuck were unhappy with, Zanuck saw no other choice but to fire Mamoulian and replace him with the only person who knew the project well enough to step into the breach: Preminger. Had this act of improvisation not taken place—the bringing back to life of Preminger as a director—the film as it exists today would never have been realized.

According to *Cahiers* critic Jacques Rivette, Preminger's creative vision was itself marked by just this sort of improvisation: the spontaneous emerging suddenly in the midst of what has been carefully planned—like my impression of the swing of the key in McPherson's hand. Two quotes from Rivette's review of Preminger's *Angel Face* make this point clearly:

Preminger believes first in *mise en scene,* the creation of a precise complex of sets and characters, a network of relationships, an architecture of connections, an animated complex that seems suspended in space . . . What is cinema, if not the play of the actor and actress, of hero and set, of word and face, of *hand* and *object*.[17]

The film is not so much an end as a means. Its unpredictability attracts him, the chance discoveries that mean things cannot go according to plan, on the spot *improvisation* that is born of a fortunate moment and dedicated to the fleeting existence of a place or a person.[18]

Throughout the film, several of the characters are forced into improvisation, most obviously, McPherson. When he realizes that Laura is in fact alive, he has to rethink the terms of his investigation, and he does it well. Others improvise not so well. At one point in the film, for example, Shelby Carpenter offers to assist McPherson in looking for the extra key to Laura's apartment. When he finds it in a bedside table drawer, McPherson charges that there was no such key there before and accuses Shelby of planting it. When suspicions fall heavily on him, Shelby offers an alibi for his whereabouts on the night of Laura's murder: he was at a classical music concert. When McPherson asks what the orchestra played, Shelby confidently reports they played Brahms' 1st and Beethoven's 9th. McPherson catches Shelby in his lie: on the night of the concert, the detective tells him, there was a sudden change in the program, and the orchestra played nothing but Sibelius.

In music, Nachmanovitch explains, improvisation suggests variations that have grown out of an original theme. That is, "rather than state the outlines of a theme and then grow from it a series of variations, the [composer] begins with the most far-flung and highly ornamented elaborations on an as yet unheard-of-theme."[19] The effect, Nachmanovitch explains, is not unlike that of the unraveling of a murder mystery. "As the (reverse) development proceeds, ornaments are progressively cast off, gradually revealing the simple outlines of a theme that [like Poe's purloined letter] was hidden in there all along."[20] In much the same way, he writes, "among all the diverse and confusing circumstances of a fictional murder, we seek the simplifying quotient, the whodunit. Among the welter of material that comes up in an improvisation, we seek to simplify all that doodling and noodling up and down the keyboard and find the answer, 'What is the deep structure of theme, pattern, or emotion from which all of this arises?'" This "reverse themes and variations" pattern, Nachmanovitch explains, is found, "for example in many of Sibelius' symphonies."[21]

In *Laura*, much of the emotion arises from the famous and enchanting musical theme, which is a variation on Preminger's original plan for the film's score. Preminger originally envisioned Duke Ellington's "Sophisticated Lady" as the theme for the film; however, musical director David Raksin had other ideas. Raksin approached Preminger, who reluctantly agreed to give the composer seventy-two hours to develop an alternative theme for the movie. When Raksin returned with his new theme, Preminger liked what he heard and decided to switch the theme of the film. Raksin's *Laura* theme, which we hear throughout the film in multiple variations, is one of the most famous musical themes in movie history, the result of an unforeseen change, an improvisation in everyday life.

Improvisation in music means allowing variations to wander and develop into more complex and elaborate constructions of an original theme or tonal structure. This method insists on a willingness to encourage a peripheral melody to grow and develop, unsure of where it might lead. Throughout the film, McPherson routinely jots down every extraneous detail or peripheral fact that he comes across, constantly referring back to the notes in his pocket notebook, cross-referencing clues. He is continually replaying things back in his head, trying to find the pattern that will make sense of them. It is in this notebook that he jots down information about the Black Pony liquor and the matching antique clocks in Waldo's and Laura's apartments.

The clock, very much like a metronome, ticks steadily, constantly in the background of every apartment scene, its pendulum a representative of strict, metered time. When McPherson examines Waldo's clock, he finds a door in its base for which there is no key. He improvises and breaks the door, revealing a hidden compartment. This image of the broken clock (i.e., metronome), or the shattering of strict time, recalls the opposite value of improvisation (variations on fixed time, peripheral melodies). By homing in on peripheral facts that appear random, then turning them over and over again in his head, McPherson is able to realize a pattern that was hidden there all along, and in plain sight: the clocks. Finding Waldo's clock empty, McPherson realizes that the murder weapon he seeks is hidden in Laura's matching clock. There is the "shock of recognition" that Nachmanovitch describes, when "the fundamental motif finally bursts forth." This realization sends McPherson back to Laura's apartment for the climactic conclusion and the uncovering of the truth.

The clock and the key, then, are symbols for the two male characters and their ways of thinking. Waldo, like the clock, holds himself rigidly, royally, proudly erect, in complete control of his body at all times. McPherson wanders, paces, swings his key in his hand. These gestures are crucial, for as Nachmanovitch suggests, "the minute particulars of body, speech, mind, and movement are . . . the vehicle[s] through which the self moves and manifests itself."[22] The swing of the key is a visual pattern embodying the character and investigative style of McPherson as he searches for the truth. Nachmanovitch sums up his book's argument in chapter 20, entitled "Quality." "This whole enterprise of improvisation in life and art, or recovering free play and awakening creativity, is about allowing ourselves to be true to ourselves and our vision, true to the undiscovered wholeness that lies beyond the self and the vision we have today. That is what quality is all about: truth."[23]

The epigram beneath the chapter's title reads:

"It don't mean a thing
   if it ain't got that swing."

* * *

Judy's Lips

In the opening scene of *Rebel Without a Cause* (1955), the film's three principal characters—teenagers Jim (James Dean), Judy (Natalie Wood), and Plato (Sal Mineo)—are in custody at the police station, where each is questioned in turn by a sympathetic juvenile officer. During her conversation with the detective, Judy delivers a monologue describing the traumatic encounter with her father that precipitated the act of juvenile delinquency that has landed her in jail that night. Extremely distraught, Judy tells of her father's violent reaction to her appearance earlier in the evening: he grabbed her face and rubbed her lipstick off so roughly that she exclaims, "I thought he'd rub off my lips!" As she tells this story, the camera frames her tightly, and the viewer's eye is unavoidably drawn to the bright, glossy, red lipstick she is wearing, the redness of which is all the more heightened by its proximity to her red overcoat. The combination of this CinemaScope close-up, Judy's bizarre and disquieting story, and the supersaturated red lipstick, bestows this moment with a hallucinatory charge.

The first few drafts of the screenplay for *Rebel Without a Cause* were filled with lengthy Surrealist scenes that were intended to dramatize the various anxieties of the three main characters. The scenes were to utilize slow motion and other camera trickery, as well as some rather heavy-handed Freudian symbolism, in order to reveal the family dysfunction that is at the source of the teenagers' distress. Though none of these strange scenes was shot, a close analysis of the finished film in conjunction with the screenplay reveals that the overwrought imagery and emotionalism of these deleted scenes has, in fact, made its way into the film in unexpected and provocative ways. One place is in Judy's lips.

The first of these Surrealist scenes was to occur during the film's opening sequence, at the police station. The screenplay describes it thus:

The wall behind JUDY DISSOLVES and becomes instead a long row of prison cells in some subterranean dungeon. A door at the far end opens, letting in a scar of light. The girl in the cell behind JUDY'S CLOSEUP rises and comes to the grate. It is also JUDY, but in prison clothes. CAMERA enters the scene. Two visitors come down the aisle carrying lanterns—they are JUDY'S PARENTS. [. . .] They arrive at JUDY'S cell. She looks at them, concerned. Then the FATHER flashes a wonderful smile and JUDY smiles too. He opens the cell door, which requires no key, and kisses her. JUDY throws an anxious look at her MOTHER, then takes her FATHER'S face tenderly between her hands and kisses him on the forehead. The kiss leaves a large and vivid scarlet impression. He is startled and JUDY looks at him, frightened. The MOTHER takes a handkerchief from her bag and wipes the kiss away, then wipes JUDY'S lips until they are white.[24]

Though it might at first seem that this scene has been completely eliminated, the film has in fact distilled the screenplay's Surrealist sequence into a single moment (an image and a line of dialogue), one that furthermore manages to retain and even intensify the energized conflict of the fantasy sequence. The violence of the screenplay's image of the red of Judy's lip print being forcibly removed by her mother, as a way to somehow suppress the scarlet impression left by her incestuous desire, has been condensed in the film into a highly charged scene in which Judy's bright red, almost too-present lips describe her father's brutal attempt to make them disappear. Both in terms of its visual effect and its dramatic conflict, the moment as filmed has the force of a dream image, which in many ways it is, condensing and intensifying the earlier version as it does.

These Surrealist-inspired scenes were conceived by director Nicholas Ray and scripted (somewhat reluctantly), under Ray's supervision, by screenwriter Stewart Stern; and their presence inevitably prompts one to ask: What would bring Ray—who was apparently in line with the studio's plan to produce a big-budget social problem film with one of its hottest young stars, James Dean—to fill his screenplay with such obscure and often disturbing images? In fact, while this kind of explicit borrowing of Surrealist imagery by Hollywood cinema may have been rare in the 1950s, it was not unprecedented. A famous example can be found in Alfred Hitchcock's *Spellbound* (1945), whose hallucinatory dream sequence had been designed by Salvador Dali. Ray could hardly have missed *Spellbound,* so he could have reasonably assumed that his odd scenes had a chance of being filmed.

Also, *Spellbound* reminds us that, during the postwar years, Hollywood had a short-lived preoccupation with Freudian psychoanalysis, and it is clear that the unfilmed Surrealist sequences from *Rebel Without a Cause* are just as beholden to a psychoanalytic understanding of family trauma as they are to the Surrealist play with cinematic form. It is possible to cite other high-profile domestic melodramas released around the same time as *Rebel* that trade heavily in psychoanalytic concepts such as hysteria and repression: *All That Heaven Allows* (1955), *The Cobweb* (1955), and *Written on the Wind* (1956), for example. Furthermore, what *Rebel*'s script reminds us of, and what *Spellbound* makes absolutely explicit, is the connection between psychoanalysis and Surrealism. For it was after reading Freud's writings on the logic of dreamwork that André Breton invented Surrealism, with its various games and methods for unlocking the marvelous power of the unconscious.

With this connection, we return to Judy's lips, for in Surrealist art there are several antecedents for this nexus of sexualized and violent imagery centered on the lips. The most famous of these is perhaps the disturbing disappearance of the hero's lips in *Un Chien Andalou* (1929). In this scene, the film's heroine enters the room and watches stunned as the hero wipes his own lips off his face. Salvador Dali and Luis Buñuel play out the sexual implications of their scene when the hero's missing lips are replaced (via a cinematic theft) by the heroine's underarm hair. The trade of lips for what is essentially pubic hair unlocks the lips' second meaning as labia, and when the heroine vigorously and defiantly applies lipstick in retaliation for the hero's tomfoolery, she opens up another doubling of language or visual pun: in so stridently asserting her gender with lipstick, the heroine suggests that the hero has "volé son sexe," which in French can mean that he has stolen her genitals.

Yet another visual antecedent appears in Jean Cocteau's *Blood of a Poet* (1930). In that film's opening scene, a young artist in his garret draws a portrait whose lips begin to move. Horrified, he vigorously wipes the mouth from the drawing, but soon discovers that the lips have transferred onto the palm of his hand, where they continue to move; later, he awakes from a sleep to find an armless, Greek-style statue in his room, and when he wipes the lips off his hands and onto the statue's face, it begins to speak. "Do you think it's that simple to get rid of a wound, to close the mouth of a wound?" she asks the artist. Here again, the sexual implications in the double meaning of the term "lips" are played upon: the lips of the mouth, the lips as labia, the vagina as wound that does not heal. Both these scenes invoke female sexuality as a potential threat, and it is clear from other scenes in *Rebel* that it is precisely Judy's burgeoning sexuality that her father seems most uncomfortable with. It is this fear that prompts his violent action of wiping away of her rid lipstick, the attack on this signifier being a transparent attempt to wipe away her developing womanhood.

Surrealism's interest in this image of disembodied lips—and in its sexual implications and associations—extended well beyond the cinema, and it figured perhaps most prominently in Man Ray's work, for example in the solarized photograph from his book, *The Age of Light* (1934), his drawing, *Kiki's lips* (1925), and perhaps most famously in his painting, *Observatory Time—The Lovers* (1932–34). This painting, which is often referred to as "The Lips," and which Man Ray himself nicknamed "My Lovers," has been described as "the quintessential Surrealist painting."[25] The contours of the giant lips, floating in clouded blue sky over a wooded ridge, were intended by Man Ray to evoke the image of a man and woman locked in sexual embrace (again, the lips as an emblem of erotic desire): "Your mouth becomes two bodies," he wrote, "separated by a long, undulating horizon. Like the earth and the sky, like you and me."[26] In addition to their disembodied existence, made flagrantly dramatic by their scale in the painting, the color of the lips strikes one, as Neil Baldwin has noted, as "redder than any lipstick-reddened lips could possibly be."[27]

Within their color-saturated context, Judy's shimmering, crimson lips inevitably echo these recurring images of disembodied lips in Surrealist art. For although they are not exactly disembodied, Judy's lips register as such. *Rebel Without a Cause* takes full advantage of Warnercolor's dense, lush palette by organizing fields of meaningfully contrasted color. Red is especially privileged in *Rebel*, and in this scene, Judy's lips are made to stand out in sharp relief against her white skin, attaining as they do a strange, almost disembodied status within the film's fractional color scheme.

These connections between this moment in *Rebel Without a Cause* and Surrealist iconography have alerted us more precisely to the nature of the latent forces at work in this scene—forces that were sensed, but whose origin was not explicitly locatable or explainable. But we have in fact only begun to scratch the surface of the ways in which Surrealism is imbedded in this image of Judy's lips and in the film as a whole. The clue that there is more is left untapped: the only other conspicuous element of Man Ray's painting is the Paris Observatory, a structure that bears a striking resemblance to Los Angeles's Griffith Park Observatory, whose domed planetarium is a key setting in *Rebel Without a Cause*.

The observatory depicted in the painting, located in the Luxembourg Gardens, is one that Man Ray strolled past regularly during the 1920s and 30s, when he lived in Paris. Built in the seventeenth century, the observatory was constructed so that its walls are situated precisely to line up with the points of the compass. It was here that "scientists and astronomers first calculated the true dimensions of the solar system," and here that, since 1919, the headquarters of the International Time Bureau has been housed.[28] Arturo Schwarz alerts us to a trans-Atlantic link, for he reports that the painting's title was inspired by "the American speaking clock of the 1930s—one dialed to hear: United States Observatory Time . . . eight forty-five, etc."[29] But it is equally clear that, for Man Ray, the reference to time is less concrete than symbolic.

"Observatory Time" is not the time gauged on a clock: it is eternal time. The floating lips as bodily embrace is an image designed to stress "the cosmic dimensions of love," for the way that they defy "time, space, and gravity."[30]

It is precisely this concept of time—eternal time, where space and time collapse into one another, giving a glimpse of eternity—that is the subject of the lecturer's talk in the planetarium scene in *Rebel Without a Cause*. As the students lean back in their chairs, gazing up at the display in the planetarium ceiling, the lecturer intones, "Long after the Earth is gone the stars will still be there, moving through their ancient rhythms. The familiar constellations that illuminate our night will seem as they've always seemed: eternal, unchanged, and little moved by the shortness of time between our planet's birth and its demise." It is the promise of this eternity that the teenagers of *Rebel* long for, and it is its threat that they fear. Devoid of love, the youths' fear comes out as anger, fury, violence; enveloped in love, their hope expresses itself as connection, passion, tenderness. The red of Judy's lips and Jim's iconic jacket embodies both possibilities. Because these themes form the emotional core of the film, screenwriter Stewart Stern argued against a film title that emphasized juvenile delinquency, preferring instead one that referenced the observatory.

These themes were present in *Rebel*'s original source, a seventeen-page "original story idea" by Nicholas Ray entitled "The Blind Run." Because his story involved troubled teens, Ray's agent Lew Wasserman hooked Ray up at Warner Brothers, who wanted to develop a nonfiction book about juvenile delinquency entitled *Rebel Without a Cause: The Story of a Criminal Psychopath*, written by Robert Lindner, who was a psychoanalyst. Ray borrowed freely from the book as it suited him, constructing as he did a much more sympathetic attitude toward his young delinquents. It was Ray who conceived of using a planetarium as an important setting (the first reference to it in the production notes is in a scene written by Ray himself), and he further insisted that the building serve as the location for the film's climax. Though one of the writers, Irving Schulman, disagreed, Ray argued: "This was a crucial point for me, because it symbolized the more violent statement, the more sweepingly developed conflict that I was searching for. [Plato's return to and breaking into the planetarium] was a gesture of anger and desperation."[31] It was his cry of pain in the face of an eternity in which he stood as an outcast, marginalized and ostracized, alone and unloved. But the planetarium not only marks the place of Plato's violent death; it also marks the point of loving reunion—between Jim and Judy, and between Jim and his parents.

Observatory Time—The Lovers can be traced to one evening in the early 1920s, when Man Ray was at a dinner party with friends at a "very smart" Parisian restaurant. Obliged to leave early, Man was saying his goodbyes when his sometime model and lover, Alice "Kiki" Prin, pressed her lips onto his shirt collar. Later, "he saw in a mirror that a splendid impression of Kiki's lips stood out boldly on the impeccable whiteness of his collar. [The vivid impression] set Man dreaming of lips detached and floating with the breeze."[32] Again, the link to *Rebel*, especially the unfilmed fantasy sequence is notable: the imprint of red lips, disembodied, and the unmistakable signifier of sexual desire. Man Ray became obsessed with the image of Kiki's lipstick imprint on his collar, and it stayed with him for a decade, but he was not prompted to paint it until his breakup with another lover/model, Lee Miller. Man had always been fascinated by the fragmented female body and had used Miller as a subject many times before—a cut-out photograph of her eye had been attached to a metronome in Man Ray's *Object to Be Destroyed* (1923), yet another work incorporating the theme of time—so when he finally decided to paint the picture, the lips became those of Lee Miller—who, in an extraordinary coincidence, had appeared just two years earlier in Cocteau's *Blood of a Poet*, performing as the Greek statue onto whose face the artist rubs the lips that have transferred from his painting to his hand.

Work on *Observatory Time* was slow and painstaking. In his autobiography, Man Ray described his method of work on the painting, a project that took two years:

> I decided to paint the scale on a subject of superhuman proportions. I placed a canvas about eight feet long over my bed and every morning, before going to my office and studio, I worked on it for an hour or two standing on the bed in my pajamas. If there had been a color process enabling me to make a photograph of such dimensions and showing the lips floating over a landscape, I would certainly have preferred to do it that way.[33]

Man Ray's desire for a photo color process of such dimensions suggests that what he wanted was something akin to the Warnercolor and CinemaScope processes in which *Rebel Without a Cause* would be filmed. For in fact, the dimensions of *Observatory Time* ($39\frac{3}{8}'' \times 98\frac{5}{8}''$) are *exactly* the ratio (width to height) of the CinemaScope frame: 2.5:1. Just as we can read the image of Judy's lips as a radical condensation of *Rebel*'s unfilmed Surrealist sequence, so can we read *Observatory Time* and its elements—the lips, the planetarium, the title, the color, and the scale—as a radical condensation of *Rebel Without a Cause*. Twenty years later, Nick Ray would unravel this condensation, partly unconsciously, partly consciously.

Originally, *Rebel* was to be shot in black and white, but the CinemaScope company refused use of the technology for any but color films: as with Man Ray's painting, color and scale had to go together. Nicholas Ray had a strong affection for the proportions of the Scope frame, but he was almost alone among Hollywood directors in this. In contrast to someone like Fritz Lang, who famously remarked that widescreen processes were good only for filming snakes and funerals, Ray explained, "My affection for CinemaScope was initially my affection for the horizontal line as I learned it from having been apprenticed to . . . Frank Lloyd Wright."[34] In fact, during the exact period that Man Ray was at work on *Observatory Time* (1932–34), Nick spent time in residence as a fellow at Wright's Taliesin, a kind of utopian workshop/retreat on a farm some forty miles east of Madison, Wisconsin. But like Man Ray before him, who had also been offered the opportunity to train as an architect, Nick turned to the dramatic and visual arts.

These links between the two Rays (Man and Nick) and their two most famous works provides a new context for each. In effect, *Observatory Time* and *Rebel Without a Cause* serve in correspondence as what Laura Marks has called "recollection objects"—material objects that encode memory. Any object can serve this function, she explains, but what is most important about these object-images, what defines them as recollection objects, "is that they condense time within themselves, and that in excavating them we expand outward in time."[35] The recollection object, she is explains, is a "stubborn survivor from another place-time that brings its volatile contents into the present."[36] *Observatory Time* is a recollection object that looks back to the past (Man Ray's life in Paris, his love affairs with Kiki and Lee Miller) as well as to the future (*Rebel Without a Cause*), while *Rebel* looks primarily backward, but to a broad Surrealist past, one including but expanding beyond Man Ray's painting.

Recollection objects function to condense the past—in ways that are partly clear and articulable, as well as in ways that are less direct, more mysterious—and we can look to one such object as it is employed in *Rebel Without a Cause*: an object intimately related to Judy's lips. The first time in the film that we see Judy, she is seated on a bench in the police station waiting room, holding a compact mirror and touching up her lipstick. Later in this sequence, after she has reported to the juvenile officer about her father's violent wiping off of her lipstick, she inadvertently leaves the compact in a chair in the inner office. A few minutes later, Jim is escorted into the same office and, sitting in the same chair, discovers the compact, which he secretes into his pocket, a kind of souvenir of his non-encounter with the beautiful young girl he has noticed. Both the camera (in a tilt and dolly-in, accompanied by a swelling of soundtrack music) and then Jim are clearly but inexplicably aware of the compact as a powerful and important object.

When Jim and Judy meet for the first time several days later, it is unclear whether or not she remembers him from the police station. Later in the film—significantly, in the first sequence at the planetarium—she indicates some recognition in a gesture that is remarkable for the density of meaning it conveys. Judy looks at herself in the mirror of another compact—one she is presumably using because she has misplaced the first—and then she touches her lips and looks at Jim with something like the shock, or disquiet, of recognition. Judy's troubled expression as she touches her lips, then glances up at Jim, suggests that something happens to her in this moment—perhaps something similar to what happens to Jim when he finds this mysteriously talismanic object. It's unclear whether it is the fact that she is holding what is, in the film's logic, the wrong compact that reminds her of the visit to the police station, causing her to touch her own lips in remembering her own traumatic encounter with her father, or whether it is simply the sight of her own reflection that begins this chain of associations, both for her and for the spectator. But either way, the chain of associations is set in motion and the compact's status as a recollection object is made clear.

It is also possible to extend this chain of associations beyond the context of the film's fiction to show the ways that an object—or the ways that a film as an object—can hold memories far beyond what is offered internally. When Jim finds Judy's compact, he effectively trades for it the toy mechanical monkey that he has found in the film's credit sequence. In the opening shot of the film, the drunken Jim lies down in the street beside the monkey. First, he winds it up and watches it clap its cymbals; then he lays it on its back, places a crumpled piece of newspaper over it like a blanket, moves a piece of yellow ribbon near its head, and curls up beside it to sleep. In the next scene, when he is brought into the police station, the cops start to take the monkey away, but Jim pleads with them, "Can I keep it?" But once Jim finds Judy's compact, the monkey disappears from the film. This trading of a child's toy for the compact—an object that relates to beauty, physical appearance, the awakening of sexual desire—appropriately and immediately establishes Jim's psychological and emotional state.

But where did the monkey come from? It would seem that it came from yet another of the film's repressed scenes—but one that was less a dream fantasy than something more realistic and nightmarish. Originally, the film was to be set at Christmastime, and one early version of the script had the film opening with a scene of Buzz, Judy's hoodlum boyfriend, and some of his friends assaulting a man who is on his way home from Christmas shopping. As they beat the man and tear at his packages, the toy monkey falls to the street; later that night, Jim happens upon it. This destruction is continued later, when some kids are shown burning a Christmas tree.[37]

These bizarre scenes of Christmastime violence echo a real event that occurred some twenty-five years earlier, when Luis Buñuel had been invited to Hollywood by MGM to observe production at their studios. While in California, Buñuel met a number of the major stars of the time, including Charlie Chaplin, with whom he became somewhat friendly, and one of his most outrageous acts involved the Little Tramp. Having been invited to a Christmas party where Chaplin and Georgia Hale were also in attendance, Buñuel writes in his autobiography,

We all bought a present that was supposed to have cost somewhere between twenty and thirty dollars, hung them on the tree, and began drinking. [. . .]

"Listen," I whispered to Ugarte and an actor named Peña at the dinner table, "when I blow my nose, that's the signal to get up. Just follow me and we'll take that ridiculous tree to pieces!"

Which is exactly what we did, although it's not easy to dismember a Christmas tree. In fact, we got a great many scratches for some rather pathetic results, so we resigned ourselves to throwing the presents on the floor and stomping on them.[38]

Apparently, the intense violence in *Rebel*'s scripted scene, and the profaning of the sacred that it implied, was too much for the studio. So for some odd reason—perhaps a kind of refusal to completely abandon the profanation that was intended in these Christmas scenes, or to further repress them—the time of the film was switched from Christmas to Easter. Curiously, the scene of Buzz and his hoodlum friends beating the man with the packages remained in this version of the script, though it did not make it into the final film.[39] Few people would remember that *Rebel* is set at Eastertime; indeed, there is only one reference to it in the entire film. In the opening scene of Judy talking with the juvenile detective, she tearfully reports, "We were all together. We were gonna celebrate Easter. We were gonna catch a double bill. Big deal." With this covert reference to the repressed scenes of holiday violence, and its immediate proximity to the report of the father's violent wiping of Judy's lips, the web of Surrealist references is particularly dense.

Was anyone alert to these references at the time of the film's release? Perhaps only the critics at *Cahiers du Cinéma*, who were among the first to give serious praise to Ray's work. From the beginning, the links between his films and the world of Surrealist art were acknowledged. Ray's first film, *They Live by Night* (released in France as *Les Amants de la nuit*, or "Lovers of the Night"), was presented at the Festival du Film Maudit at Biarritz, organized by André Bazin and the film society Objectif 49. This event was presided over by Jean Cocteau, and its catalogue closed with a poem by Lautréamont, the great precursor of Surrealism. François Truffaut repeatedly noted the similarities between the world of Nicholas Ray and the world of Surrealism: he wrote of *Johnny Guitar* that it was "the *Beauty and the Beast* of Westerns, a Western dream";[40] he compared B*igger Than Life* to Luis Buñuel's *El*;[41] and when *Rebel Without a Cause* was released, Truffaut wrote, "Cocteau and *Les Enfants Terribles* . . . comes to mind. [. . .] Like Cocteau, there is a sense of realism in

Ray's work, which violently bursts to the surface, and ricochets back and forth in a flurry of words, a theatrical realism that possesses the sudden energy of a musical beat."[42] But perhaps most remarkable was Eric Rohmer's review: his description of the film serves also as an uncanny description of Man Ray's painting.

Just as he is a poet of violence, Nicholas Ray is perhaps the only poet of love; it is the fascination peculiar to both feelings that obsesses him. [. . . .] Neither fury nor cruelty, but that special intoxication into which we are plunged by a violent physical act, situation or passion. Not desire, like the majority of his compatriots in the cinema, but the mysterious affinity that locks two human beings together. To all this I would add a feeling for nature, discernible in the background. [. . .] Here, everything is circular, from the gestures of love to the movement of the stars.[43]

N O T E S

Introduction

1. Susan Sontag, "The Decay of Cinema," *New York Times Magazine*, February 25, 1996.

2. David Denby, "The Moviegoers: Why Don't People Like the Right Movies Anymore?" *New Yorker*, April 6, 1998, 95; Stanley Kauffmann, "A Lost Love," *New Republic*, September 8 and 15, 1997, 28.

3. Sontag, 61.

4. Antoine de Baecque and Thierry Frémaux, "La Cinéphilie ou L'Invention d'Une Culture," *Vingtième Siècle* 46 (April–June 1995): 135. Trans. Timothy Barnard.

5. Ibid., 134.

6. Ibid.

7. Ibid., 137.

8. Ibid., 133.

9. Quoted in Jean-André Fieschi, "Jacques Rivette," in *Cinema: A Critical Dictionary*, ed. Richard Roud (New York: Viking, 1980), 874.

10. Dudley Andrew, "The 'Three Ages' of Cinema Studies and the Age to Come," *PMLA* 115, no. 3 (May 2000): 341–351.

11. Raymond Bellour has further distinguished between the 1950s French cinephilia, which was oriented primarily toward Hollywood cinema, and the more internationalized cinephilia of the 1960s, which included the French New Wave as part of its object of obsession. See *Movie Mutations: The Changing Face of World Cinephilia*, ed. Jonathan Rosenbaum and Adrian Martin (London: BFI, 2003), 29. Clearly, the first of these manifestations of cinephilia is embedded in the latter. This study considers both these historical moments, as well as the earlier moment in the 1920s.

12. Ibid., 343.

13. Ibid., 345.

14. Ibid., 346.

15. De Baecque and Frémaux, 134.

16. Ibid., 135.

17. Jean Douchet, "La fabrique du regard," *Vertigo* 10 (1993): 34. Trans. Timothy Barnard.

18. De Baecque and Frémaux, 135.

19. Bazin, quoted in de Baecque and Frémaux, 134.

20. De Baecque and Frémaux, 139.

21. Ibid., 137.

22. Paul Willemen, "Through the Glass Darkly: Cinephilia Reconsidered," in *Looks and Frictions* (Bloomington: Indiana University Press, 1994), 232.

23. Geoffrey Nowell-Smith, "On History and the Cinema," *Screen* 31, no. 2 (Summer 1990): 170.

24. Miriam Hansen, Introduction to Siegfried Kracauer's *Theory of Film: The Redemption of Physical Reality* (Princeton: Princeton University Press, 2000), x.

1. The Desire for Cinema

1. Andrew Sarris, *The Primal Screen* (New York: Simon and Schuster, 1973), 81.

2. Antoine de Baecque and Thierry Frémaux, "La Cinéphilie ou L'Invention d'Une Culture," *Vingtième Siècle* 46 (April–June 1995): 133. Trans. Timothy Barnard.

3. Both these essays are collected in Bazin's *What Is Cinema?* vol. 1, ed. and trans. Hugh Gray (Berkeley: University of California Press, 1967).

4. Thomas Elsaesser, "Two Decades in Another Country," in *Superculture: American Popular Culture and Europe,* ed. C. W. E. Bigsby (Bowling Green: Bowling Green University Press, 1975), 203.

5. Paul Willemen, "The Desire for Cinema: An Edinburgh Retrospective," *Framework* 19 (1982): 49.

6. Dominique Païni, "La cinéphilie au risque du patrimonie," *Cahiers du Cinéma* 498 (January 1996): 54. Trans. Timothy Barnard.

7. Ibid.

8. S. J. Freedberg, "Berenson, Connoisseurship, and the History of Art," *New Criterion* 7, no. 6 (February 1989): 10.

9. Ibid.

10. Hilton Kramer, "Grappling with the Mysteries of Taste," *New York Times,* February 11, 1979: D29.

11. Freedberg, 10.

12. John Hess has argued that it was not any worldview, but a very specific one—namely, existentialist—that was valued. See his essay "*La Politique des auteurs:* Part One: World View as Aesthetic," *Jump Cut,* no. 1 (May–June 1974).

13. André Bazin, "On the *politique des auteurs,*" in *Cahiers du Cinéma, the 1950s: Neo-Realism, Hollywood, New Wave,* ed. Jim Hillier (Cambridge: Harvard University Press, 1985).

14. David Bordwell, *On the History of Film Style* (Cambridge: Harvard University Press, 1997). See chap. 3, "Against the Seventh Art: André Bazin and the Dialectical Program."

15. Freedberg, 15.

16. Rosalind Krauss, "The Ministry of Fate," in *A New History of French Literature,* ed. Denis Hollier (Cambridge: Harvard University Press, 1989).

17. André Malraux, *The Voices of Silence,* trans. Stuart Gilbert (Princeton: Princeton University Press, 1978). "Museum without Walls" is the first of four sections.

18. Bordwell, 81. The reference here should be to Jacques Rivette, not Luc Moullet. See the exchanges on Japanese cinema by Moullet, André Bazin, and Rivette in *Cahiers du Cinéma, the 1950s,* 260–265.

19. Dominique Païni, "Le cinéphile, la mélancolie, et la Cinémathèque," *Vertigo* 10 (1993): 62. Trans. Timothy Barnard.

20. Malraux, 19.

21. Dudley Andrew, "Jules, Jim, and Walter Benjamin," in *The Image in Dispute,* ed. Andrew (Austin: University of Texas Press, 1997), 35.

22. Luc Moullet, "Confession impudique d'un vieux cinéphile," *Cahiers du Cinéma* 497 (December 1995): 67. Trans. Timothy Barnard.

23. Ibid.

24. Ibid.

25. Marc Vernet, "The Fetish in the Theory and History of the Cinema," in *Endless Night: Cinema and Psychoanalysis, Parallel Histories,* ed. Janet Bergstrom (Berkeley: University of California Press, 1999).

26. Robert B. Ray, "Film Studies/Crisis/Experimentation," *Film Criticism* 17, nos. 2–3 (Winter–Spring 1993): 58.

27. For a particularly detailed and provocative account of the memory of a movie, see 25–28 of Edward Casey, *Remembering* (Bloomington: Indiana University Press, 1987).

28. Thomas Elsaesser, "Rivette and the End of Cinema," *Sight and Sound* (April 1992): 22.

29. Walter Benjamin, "The Work of Art in the Age of Mechanical Reproduction," in *Illuminations,* ed. Hannah Arendt, trans. Harry Zohn (New York: Schocken Books, 1969), 220.

30. De Baecque and Frémaux, 133–134.

31. One of the finest discussions of the transformations in cinephilia as a result of television and, especially, home video, can be found in Barbara Klinger, "The Contemporary Cinephile: Film Collecting in the Post-Video Era," in *Hollywood Spectatorship: Changing Perceptions of Cinema Audiences,* ed. Melvyn Stokes and Richard Maltby (London: BFI, 2001): 132–151.

32. Adrian Martin, *Movie Mutations: The Changing Face of World Cinephilia,* ed. Jonathan Rosenbaum and Adrian Martin (London: BFI, 2003), 6–7. Originally published in *Film Quarterly* 52, no. 1 (Fall 1998): 43.

33. Stanley Kauffmann, "A Lost Love," *New Republic,* September 8 and 15, 1997, 28. Kauffmann's essay on the death of cinephilia was inspired by Sontag's piece, as was James Wolcott's "Waiting for Godard," *Vanity Fair,* April 1997.

34. Andrew Sarris, *The American Cinema: Director and Directions 1929–1968* (Chicago: University of Chicago Press, 1968).

35. See, for example, Pierre Sorlin, "Endgame?" *Screening the Past,* 6. http://www.latrobe.edu.au/screeningthepast/ (access date: 1999).

36. Thomas Elsaesser, " 'One Train May Be Hiding Another': Private History, Memory, and National Identity," *Screening the Past,* 5, www.latrobe.edu.au/screening the past/ (access date: 1999). This essay originally appeared in *The Low Countries: Arts and Society in Flanders and the Netherlands—A Yearbook, 1996–1997* (Rekkem: Flemish Nederlands Foundation Ons Erfdeel, 1997).

37. Chap. 9 of John Belton's *Widescreen Cinema* (Cambridge: Harvard University Press, 1992) provides a superb and suggestive account of the new demands that widescreen formats brought to film spectators in the 1950s. In *A Cinema without Walls* (New York: Routledge, 1991), Timothy Corrigan argues that the "glance aesthetics" that governs the viewing of contemporary films was brought about in large part by the increased importance of the television viewing of motion pictures.

38. Malcolm Imrie, Introduction to Serge Daney, "Falling Out of Love," *Sight and Sound* (July 1992): 14.

39. Daney, 15.

40. Ibid., 14.

41. Ibid., 15.

42. E. H. Gombrich, *Art and Illusion: A Study in the Psychology of Pictorial Representation* (Princeton: Princeton University Press, 1969).

43. Christian Metz, *The Imaginary Signifier: Psychoanalysis and the Cinema*, trans. Celia Britton, Annwyl Williams, Ben Brewster, and Alfred Guzzetti (Bloomington: Indiana University Press, 1977), 10

44. Daney, 15.

45. Willemen, "Through the Glass Darkly: Cinephilia Reconsidered," *Looks and Frictions* (Bloomington: Indiana University Press, 1994), 228.

46. Païni, "La cinéphilie au risque du patrimonie," 54.

47. A fine selection of essays reflecting this theoretical position can be found in *Narrative, Apparatus, Ideology*, ed. Philip Rosen (New York: Columbia University Press, 1986). This volume includes: Jean-Louis Baudry, "Ideological Effects of the Basic Cinematic Apparatus," Jean-Louis Comolli, "Technique and Ideology: Camera, Perspective, Depth of Field," and Laura Mulvey, "Visual Pleasure and Narrative Cinema."

48. Metz, 15.

49. Ibid., 16.

50. In chap. 8 of *Downcast Eyes: The Denigration of Vision in Twentieth-Century French Thought* (Berkeley: University of California Press, 1993), Martin Jay dubs the Metzian-influenced ideological/semiotic project as "cinephobic."

51. Peter Wollen, "Afterword: Lee Russell Interviews Peter Wollen," in *Signs and Meaning in the Cinema*, expanded ed. (London: BFI, 1998), 155.

52. Willemen, "Through the Glass Darkly," 232.

53. Sylvia Harvey, "What Is Cinema? The Sensuous, the Political, and the Abstract," in *Cinema: The Beginnings and the Future*, ed. Christopher Williams (London: University of Westminster Press, 1996), 231–232.

54. Ibid., 233.

2. The Cinephiliac Moment and Panoramic Perception

1. Jean Renoir, *My Life and My Films*, trans. Norman Denny (New York: Atheneum, 1974), 18.

2. Ibid.

3. Paul Willemen, "Through the Glass Darkly: Cinephilia Reconsidered," in *Looks and Frictions* (Bloomington: Indiana University Press, 1994), 231.

4. Noel King, in Willemen, 227.

5. Ibid., 235.

6. Ibid., 237.

7. Ibid., 245.

8. Ibid., 234–235.

9. David Thomson, *A Biographical Dictionary of Film*, 3rd ed. (New York: Knopf, 1994), 614.

10. Manny Farber, *Negative Space* (New York: DaCapo Press, 1998), 17.

11. Ibid., 21.

12. Ibid., 6.

13. Greg Taylor, *Artists in the Audience: Cults, Camp, and American Film Criticism* (Princeton: Princeton University Press, 1999), 79.

14. Roger Cardinal, "Pausing Over Peripheral Detail," *Framework* 30/31 (1986): 118.

15. Ibid.

16. James Naremore, *Acting in the Cinema* (Berkeley: University of California Press, 1988), 214–215.

17. Cardinal, 119.

18. Willemen, 233–234.

19. Ibid., 232.

20. David Bordwell, *Narration in the Fiction Film* (Madison: University of Wisconsin Press, 1985), 53. See also Kristin Thompson, "The Concept of Cinematic Excess," in *Narrative, Apparatus, Ideology,* ed. Philip Rosen (New York: Columbia University Press, 1986).

21. Raymond Durgnat, David Ehrenstein, and Jonathan Rosenbaum, "Obscure Objects of Desire," *Film Comment* (July–August 1978): 61. In this case, the viewer obsessed with the color of Cary Grant's socks is Gilbert Adair.

22. Lesley Stern, "I Think, Sebastian, Therefore, I . . . Somersault," *Paradoxa* 3, nos. 3–4 (1997): 350.

23. Cardinal, 114.

24. Walker Percy, *The Moviegoer* (New York: Knopf, 1960), 7.

25. Stern, 348.

26. Roland Barthes, "The Third Meaning," in *Image/Music/Text,* trans. Stephen Heath (New York: Hill and Wang, 1977), 64–65.

27. Roland Barthes, *Camera Lucida,* trans. Richard Howard (New York: Hill and Wang, 1981), 55.

28. Gregory Ulmer, "Fetishism in Roland Barthes's Nietzschean Phase," *Papers on Language and Literature* 14, no. 3 (Summer 1978): 334–355.

29. Roland Barthes, *The Pleasure of the Text,* trans. Richard Miller (New York: Hill and Wang, 1975), 56–57.

30. Ibid., 56.

31. Durgnat et al., 61.

32. Willemen, 237.

33. Walter Pater, *The Renaissance: Studies in Art and Poetry,* in *Selected Writings of Walter Pater,* ed. Harold Bloom (New York: Columbia University Press, 1974), 17.

34. Ibid.

35. Harold Bloom, Introduction to *Selected Writings of Walter Pater,* xiii.

36. Quoted in Bloom's Introduction, xiii–xiv.

37. Quoted in Bloom's Introduction, xx.

38. Pater, 60.

39. Bloom, xxiv.

40. Pater, 60.

41. Bloom, Introduction to *Selected Writings,* xiii.

42. Leo Charney has explained that Pater's position is part of a pattern of attempts in early modernity to recover a lost sense of the present through a focus on momentary experience. See *Empty Moments: Cinema, Modernity, and Drift* (Durham, N.C.: Duke University Press, 1998).

43. Pater, 52.

44. Ibid.

45. Willemen, 248.

46. Willemen, 243.

47. Peter Wollen, *Signs and Meaning in the Cinema,* expanded ed. (London: BFI, 1998).

48. Ibid., 122.

49. Quoted in ibid., 124.

50. André Bazin, "The Ontology of the Photographic Image," in *What Is Cinema?* vol. 1, ed. and trans. Hugh Gray (Berkeley: University of California Press, 1971), 12.

51. Ibid.

52. Willemen, 227.

53. Ibid., 243.

54. Ibid., 238.

55. Laura Mulvey, "The Index and the Uncanny," in *Time and the Image,* ed. Carolyn Bailey Gill (New York: Manchester University Press, 2000).

56. Jean-Luc Godard, *Godard on Godard,* trans. and ed. Tom Milne (New York: DaCapo, 1972), 223.

57. A superb discussion of classical Hollywood's continuity system, and the way in which it turned fragmented discontinuity into an apparently seamless continuity, can be found in chap. 1 of Robert Ray, *A Certain Tendency of the Hollywood Cinema 1930–1980* (Princeton: Princeton University Press, 1985).

58. Noël Burch, *Theory of Film Practice,* trans. Helen R. Lane (Princeton, N.J.: Princeton University Press, 1981), 112.

59. Christian-Marc Bosséno, "La Place du Spectateur," *Vingtième Siècle* 46 (April–June 1995), 152–153. Trans. Timothy Barnard.

60. Willemen, 235.

61. Dudley Andrew discusses the influence on André Bazin of theories of phenomenology, especially Henri Bergson's writings, in *André Bazin* (New York: Columbia University Press, 1978). See also Andrew's *The Major Film Theories* (New York: Oxford University Press, 1976). The influence of existentialism on the young critics at *Cahiers du Cinéma* has been explored, most famously, by John Hess, "*La Politique des auteurs:* Part One: World View as Aesthetic," *Jump Cut* 1 (May–June 1974); and "Part Two: Truffaut's Manifesto," *Jump Cut* 2 (July–August 1974).

62. Dudley Andrew, "The Neglected Tradition of Phenomenology in Film Theory," *Wide Angle* 2 (1978): 44–49.

63. Vivian Sobchack, "The Active Eye: A Phenomenology of Cinematic Vision," *Quarterly Review of Film and Video* 12, no. 3 (1990): 24.

64. Vivian Sobchack, *The Address of the Eye: A Phenomenology of Film Experience* (Princeton, N.J.: Princeton University Press, 1992), 34.

65. Cardinal, 118.

66. Ibid.

67. Ibid., 124.

68. Kaja Silverman, *Threshold of the Visible World* (New York: Routledge, 1995), 181.

69. Wolfgang Schivelbusch, *The Railway Journey* (Berkeley: University of California Press, 1986).

70. Ibid., 58.

71. Ibid., 61.

72. Ibid., 58.

73. See, for example, Tom Gunning, "An Aesthetics of Astonishment: Early Film and the (In)Credulous Spectator," *Art & Text* 34 (Spring 1989); Anne Friedberg, *Window Shopping: Cinema and the Postmodern* (Berkeley: University of California Press, 1993); Jacques Aumont, "The Variable Eye, or the Mobilization of the Gaze," in *The Image in Dispute,* ed. Dudley Andrew (Austin: University of Texas Press, 1997); Lynne Kirby, *Parallel Tracks: The Railroad and Silent Cinema* (Durham, N.C.: Duke University Press, 1997); Scott Bukatman, "Zooming Out: The End of Offscreen Space," in *The New American Cinema,* ed. Jon Lewis (Durham, N.C.: Duke University Press, 1998).

74. Schivelbusch, 66.

75. Mary Ann Doane, " . . . when the direction of the force acting on the body is changed," *Wide Angle* 7, nos. 1 and 2 (1985): 44.

76. Ibid., 43.

77. Cited in Schivelbusch, 57–58.

78. Schivelbusch, 61.

79. A detailed exploration of the links between the nineteenth-century *flâneur* and the twentieth-century cinemagoer can be found in Anne Friedberg, *Window Shopping.*

80. Tom Gunning, "From the Kaleidoscope to the X-Ray: Urban Spectatorship, Poe, Benjamin, and *Traffic in Souls* (1913)," *Wide Angle* 19, no. 4 (October 1977): 28.

81. Dominique Païni, "La cinéphilie au risque du patrimonie," *Cahiers du Cinéma* 498 (January 1996): 57.

82. Durgnat et al., 61.

83. Jean Douchet, "La fabrique du regard," *Vertigo* 10 (1993): 34. Trans. Timothy Barnard.

84. Bosséno, 153.

85. François Truffaut, "A Full View," in *Cahiers du Cinéma, the 1950s: Neo-Realism, Hollywood, New Wave,* ed. Jim Hillier (Cambridge: Harvard University Press, 1985), 273.

86. André Bazin, quoted in *Cahiers du Cinéma, the 1950s,* 271.

87. Rivette, "The Age of *metteurs en scène,*" in *Cahiers du Cinéma, the 1950s,* 278.

88. François Truffaut, *The Early Film Criticism of François Truffaut,* ed. Wheeler Winston Dixon (Bloomington: Indiana University Press, 1993), 27.

It is also worth noting that the *Cahiers* criticism of 3-D echoes the complaints of some about the nineteenth-century panorama's poor simulation of depth (when compared to its successful simulation of breadth). Antonia Lant has summarized nineteenth-century critic Adolf Hildebrand: "Panoramas, in combing deep, distant, painted scenes with real foreground objects, 'brought forth an unpleasant feeling, a sort of dizziness' in the 'sensitive observer' trying to reconcile multiple, incommensurate clues to coded depth as he or she scanned from the near to the distant and back." Antonia Lant, "Haptical Cinema," *October* 74 (Fall 1995): 54. Just as Rivette complained of the distorted depth and perspective of 3-D, Truffaut, in his review of *Man in the Dark,* argued: "It is perfectly clear that, in life, we don't see 'in relief': our sight adjusts to whatever is of concern at the moment, and seeing clearly both backgrounds and foregrounds, whatever their depth, is all the more disconcerting."

89. Roland Barthes, "On CinemaScope," quoted in Jonathan Rosenbaum, *Placing Movies* (Berkeley: University of California Press, 1995), 101.

90. Rosenbaum's essay, "Barthes and Film: 12 Suggestions," anthologized in the above-cited *Placing Movies,* is one of the best essays in print on Barthes's conflicted relationship with cinema.

91. Béla Balázs, *The Theory of the Film* (North Stratford, N.H.: Ayer Company Publishers, 1972), 139–142.

92. Ibid., 55.

93. Jean-Luc Godard, *Godard on Godard,* trans. Tom Milne (New York: Da Capo Press, 1972).

94. André Bazin, *The Cinema of Cruelty,* trans. Sabine d'Estrée (New York: Seaver Books, 1982), 20.

95. Willemen, 239–240.

96. Noel King, in ibid., 235.

97. Bill Nichols, *Representing Reality* (Bloomington: Indiana University Press, 1991), 141.

98. Adrian Martin, "The Body Has No Head: Corporeal Figuration in Aldrich," *Screening the Past* 10, http://www.latrobe.edu.au/www/screeningthepast/firstrelease/fr0600/amfr10b (access date: 2000).

99. Nicole Brenez's work has been collected in a volume entitled *De la figure en général et du corps en particulier: l'invention figurative au cinema* (Paris: De Boeck

Université, 1998). One of her articles, "Ultimate Journey: Remarks on Contemporary Theory," can be found in *Screening the Past* 2, http://www.latrobe.edu.au/www/ screeingthepast/reruns/brenez (access date: 1997).

For discussions of Brenez's work, see William Routt, "For Criticism," *Screening the Past* 9, http://www.latrobe.edu.au/www/screeningthepast/shorts/reviews/rev0300/ wr1br9a (access date: 2000); and Adrian Martin, "Ultimatum: An Introduction to the work of Nicole Brenez," *Screening the Past* 2, http://www.latrobe.edu.au/www/ screeningthepast/reruns/brenezintro (access date: 1997).

100. Martin, 4–5.

101. Thomson, 29.

102. Schivelbusch, 55.

103. Jonathan Crary, *Techniques of the Observer* (Cambridge: MIT Press, 1992), 79.

104. Ibid.

105. Walter Benjamin's discussion of modernity, shock, and the stimulus shield can be found in "On Some Motifs in Baudelaire," in *Illuminations,* ed. Hannah Arendt, trans. Harry Zohn (New York: Schocken Books, 1969).

106. Susan Buck-Morss, "Aesthetics and Anaesthetics: Walter Benjamin's Artwork Essay Reconsidered," *October* 62 (Fall 1992), 4–5.

107. Schivelbusch, 63.

108. Cited in ibid., 62.

109. Cited in ibid., 63.

110. Cardinal, 124.

111. Stern, 361.

112. Cardinal, 124.

113. Walter Benjamin, "On the Mimetic Faculty," in *Reflections,* ed. Peter Demetz, trans. Edmund Jephcott (New York: Schocken Books, 1978).

114. Michael Taussig, *Mimesis and Alterity: A Particular History of the Senses* (New York: Routledge, 1993), 21.

115. Walter Benjamin, "Little History of Photography," in *Selected Writings,* vol. 2: *1927–1934,* gen. ed. Michael W. Jennings (Cambridge: Harvard University Press, 1999), 510.

116. Walter Benjamin, "The Work of Art in the Age of Mechanical Reproduction," in *Illuminations,* ed. Hannah Arendt, trans. Harry Zohn (New York: Schocken Books, 1969), 238.

117. Benjamin, "Little History of Photography," 510.

118. Taussig, 25.

119. Ibid., 23.

120. Laura Marks, *The Skin of the Film: Intercultural Cinema, Embodiment, and the Senses* (Durham, N.C.: Duke University Press, 2000), 85. William Pietz, "The Problem of the Fetish, I," *Res* 9 (Spring 1985); "The Problem of the Fetish, II," *Res* 13 (Spring 1987); "The Problem of the Fetish, IIIa," *Res* 16 (Autumn 1988).

121. Marks, 85–86.

122. André Bazin, "*Umberto D:* A Great Work," *What Is Cinema?* vol. 2, ed. and trans. Hugh Gray (Berkeley: University of California Press, 1971), 81.

123. Ibid., 82.

3. André Bazin and the Revelatory Potential of Cinema

1. Colin MacCabe, "On the Eloquence of the Vulgar," in *The Eloquence of the Vulgar* (London: BFI, 1999), 150.

2. Dudley Andrew, *André Bazin* (New York: Oxford University Press, 1999), 53.

3. Though Raymond Durgnant argues that "a certain 'fetishism' often cramps Bazin's intelligence." *Films and Feelings* (Cambridge: MIT Press, 1971), 29.

4. François Truffaut, "Foreword," in André Bazin, *What Is Cinema?* vol. 2, ed. and trans. Hugh Gray (Berkeley: University of California Press, 1971), vi.

5. Ibid.

6. André Bazin, "The Ontology of the Photographic Image," *What Is Cinema?* vol. 1, ed. and trans. Hugh Gray (Berkeley: University of California Press, 1971), 10.

7. Ibid., 11.

8. Ibid., 12.

9. Ibid., 13.

10. Ibid.

11. Ibid., 14.

12. See, for example, Mary Ann Doane, *The Emergence of Cinematic Time* (Cambridge: Harvard University Press, 2003); Miriam Bratu Hansen's introduction to Siegfried Kracauer's *Theory of Film* (Princeton, N.J.: Princeton University Press, 1997); Philip Rosen, *Change Mummified* (Minneapolis: University of Minnesota Press, 2001).

13. Bazin, "The Ontology of the Photographic Image," 15.

14. André Bazin, *Jean Renoir,* ed. François Truffaut, trans. W. W. Halsey II and William H. Simon (New York: Touchstone, 1971), 28.

15. Dai Vaughan, *For Documentary* (Berkeley: University of California Press, 1999), 4–5. See also Anthony Guneratne, "The Birth of a New Realism: Photography, Painting and the Advent of Documentary Cinema," *Film History* 10 (1998): 165–187.

16. Philip Rosen, "History of Image, Image of History: Subject and Ontology in Bazin," *Wide Angle* 9, no. 4 (1988): 9.

17. Ibid.

18. Ibid., 31.

19. That is, these experiences are not aesthetic in the fine arts–appreciation sense of the term; but as we saw in chapter 2, they are aesthetic in the bodily sense of the term.

20. Paul Willemen, "Through the Glass Darkly: Cinephilia Reconsidered," in *Looks and Frictions* (Bloomington: Indiana University Press, 1994), 253.

21. Sergei Eisenstein, "Through Theater to Cinema," in *Film Form,* ed. and trans. Jay Leyda (New York: Harcourt Brace Jovanovich, 1949), 3.

22. Ibid. See also "The Cinematographic Principle and the Ideogram" and "Dickens, Griffith, and the Film Today," both in *Film Form.*

23. Bazin, "The Ontology of the Photographic Image," 15.

24. André Bazin, "The Evolution of the Language of Cinema," *What Is Cinema?* vol. 1, 24.

25. Ibid.

26. Ibid.

27. André Bazin, "William Wyler, or the Jansenist of Directing," in *Bazin at Work,* ed. Bert Cardullo, trans. Alain Piette (New York: Routledge, 1997), 4.

28. Annette Michelson, Introduction to Noël Burch, *Theory of Film Practice* (Princeton, N.J.: Princeton University Press, 1981), xi. Review of *What Is Cinema?, Artforum* 1, no. 10 (1968): 67–71.

29. Andrew, 58–59.

30. Quoted in Colin MacCabe, *Godard: Portrait of the Artist at Seventy* (New York: Farrar, Straus and Giroux, 2003), 48.

31. André Bazin, *The Cinema of Cruelty* (New York: Seaver Books, 1982), 57. Bazin's claim that Buñuel's were "the only cinematic productions of major quality inspired by surrealism" must surely be taken in the strictest sense. Bazin also held Jean Vigo in the highest esteem, and presented a restored version of *L'Atalante* at the Biarritz Festival.

32. Bazin, *Jean Renoir,* 85–86.

33. Alexander Astruc, "The Birth of a New Avant-Garde: *La Caméra-stylo,*" in *The New Wave,* ed. Peter Graham (New York: Doubleday, 1968), 18.

34. Bazin, "The Ontology of the Photographic Image," 13.

35. Bazin, *Jean Renoir,* 82.

36. Ibid., 84.

37. André Bazin, "A propos de Jean Painlevé," *Qu'est-ce que le cinéma?* vol. 1: *Ontologie et Langage,* 37. Trans. Timothy Barnard.

38. André Breton, "Manifesto of Surrealism," in *Manifestoes of Surrealism,* trans. Richard Seaver and Helen R. Lane (Ann Arbor: University of Michigan Press, 1972), 26.

39. Quoted in Rosalind E. Krauss, "The Photographic Conditions of Surrealism," in *The Originality of the Avant-garde and Other Modernist Myths* (Cambridge: MIT Press, 1986), 103.

40. Breton, 29.

41. Adrian Martin. "The Artificial Night: Surrealism and Cinema," in *Surrealism: Revolution by Night* (Melbourne: National Gallery of Australia, 1993), 192.

42. See Paul Hammond, ed., *The Shadow and Its Shadow: Surrealist Writings on the Cinema* (London: Polygon, 1991), 42–43.

43. Hubert Damisch, "Five Notes for a Phenomenology of the Photographic Image," *October* 5 (Summer 1978): 72.

44. Breton, 27–28.

45. André Breton, "Surrealist Situation of the Object," *Manifestoes of Surrealism.*

46. Ibid., 3.

47. Martin Heidegger, *The Question Concerning Technology,* trans. William Lovitt (New York: Garland, 1977).

48. Walter Benjamin, "Surrealism: The Last Snapshot of the European Intelligentsia," in *Selected Writings,* vol. 2: *1927–1934,* gen. ed. Michael W. Jennings (Cambridge: Harvard University Press, 1999), 210.

49. Walter Benjamin, "The Work of Art in the Age of Mechanical Reproduction," in *Illuminations,* ed. Hannah Arendt, trans. Harry Zohn (New York: Schocken Books, 1969), 235.

50. Ibid., 236.

51. Louis Aragon, "On Décor," in *The Shadow and Its Shadow,* ed. Paul Hammond, 57.

52. André Bazin, "An Aesthetic of Reality," in *What Is Cinema?* vol. 2, ed. and trans. Hugh Gray (Berkeley: University of California Press, 1971), 37.

53. Ibid., 37–38.

54. Peter Wollen, "Introduction to Citizen Kane," in *Readings and Writings: Semiotic Counter-Strategies* (London: Verso, 1982), 51.

55. Kristin Ross, *Fast Cars, Clean Bodies: Decolonization and the Reordering of French Culture* (Cambridge: Harvard University Press, 1995), 180.

56. André Bazin, "Charlie Chaplin," in *What Is Cinema?* vol. 1, 145.

57. Ibid., 146.

58. Bill Brown, "How to Do Things with Things (A Toy Story)," *Critical Inquiry* 24, no. 4 (Summer 1998): 935–964.

59. Ibid., 953.

60. Bazin, "An Aesthetic of Reality," 35.

61. Bazin, *Jean Renoir,* 86.

62. André Bazin, "*Umberto D:* A Great Work," in *What Is Cinema?* vol. 2, 82.

63. Sigmund Freud, "The 'Uncanny,'" in *The Complete Psychological Works of Sigmund Freud,* vol. 17, trans. James Strachey (London: Hogarth Press, 1955), 236, 234.

64. Lesley Stern, "I Think, Sebastian, Therefore . . . I Somersault," *Paradoxa* 3, no. 3–4 (1997): 351, 357.

65. Freud, 226.

66. William Paul, "Uncanny Theater: The Twin Inheritances of the Movies," *Paradoxa* 3, no. 3–4 (1997): 321–347.

67. André Bazin, "Cabiria: Voyage to the End of Neo-Realism," in *What Is Cinema?* vol. 2, 88.

68. Margaret Cohen, *Profane Illumination* (Berkeley: University of California Press, 1993).

69. André Breton, *Nadja,* trans. Richard Howard (New York: Grove Press, 1960), 19.

70. Ibid., 89.

71. Anna Balakian, *Surrealism: The Road to the Absolute* (Chicago: University of Chicago Press, 1986), 125. Adam Rifkin has argued the opposite, that "the chance discovery" typical of Breton's surrealism "actually became the masquerade for the fear of the aleatoric." *Street Noises: Parisian Pleasure 1900–40* (New York: Manchester University Press, 1993), 125.

72. Breton, *Nadja,* 19.

73. Ibid., 78.

74. Wollen, 52.

75. Rosen, 11.

76. E. H. Gombrich, *Art and Illusion: A Study in the Psychology of Pictorial Representation* (Princeton, N.J.: Princeton University Press, 1960).

77. Bazin, "William Wyler," 7.

78. Ibid., 9.

79. Bazin, "An Aesthetic of Reality," 32.

80. André Bazin, "In Defense of Rossellini," in *What Is Cinema?* vol. 2, 101.

81. Gombrich, 232, 385.

82. Rosen, 9.

83. Bazin, "The Ontology of the Photographic Image," 13.

84. Amédée Ayfre, "Neo-Realism and Phenomenology," in *Cahiers du Cinéma, the 1950s: Neo-Realism, Hollywood, New Wave,* ed. Jim Hillier (Cambridge: Harvard University Press, 1985), 182.

85. Ibid., 186.

86. Gombrich, 173.

87. Quoted in Fereydoun Hoveyda and Jacques Rivette, "Interview with Roberto Rossellini," in *Cahiers du Cinéma, the 1950s,* 213.

88. Peter Galassi, *Before Photography* (New York: Museum of Modern Art, 1981), 20.

89. Jacques Aumont, "The Variable Eye, or the Mobilization of the Gaze," in *The Image in Dispute: Art and Cinema in the Age of Photography,* ed. Dudley Andrew (Austin: University of Texas Press, 1997), 232.

90. Galassi, 20.

91. Ibid., 25.

92. Gombrich, 385.

93. Roland Barthes, *Camera Lucida,* trans. Richard Howard (New York: Hill and Wang, 1981), 34.

94. Bazin, *Jean Renoir,* 32.

95. Ibid., 84.

96. Quoted in Jean Narboni, "The Critical Years: Interview with Eric Rohmer," in Eric Rohmer, *The Taste for Beauty,* ed. Jean Narboni, trans. Carol Volk (New York: Cambridge University Press, 1989), 11.

97. Quoted in Bazin, *Jean Renoir,* 17.

98. François Truffaut, *The Films in My Life*, trans. Leonard Mayhew (New York: Simon and Schuster, 1975).

99. André Malraux, "Sketch for a Psychology of the Moving Pictures," in *Reflections on Art*, ed. Susanne K. Langer (Baltimore: Johns Hopkins University Press, 1958).

100. Ibid., 322.

101. Noël Burch, *Theory of Film Practice*, 105.

102. Gombrich, 189.

103. Jacques Rivette, "Letter on Rossellini," in *Cahiers du Cinéma, the 1950s*, 194.

104. Ibid., 197.

105. Gérard Gozlan, "In Praise of André Bazin," in *The New Wave*, 54.

106. Eric Rohmer, "The Land of Miracles," in *Cahiers du Cinéma, the 1950s*, 206.

107. Gilbert Adair, *Flickers: An Illustrated Celebration of 100 Years of Cinema* (London: Faber & Faber, 1995), 186.

108. Ibid.

109. Ibid., 186–187.

110. Ibid., 112.

111. Ibid.

112. Quoted in V. F. Perkins, *Film as Film* (Baltimore: Penguin Books, 1972), 30.

4. *Cahiers du Cinéma* and the Way of Looking

1. Jim Hillier, ed., *Cahiers du Cinéma, the 1950s: Neo-Realism, Hollywood, New Wave* (Cambridge: Harvard University Press, 1985), 75.

2. Paul Willemen, "Through the Glass Darkly: Cinephilia Reconsidered," in *Looks and Frictions* (Bloomington: Indiana University Press, 1994), 235.

3. Jean-Luc Godard, *Godard on Godard*, ed. and trans. Tom Milne (New York: Da Capo, 1972), 62.

4. Ibid., 63.

5. Ibid., 133–134.

6. François Truffaut, *The Films in My Life*, trans. Leonard Mayhew (New York: Simon and Schuster, 1975), 70.

7. Ibid., 27–28.

8. Ibid., 38.

9. François Truffaut, *Correspondence 1945–1984*, ed. Gilles Jacob and Claude de Givray, trans. Gilbert Adair (New York: Noonday Press, 1990), 35.

10. Willemen, 235.

11. Ibid.

12. Ibid.

13. Hillier, 76.

14. François Truffaut, "A Wonderful Certainty," in *Cahiers du Cinéma, the 1950s*, 107.

15. Jean-Luc Godard, "Nothing but Cinema," in *Cahiers du Cinéma, the 1950s*, 117.

16. Ibid.

17. Jacques Rivette, "On Imagination," in *Cahiers du Cinéma, the 1950s*, 105.

18. Truffaut, "A Wonderful Certainty," 108.

19. Rivette, "On Imagination," 105.

20. Ibid., 104–105.

21. Fereydoun Hoveyda, "Sunspots," in *Cahiers du Cinéma, the 1960s: New Wave, New Cinema, Reevaluating Hollywood*, ed. Jim Hillier (Cambridge: Harvard University Press, 1986), 142.

22. Rivette, "On Imagination," 105.

23. Hillier, *Cahiers du Cinéma, the 1950s*, 225.

24. Rivette, "On Imagination," 105.

25. Jean-Luc Godard, "Beyond the Stars," in *Cahiers du Cinéma, the 1950s*, 118.

26. Rivette, "On Imagination," 104.

27. Hillier, 9.

28. Jim Hillier, "Introduction: *Cahiers du Cinéma* in the 1960s," in *Cahiers du Cinéma, the 1960s*, 2.

29. David Bordwell and Kristin Thompson, *Film Art: An Introduction*, 5th ed. (New York: McGraw-Hill, 1997), 169.

30. Louis Giannetti, *Understanding Movies*, 9th ed. (Upper Saddle River, N.J.: Prentice-Hall, 2002), 538.

31. A fine discussion of different understandings and uses of the term *mise-en-scène* can be found in Adrian Martin's essay "*Mise en scene* Is Dead, or The Expressive, The Excessive, The Technical and The Stylish," *Continuum: The Australian Journal of Media and Culture* 5, no. 2 (1990), http://kali.murdoch.edu.au/~cntinuum (access date: 1998). See also John Gibbs, *Mise-en-Scène: Film Style and Interpretation* (New York: Wallflower Press, 2002).

32. Paul Mayersberg, "From *Laura* to *Angel Face*," in *Movie Reader*, ed. Ian Cameron (New York: Praeger, 1972), 44.

33. Martin, 10.

34. Robin Wood, "Attitudes in *Advise and Consent*," in *Movie Reader*, 56.

35. Ibid., 54.

36. This hermeneutic approach to details of gesture would remain the standard at *Movie* well beyond this heady moment of intense polemicization about auteurism and *mise-en-scène*. In *Movie*, nos. 34/35 (1990), V. F. Perkins began an essay with a several-hundred-word analysis of "two swift gestures" made by Barbara Bel Geddes in a scene from Max Ophuls's *Caught*. "It is necessary to reflect on what gestures mean and where they come from," he argues. On the other hand, he notes, "A moment-by-moment plot of the intricately patterned and unavoidably meaningful eye movements performed by Bel Geddes and [Robert] Ryan would be tedious and unrevealing." "Must We Say What They Mean? Film Criticism and Interpretation," *Movie*, nos. 34/35 (1990): 1.

37. Pam Cook, "*Movie* and *Mise-en-Scène* Analysis," in *The Cinema Book*, 2nd ed., ed. Pam Cook and Mieke Bernink (London: BFI, 1999), 269.

38. Wood, 54.

39. John Caughie, ed., *Theories of Authorship* (London: Routledge & Kegan Paul, 1981), 48.

40. Andrew Sarris, "Preminger's Two Periods: Studio and Solo," *Film Comment* 3, no. 3 (Summer 1965): 13.

41. Andrew Sarris, "Review of *Bunny Lake Is Missing*," in *Confessions of a Cultist* (New York: Simon and Schuster, 1970), 214.

42. It should be remembered that "Notes on the *Auteur* Theory in 1962" was fashioned as a kind of rebuttal to Bazin's essay criticizing *la politique*. Sarris's essay is anthologized in his collection, *The Primal Screen* (New York: Simon and Schuster, 1973).

43. Martin, 5.

44. Jacques Rivette, "The Essential," in *Cahiers du Cinéma, the 1950s*, 133.

45. Ibid., 134.

46. Ibid., 132.

47. Ibid., 134.

48. Ibid., 133.

49. André Bazin, *Jean Renoir*, ed. François Truffaut, trans. W. W. Halsey and William H. Simon (New York: Touchstone, 1971), 32.

50. Rivette, "The Essential," 134.

51. Ibid., 133.
52. Ibid.
53. Ibid., 134.
54. William Routt, "L'Evidence," *Continuum: The Australian Journal of Media and Culture* 5, no. 2 (1990), http://kali.murdoch.edu.au/~cntinuum (access date: 1998).
55. Ibid., 12.
56. Ibid., 9.
57. Ibid., 8.
58. Ibid., 9.
59. Ibid., 12.
60. Ibid., 10.
61. Ibid., 12.
62. Ibid., 11.
63. Ibid., 15.
64. Rivette, "The Essential," 135.
65. Routt, 16.
66. Quoted in Martin, 30.
67. Quoted in Peter Wollen, "Fashion Notes," *Framework* 4, no. 1 (1999): 2.
68. Quoted in Richard Abel, *French Cinema: The First Wave* (Princeton, N.J.: Princeton University Press, 1984), 249.
69. A fine summary of the film society movement during this period can be found in Part 3 of Abel's *French Cinema: The First Wave.*
70. David Bordwell, "French Impressionist Cinema: Film Culture, Film Theory and Film Style" (Ph.D. thesis, University of Iowa, 1974).
71. Paul Willemen, "Through the Glass Darkly," 233.
72. Willemen notes that, "In an angry letter to Delluc's own magazine, *Cinéa,* [Louis] Feuillade had protested against the impressionists' appropriation of a term that had appeared in the 1874 edition of the *Larousse* dictionary." Paul Willemen, *"Photogénie* and Epstein," in *Looks and Frictions,* 126.
73. Quoted in Abel, *French Cinema: The First Wave,* 292.
74. Ibid., 315.
75. Jean Epstein, "Magnification," in *French Film Theory and Criticism, 1907–1939,* vol. 1, ed. Richard Abel (Princeton, N.J.: Princeton University Press, 1988), 236.
76. Ibid.
77. Epstein, "On Certain Characteristics of *Photogénie,*" in *French Film Theory and Criticism, 1907–1939,* vol. 1, 317.
78. Ibid.
79. Ibid.
80. Jean Epstein, "The Senses I (b)," in *French Film Theory and Criticism, 1907–1939,* vol. 1, 243. Epstein's enthusiasm for Hayakawa was not uncommon among the Impressionists. Louis Delluc called him "a phenomenon" and placed him in the company of Charles Chaplin. See Louis Delluc, "Beauty in the Cinema," also in *French Film Theory and Criticism,* 138.
81. Ibid.
82. Malcolm Turvey, "Jean Epstein's Cinema of Immanence: The Rehabilitation of the Corporeal Eye," *October* 83 (Winter 1998): 34.
83. Martin Jay, *Downcast Eyes: The Denigration of Vision in Twentieth Century French Thought* (Berkeley: University of California Press, 1994).
84. Turvey, 35.
85. Epstein, "On Certain Characteristics of *Photogénie,*" 317–318.
86. Willemen, *"Photogénie* and Epstein," 126.

87. Ibid.

88. Ibid.

89. Quoted in Willemen, "*Photogénie* and Epstein," 127.

90. Ibid., 127.

91. Alexander Astruc, "The Birth of a New Avant-Garde: *La Caméra-stylo,*" in *The New Wave,* ed. Peter Graham (New York: Doubleday, 1968).

92. François Truffaut, "A Certain Tendency of the French Cinema," in *Movies and Methods,* ed. Bill Nichols (Berkeley: University of California Press, 1976), 233.

93. Ibid., 232.

94. Ibid.

95. Alexandre Astruc, "What is *mise en scène?*" in *Cahiers du Cinéma, the 1950s,* 266.

96. Ibid.

97. Serge Daney, "Interview: *Les Cahiers du Cinéma* 1968–1977," *The Thousand Eyes,* no. 2 (1977), 20–21.

98. Jacques Rivette, "The Hand," in *Cahiers du Cinéma, the 1950s,* 141.

99. Ibid., 140.

100. Ibid., 142.

101. Ibid., 141.

102. Jacques Rivette, "Letter on Rossellini," in *Cahiers du Cinéma, the 1950s,* 197.

103. Ibid., 196.

104. Ibid.

105. Ibid.

106. Rivette, "The Hand," 142.

107. Rivette, "Letter on Rossellini," 197.

108. Ibid., 200.

109. Jean-André Fieschi, "Jacques Rivette," in *Cinema: A Critical Dictionary,* ed. Richard Roud (New York: Viking Press, 1980), 875.

110. Rivette, "Letter on Rossellini," 203.

111. Rivette, "The Essential," 134.

112. Jonathan Rosenbaum, in Rosenbaum, Lauren Sedofsky, and Gilbert Adair, "Phantom Interviewers over Rivette," *Film Comment* (September–October 1974): 18.

113. Quoted in Jean-André Fieschi, 872.

114. Quoted in Rosenbaum, 22.

115. Fieschi, 874.

116. Gilbert Adair, in "Phantom Interviewers over Rivette," *Film Comment* (September–October 1974): 20.

117. Thomas Elsaesser, "Rivette and the End of Cinema," *Sight and Sound* (April 1992): 22.

118. Quoted in Fieschi, 874.

119. Tom Gunning, "The Cinema of Attractions: Early Cinema, Its Spectator and the Avant-Garde," *Wide Angle* 8, nos. 3 and 4 (1986): 64.

120. Ibid., 66.

121. Ibid.

122. The most famous proclamation of this opposition came from Jean-Luc Godard: "Cinema, Truffaut said, is spectacle—Méliès—and research—Lumière." *Godard on Godard,* 181.

123. An excellent discussion of these developments can be found in Noël Burch's entry, "Fritz Lang: German Period," in Richard Roud's *Cinema: A Critical Dictionary.*

124. Gunning, 68.

125. Peter Wollen, "The Two Avant-gardes," in *Readings and Writings: Semiotic Counter-Strategies* (London: Verso, 1982).

126. Gunning, 68.

127. Jonathan Rosenbaum, "Work and Play in the House of Fiction," in *Placing Movies* (Berkeley: University of California Press, 1995), 149.

128. Ibid.

129. Noël Burch, *Life to Those Shadows* (Berkeley: University of California Press, 1990), 154.

130. Ibid.

131. Jean-Luc Godard, *Godard on Godard*, 173.

132. Richard Roud, *Cinema: A Critical Dictionary*, 877.

133. Adair, 21.

134. Dominique Païni, "Le cinéphile, la mélancholie, et la Cinémathèque," *Vertigo* 10 (1993): 62. Trans. Timothy Barnard.

135. See Richard Roud's entry, "Louis Feuillade and The Serial," in his *Cinema: A Critical Dictionary*, 348–359.

136. Ibid., 348.

137. Dominique Païni, "La cinéphilie au risque du patrimonie," *Cahiers du cinéma* 498 (January 1996): 57. Trans. Timothy Barnard.

5. Film and the Limits of History

1. Susan Buck-Morss, "Aesthetics and Anaesthetics: Walter Benjamin's Artwork Essay Reconsidered," *October* 62 (Fall 1992): 16.

2. See, for example, Eduardo Cadava, *Words of Light: Theses on the Photography of History* (Princeton, N.J.: Princeton University Press, 1997).

3. See Miriam Hansen's introduction to the recent edition of Kracauer's *Theory of Film: The Redemption of Physical Reality*.

4. Siegfried Kracauer, *Theory of Film* (Princeton, N.J.: Princeton University Press, 2000), xlix.

5. Hansen, Introduction to *Theory of Film*, x.

6. Kracauer, 60.

7. Ibid.

8. Gertrud Koch, *Siegfried Kracauer: An Introduction*, trans. Jeremy Gaines (Princeton, N.J.: Princeton University Press, 2000), 105.

9. Kracauer, 56–57.

10. Ibid., 96.

11. Heide Schlüpmann, "Phenomenology of Film: On Siegfried Kracauer's Writings of the 1920s," *New German Critique* 40 (Winter 1987): 109–110.

12. Kracauer, 170.

13. Ibid., 165.

14. Ian Aitken has drawn just this link between Kracauer's film theory and the legacy of Surrealism. See "Distraction and Redemption: Kracauer, Surrealism, and Phenomenology," *Screen* 39, no. 2 (Summer 1998): 124–140.

15. Koch, 103.

16. Kracauer, 158.

17. This term, cited by Miriam Hansen, is used by Kracauer in an early draft of material that would eventually become *Theory of Film*. See Hansen's essay "'With Skin and Hair': Kracauer's Theory of Film, Marseille 1940," *Critical Inquiry* 19, no. 3 (Spring 1993): 437–469.

18. Quoted in Hansen, Introduction to *Theory of Film*, xxi.

19. Kracauer, 158–159.

20. Hansen, x.

21. Siegfried Kracauer, "Photography," in *The Mass Ornament* (Cambridge: Harvard University Press, 1995), 49.

22. Ibid., 50.

23. Ibid., 62.

24. Ibid., 62.

25. Quoted in Gertrud Koch, 96.

26. Walter Benjamin, "Little History of Photography," *Selected Writings*, vol. 2: *1927–1934*, gen. ed. Michael W. Jennings (Cambridge: Harvard University Press, 1999), 510.

27. Ibid., 514.

28. Ibid., 510.

29. Ibid., 512.

30. Walter Benjamin, "The Work of Art in the Age of Mechanical Reproduction," in *Illuminations*, ed. Hannah Arendt, trans. Harry Zohn (New York: Schocken Books, 1969), 235–237.

31. Sigmund Freud, "On Beginning the Treatment," in *Therapy and Technique* (New York: W. W. Norton, 1963), 147.

32. Ibid.

33. Benjamin, "Little History of Photography," 518–519.

34. Miriam Hansen, "Benjamin, Cinema, and Experience: 'The Blue Flower in the Land of Technology,'" *New German Critique* 40 (Winter 1987): 189.

35. Walter Benjamin, "On Some Motifs in Baudelaire," in *Illuminations*, 188.

36. Benjamin, "Little History of Photography," 512.

37. Hansen, "Benjamin, Cinema, and Experience," 188.

38. Benjamin, "On Some Motifs in Baudelaire," 188.

39. Hansen, "Benjamin, Cinema, and Experience," 200.

40. Benjamin, "On Some Motifs in Baudelaire," 158.

41. Ibid.

42. See Benjamin's discussion in "The Image of Proust," in *Illuminations*, 214.

43. Edward S. Casey, "The Memorability of the Filmic Image," *Quarterly Review of Film Studies* 6, no. 3 (Summer 1981): 261.

44. Hansen, "Benjamin, Cinema, and Experience," 209.

45. Walter Benjamin, "Theses on the Philosophy of History," *Illuminations*, 262.

46. Ibid.

47. Ibid., 254.

48. Ibid., 255.

49. Hansen, "Benjamin, Cinema, and Experience," 194.

50. Ibid., 194–195.

51. Ibid., 217–218.

52. François Truffaut, *The Films in My Life*, trans. Leonard Mayhew (New York: Simon and Schuster, 1975), 3–4.

53. Jonathan Rosenbaum, "Putting Back the Ritz," in *Seeing in the Dark: A Compendium of Cinemagoing*, ed. Ian Breakwell and Paul Hammond (London: Serpent's Tail, 1990), 48.

54. Tom Gunning, "From the Kaleidoscope to the X-Ray: Urban Spectatorship, Poe, Benjamin, and *Traffic in Souls* (1913)," *Wide Angle* 19, no. 4 (October 1997): 28.

55. The *badaud*, it would seem, experiences what Scott Bukatman has described as "kaledioscopic" perception, a term he relates not to panoramas, but to phantasmagorias, another nineteenth-century visual entertainment form discussed by Benjamin. This mode, "comprised of equal parts delirium, kinesis, and immersion," finds its contemporary manifestation in special effects spectacles and rides. Scott Bukatman, "The

Ultimate Trip: Special Effects and Kaleidoscopic Perception," *Iris,* no. 25 (Spring 1998): 75–97.

56. Walter Benjamin, "The Paris of the Second Empire in Baudelaire," in *Charles Baudelaire: A Lyric Poet in the Era of High Capitalism,* trans. Harry Zohn (London: NLB, 1973), 69. One of the best discussions the *flâneur,* the detective, and issues of legibility and illegibility in the modern European cities of the mid-nineteenth century can be found in chap. 2 of Robert B. Ray's *The Avant-garde Finds Andy Hardy* (Cambridge: Harvard University Press, 1995).

57. Paul Willemen, "Through the Glass Darkly," in *Looks and Frictions* (Bloomington: Indiana University Press/BFI, 1994), 233.

58. Walter Benjamin, *The Arcades Project,* ed. Rolf Tiedemann, trans. Howard Eiland and Kevin McLaughlin (Cambridge: Harvard University Press, 1999), 208, 209.

59. Ibid., 204–205.

60. Walter Benjamin, "Edward Fuchs: Collector and Historian," *New German Critique* 5 (Spring 1975): 27–58.

61. Benjamin, *The Arcades Project,* 211.

62. Ibid.

63. Ibid., 205.

64. Ibid., 206–207.

65. Jean-Louis Leutrat, "Traces That Resemble Us: Godard's *Passion,*" *Sub-Stance* 51 (1986): 36.

66. Roger Cardinal, "Pausing over Peripheral Detail," *Framework* 30/31 (1986): 118.

67. Susan Pearce, *On Collecting: An Investigation into Collecting in the European Tradition* (London: Routledge, 1995), 32.

68. John Windsor, "Identity Parades," in *Cultures of Collecting,* ed. John Elsner and Roger Cardinal (Cambridge: Harvard University Press, 1994), 50.

69. Pearce, 32.

70. Windsor, 50.

71. Pearce, 32.

72. Windsor, 50.

73. Roger Cardinal, 118.

74. Robert C. Allen and Douglas Gomery, *Film History: Theory and Practice* (New York: McGraw-Hill, 1985), 6.

75. Ibid., 7.

76. Keith Jenkins, *Re-Thinking History* (New York: Routledge, 1991).

77. Allen and Gomery, 15.

78. Ibid., 17.

79. See, for example, their discussion of the first commercial exhibition of motion pictures in the United States, 18–20.

80. Hayden White, *Tropics of Discourse: Essays in Cultural Criticism* (Baltimore: Johns Hopkins University Press, 1978), 43.

81. Ibid., 42.

82. Ibid., 43.

83. Ibid.

84. Ibid.

85. Antoine de Baecque and Thierry Frémaux, "La Cinéphilie ou L'Invention d'Une Culture," *Vingtième Siècle* 46 (April–June 1995): 136. Trans. Timothy Barnard.

86. Ibid., 137.

87. Ibid.

88. Ibid., 142.

89. Ibid., 136.
90. Ibid.

6. A Cinephiliac History

1. Thomas Elsaesser, "Louis Lumiére—the Cinema's First Virtualist?" in *Cinema Futures: Cain, Abel, or Cable,* ed. Elsaesser and Kay Hoffmann (Amsterdam: Amsterdam University Press, 1998), 47.

2. Ibid., 50.

3. Roland Barthes, *Mythologies,* trans. Annette Lavers (New York: Hill and Wang, 1972), 158–159.

4. Paul Willemen concludes, "Mysticism was indeed the swamp in which most of the theoretical statements of the Impressionists eventually drowned." Paul Willemen, "*Photogénie* and Epstein," in *Looks and Frictions* (Bloomington: Indiana University Press, 1994), 214.

5. Catherine Gallagher and Stephen Greenblatt, *Practicing New Historicism* (Chicago: University of Chicago Press, 2000), 52.

6. Ibid., 47.

7. Ibid.

8. Ibid., 17.

9. Ibid., 49.

10. Michel Foucault, *Michel Foucault: Power, Truth, Strategy,* ed. Meaghan Morris and Paul Patton (Sydney: Feral Publications, 1979), 158.

11. Ibid., 157.

12. One of the most famous examples is Stephen Greenblatt's essay "Fiction and Friction," which is collected in his volume *Shakespearean Negotiations* (Berkeley: University of California Press, 1988).

13. David Simpson, "Touches of the Real," *London Review of Books* 23, no. 10 (24 May 2001): 26.

14. Gallagher and Greenblatt, 15.

15. Ibid.

16. Joel Fineman, "The History of the Anecdote: Fiction and Fiction," in *The New Historicism,* ed. H. Aram Veeser (New York: Routledge, 1989), 56.

17. Paul Willemen, "Through the Glass Darkly: Cinephilia Reconsidered," in *Looks and Frictions,* 243.

18. Gallagher and Greenblatt, 67.

19. Robert Darnton, *The Great Cat Massacre* (New York: Vintage, 1985), 4–5.

20. Willemen, "Through the Glass Darkly," 235, 231.

21. Gallagher and Greenblatt, 50.

22. Fineman, 61.

23. Gallagher and Greenblatt, 51.

24. Willemen, "Through the Glass Darkly," 235.

25. Ibid., 239.

26. Roland Barthes, *Roland Barthes,* trans. Richard Howard (New York: Hill and Wang, 1977), 90.

27. Fredric Jameson, *Signatures of the Visible* (New York: Routledge, 1990), 2–3.

28. Roland Barthes, "*Longtemps, je me suis couché de bonne heure . . . ,*" in *The Rustle of Language,* trans. Richard Howard (New York: Hill and Wang, 1977), 278–279.

29. For a thorough inventory and critique of film studies' commitment to various forms of hermeneutics, see David Bordwell's *Making Meaning* (Cambridge: Harvard University Press, 1989).

30. Roland Barthes, *Camera Lucida,* trans. Richard Howard (New York: Hill and Wang, 1981), 45.

31. Roger Cardinal, "Pausing over Peripheral Detail," *Framework* 30/31 (1986): 124.

32. Lesley Stern, "I Think, Sebastian, Therefore . . . I Somersault: Film and the Uncanny," *Paradoxa* 3–4 (1997): 350.

33. Ibid., 351.

34. For a full discussion of the theory of heuretics, see Gregory Ulmer's books *Teletheory: Grammatology in the Age of Video* (New York: Routledge, 1989) and *Heuretics: The Logic of Invention* (Baltimore: Johns Hopkins University Press, 1994).

35. Robert B. Ray, *The Avant-garde Finds Andy Hardy* (Cambridge: Harvard University Press, 1995), 114–115.

36. Ibid., 116.

37. Ibid., 117.

38. Stanley Cavell, *Disowning Knowledge in Seven Plays of Shakespeare* (New York: Cambridge University Press, 1987), 3. See also William Rothman and Marian Keane's discussion in *Reading Cavell's The World Viewed: A Philosophical Perspective on Film* (Detroit: Wayne State University Press, 2000), 24–28.

39. See Sorlin's *Esthéthiques de l'audio-visuel* (Paris: Nathan, 1992).

40. These words, a summary of Sorlin's position, come from Dominique Païni, "Le cinéphile, la mélancholie et la Cinémathèque," *Vertigo* 10 (1993): 64. Trans. Timothy Barnard.

41. Lesley Chow, "Speed and Light: David Thomson on Film," *Senses of Cinema* 28 (September–October 2003). http://www.sensesofcinema.com/contents/03/28/davidthomson.html (access date: 2003).

42. Gilbert Adair, *Myths and Memories* (London: Flamingo, 1986), xiv.

43. Roland Barthes, *Roland Barthes,* trans. Richard Howard (New York: Hill and Wang, 1977), 107.

44. Ibid., 108–109.

45. Ibid., 109–110.

46. Ibid., 87.

47. Joe Brainerd, *I Remember* (New York: Penguin Books, 1995).

48. Quoted in Adair, xv.

49. Walter Benjamin, "Surrealism: Last Snapshot of the European Intelligentsia," in *Selected Writings,* vol. 2: *1927–1934,* gen. ed. Michael W. Jennings (Cambridge: Harvard University Press, 1999), 210.

50. Max Pensky, "Tactics of Remembrance: Proust, Surrealism, and the Origin of the *Passagenwerk,*" in *Walter Benjamin and the Demands of History,* ed. Michael P. Steinberg (Ithaca: Cornell University Press, 1996).

51. Benjamin, "Surrealism," 210.

52. Recall Benjamin's words, cited earlier: "Breton and Nadja are the lovers who convert everything that we have experienced on mournful railway journeys (railways are beginning to age), on Godforsaken Sunday afternoons in the proletarian quarters of the great cities, in the first glance through the rain-blurred windows of a new apartment, into revolutionary experience, if not action. They bring the immense forces of 'atmosphere' concealed in these things to the point of explosion." "Surrealism," 210.

53. Benjamin, *The Arcades Project,* ed. Rolf Tiedemann, trans. Howard Eiland and Kevin McLaughlin (Cambridge: Harvard University Press, 1999), 456.

54. Quoted in Richard Wolin, *Walter Benjamin: An Aesthetic of Redemption* (New York: Columbia University Press, 1982), 130.

55. Benjamin, *The Arcades Project,* 461.

56. Pensky, 169–170.

57. Ibid., 167.

58. Ibid.

59. Ibid., 175.

60. Benjamin, "On Some Motifs in Baudelaire," in *Illuminations,* ed. Hannah Arendt, trans. Harry Zohn (New York: Schocken Books, 1969), 158.

61. Roland Barthes, *S/Z,* trans. Richard Miller (New York: Hill and Wang, 1974), 8.

62. Michael Arnzen, "The Return of the Uncanny: Introduction," *Paradoxa* 3, nos. 3–4 (1997): 317.

63. Paul Auster, ed., *I Thought My Father Was God* (New York: Picador, 2001), xvi.

64. Paul Auster, *The Red Notebook* (New York: New Directions, 2002). See also the above-cited volume, which contains dozens of such stories submitted to Auster for NPR's National Story Project.

65. Peter Wollen, "An Alphabet of Cinema," in *Paris Hollywood: Writings on Film* (London: Verso, 2002), 3–4.

66. Ibid., 4.

67. Benjamin, *The Arcades Project,* 206.

7. Five Cinephiliac Anecdotes

1. Raymond Bellour, "The Unattainable Text," trans. Ben Brewster, in *The Analysis of Film,* ed. Constance Penley (Bloomington: Indiana University Press, 2000), 21.

2. Ibid.

3. A superb example of the ways in which re-experiencing a movie in different times and places affects our memories of the film, and changes the film itself, can be found in Jonathan Rosenbaum's *Moving Places* (Berkeley: University of California Press, 1995), especially the extraordinary second chapter, "*On Moonlight Bay* as Time Machine."

4. Stephen Prince, "The Hemorrhaging of American Cinema: *Bonnie and Clyde*'s Legacy of Cinematic Violence," in *Arthur Penn's Bonnie and Clyde,* ed. Lester Friedman (New York: Cambridge University Press, 2000), 127.

5. Pauline Kael, "Bonnie and Clyde," in *Awake in the Dark,* ed. David Denby (New York: Vintage Books, 1977), 88.

6. Lester Friedman, *Bonnie and Clyde* (London: BFI, 2000), 34.

7. Kael, 97.

8. André Bazin, "The Ontology of the Photographic Image," in *What Is Cinema?* vol. 1, ed. and trans. Hugh Gray (Berkeley: University of California Press, 1967), 9.

9. André Bazin, "Death Every Afternoon," trans. Mark A. Cohen, in *Rites of Realism,* ed. Ivone Margulies (Durham, N.C.: Duke University Press, 2003), 30.

10. Bazin, "Ontology," 15.

11. Marta Braun, *Picturing Time: The Work of Etienne-Jules Marey* (Chicago: University of Chicago Press, 1992), 57.

12. Noël Burch, *Theory of Film Practice,* trans. Helen R. Lane (Princeton, N.J.: Princeton University Press, 1969), 17.

13. James Naremore, *Acting in the Cinema* (Berkeley: University of California Press, 1988), 40.

14. Ibid., 41.

15. Stephen Nachmanovitch, *Free Play: Improvisation in Art and Life* (New York: Tarcher/Putnam, 1990), 21.

16. Ibid., 22.

17. Jacques Rivette, "The Essential," in *Cahiers du Cinéma, the 1950s,* ed. Jim Hillier (Cambridge: Harvard University Press, 1985), 135.

18. Ibid., 134.

19. Nachmanovitch, 104.

20. Ibid.

21. Ibid.

22. Ibid., 25.

23. Ibid., 177.

24. Stewart Stern, *Rebel Without a Cause Notebook,* Stewart Stern Papers, Ms. Boxes 11–12, The University of Iowa Special Collections, Iowa City, Iowa.

25. Neil Baldwin, *Man Ray: American Artist* (New York: Clarkson N. Potter, 1988), 174.

26. Quoted in Baldwin, 174.

27. Ibid., 172.

28. Baldwin, 174.

29. Arturo Schwarz, *Man Ray: The Rigour of Imagination* (New York: Rizzoli, 1977), 61.

30. Ibid.

31. Bernard Eisenschitz, *Nicholas Ray: An American Journey,* trans. Tom Milne (Boston: Faber & Faber, 1993), 236.

32. Roland Penrose, *Man Ray* (London: Thanks and Hudson, 1975), 100–101.

33. Man Ray, *Self Portrait* (Boston: Little, Brown and Co., 1963), 255.

34. Quoted in *Directing the Film,* ed. Eric Sherman (Boston: Little, Brown and Co., 1976), 128.

35. Laura U. Marks, *The Skin of the Film* (Durham, N.C.: Duke University Press, 2000), 77.

36. Ibid.

37. Ibid., 239. Later in the scripting process, as the use of CinemaScope necessitated a switch from black-and-white to color, the film's period was switched from Christmas to Easter.

38. Luis Buñuel, *My Last Sigh* (New York: Alfred A. Knopf, 1983), 133–134.

39. See *Best American Screenplays,* ed. Sam Thomas (New York: Crown Publishers, 1986), 217–218.

40. François Truffaut, *The Films in My Life* (New York: Simon and Schuster, 1975), 142.

41. Ibid., 146.

42. François Truffaut, quoted in Jean Douchet, *French New Wave,* trans. Robert Bonnono (New York: D.A.P., 1999), 71–72.

43. Eric Rohmer, "Ajax or the Cid," in *Cahiers du Cinéma, the 1950s: Neo-Realism, Hollywood, New Wave,* ed. Jim Hillier (Cambridge: Harvard University Press, 1985), 112.

SELECTED BIBLIOGRAPHY

Abel, Richard. *French Cinema: The First Wave*. Princeton, N.J.: Princeton University Press, 1984.

———. *French Film Theory and Criticism, 1907–1939*. Vol. 1. Princeton, N.J.: Princeton University Press, 1988.

Adair, Gilbert. *Myths and Memories*. London: Flamingo, 1986.

———. *Flickers: An Illustrated Celebration of 100 Years of Cinema*. London: Faber & Faber, 1995.

Allen, Robert C., and Douglas Gomery. *Film History: Theory and Practice*. New York: McGraw-Hill, 1985.

Andrew, Dudley. *André Bazin*. New York: Columbia University Press, 1978.

———. *The Major Film Theories*. New York: Oxford University Press, 1976.

———. "The Neglected Tradition of Phenomenology in Film Theory." *Wide Angle* 2 (1978): 44–49.

———. "The 'Three Ages' of Cinema Studies and the Age to Come." *PMLA* 115, no. 3 (May 2000): 341–351.

Andrew, Dudley, ed. *The Image in Dispute*. Austin: University of Texas Press, 1997.

Auster, Paul. *The Red Notebook*. New York: New Directions, 2002.

Auster, Paul, ed. *I Thought My Father Was God*. New York: Picador, 2001.

Balakian, Anna. *Surrealism: The Road to the Absolute*. Chicago: University of Chicago Press, 1986.

Balázs, Béla. *The Theory of the Film*. North Stratford, N.H.: Ayer Company Publishers, 1972.

Baldwin, Neil. *Man Ray: American Artist*. New York: Clarkson N. Potter, 1988.

Barthes, Roland. *Camera Lucida*. Trans. Richard Howard. New York: Hill and Wang, 1981.

———. *Image/Music/Text*. Trans. Stephen Heath. New York: Hill and Wang, 1977.

——. *Mythologies*. Trans. Annette Lavers. New York: Hill and Wang, 1972.

——. *The Pleasure of the Text*. Trans. Richard Miller. New York: Hill and Wang, 1975.

——. *Roland Barthes*. Trans. Richard Howard. New York: Hill and Wang, 1977.

——. *The Rustle of Language*. Trans. Richard Howard. New York: Hill and Wang, 1977.

Bazin, André. *Bazin at Work*. Ed. Bert Cardullo. Trans. Alain Piette. New York: Routledge, 1997.

——. *The Cinema of Cruelty*. Trans. Sabine d'Estrée. New York: Seaver Books, 1982.

——. *Jean Renoir*. Ed. François Truffaut. Trans. W. W. Halsey II and William H. Simon. New York: Touchstone, 1971.

——. *What Is Cinema?* Vol. 1. Ed. and trans. Hugh Gray. Berkeley: University of California Press, 1967.

——. *What Is Cinema?* Vol. 2. Ed. and trans. Hugh Gray. Berkeley: University of California Press, 1971.

Benjamin, Walter. *The Arcades Project*. Ed. Rolf Tiedemann. Trans. Howard Eiland and Kevin McLaughlin. Cambridge: Harvard University Press, 1999.

——. *Charles Baudelaire: A Lyric Poet in the Era of High Capitalism*. Trans. Harry Zohn. London: NLB, 1973.

——. "Edward Fuchs: Collector and Historian." *New German Critique* 5 (Spring 1975): 27–58.

——. *Illuminations*. Ed. Hannah Arendt. Trans. Harry Zohn. New York: Schocken Books, 1969.

——. *Reflections*. Ed. Edmund Jephcott. Trans. Peter Demetz. New York: Schocken Books, 1978.

——. *Selected Writings*. Vol. 2: *1927–1934*. Ed. Michael W. Jennings. Cambridge: Harvard University Press, 1999.

Bordwell, David. "French Impressionist Cinema: Film Culture, Film Theory and Film Style." Ph.D. thesis, University of Iowa, 1974.

——. *Making Meaning*. Cambridge: Harvard University Press, 1989.

——. *Narration in the Fiction Film*. Madison: University of Wisconsin Press, 1985.

——. *On the History of Film Style*. Cambridge: Harvard University Press, 1997.

Bosséno, Christian-Marc. "La Place du Spectateur." *Vingtième Siècle* 46 (April–June 1995): 143–154.

Brainard, Joe. *I Remember*. New York: Penguin Books, 1995.

Braun, Marta. *Picturing Time: The Work of Etienne-Jules Marey*. Chicago: University of Chicago Press, 1992.

Breakwell, Ian, and Paul Hammond, eds. *Seeing in the Dark: A Compendium of Cinemagoing*. London: Serpent's Tail, 1990.

Brenez, Nicole. *De la figure en général et du corps en particulier: l'invention figurative au cinema*. Paris: De Boeck Université, 1998.

Breton, André. *Manifestoes of Surrealism*. Trans. Richard Seaver and Helen R. Lane. Ann Arbor: University of Michigan Press, 1972.

——. *Nadja*. Trans. Richard Howard. New York: Grove Press, 1960.

Brown, Bill. "How to Do Things with Things (A Toy Story)." *Critical Inquiry* 24, no. 4 (Summer 1998): 935–964.

Buck-Morss, Susan. "Aesthetics and Anaesthetics: Walter Benjamin's Artwork Essay Reconsidered." *October* 62 (Fall 1992): 3–41.

Buñuel, Luis. *My Last Sigh*. New York: Alfred A. Knopf, 1983.

Burch, Noël. *Life to Those Shadows*. Berkeley: University of California Press, 1990.

——. *Theory of Film Practice*. Princeton, N.J.: Princeton University Press, 1981.

Cameron, Ian, ed. *Movie Reader*. New York: Praeger, 1972.

Cardinal, Roger. "Pausing over Peripheral Detail." *Framework* 30/31 (1986): 112–133.

Casey, Edward S. "The Memorability of the Filmic Image." *Quarterly Review of Film Studies* 6, no. 3 (Summer 1981): 241–264.

Caughie, John, ed. *Theories of Authorship*. London: Routledge & Kegan Paul, 1981.

Cavell, Stanley. *Disowning Knowledge in Seven Plays of Shakespeare*. New York: Cambridge University Press, 1987.

Cohen, Margaret. *Profane Illumination*. Berkeley: University of California Press, 1993.

Crary, Jonathan. *Techniques of the Observer*. Cambridge: MIT Press, 1992.

Damisch, Hubert. "Five Notes for a Phenomenology of the Photographic Image." *October* 5 (Summer 1978): 70–72.

Daney, Serge. "Falling Out of Love." *Sight and Sound* (July 1992): 14–15.

———. "Interview: *Les Cahiers du Cinéma* 1968–1977." *The Thousand Eyes*, no. 2 (1977): 18–31.

Darnton, Robert. *The Great Cat Massacre*. New York: Vintage, 1985.

De Baecque, Antoine, and Thierry Frémaux. "La Cinéphilie ou L'Invention d'Une Culture." *Vingtième Siècle* 46 (April–June 1995): 133–142.

Doane, Mary Ann. *The Emergence of Cinematic Time*. Cambridge: Harvard University Press, 2003.

———. " . . . when the direction of the force acting on the body is changed." *Wide Angle* 7, nos. 1 and 2 (1985): 42–57.

Douchet, Jean. *French New Wave*. Trans. Robert Bonnono. New York: D.A.P., 1999.

———. "La fabrique du regard." *Vertigo* 10 (1993): 33–36.

Eisenschitz, Bernard. *Nicholas Ray: An American Journey*. Trans. Tom Milne. Boston: Faber & Faber, 1993.

Eisenstein, Sergei. *Film Form*. Ed. and trans. Jay Leyda. New York: Harcourt Brace Jovanovich, 1949.

Elsaesser, Thomas. "Louis Lumière—the Cinema's First Virtualist?" In *Cinema Futures: Cain, Abel, or Cable,* ed. Thomas Elsaesser and Kay Hoffmann. Amsterdam: Amsterdam University Press, 1998.

———. "'One Train May Be Hiding Another': Private History, Memory, and National Identity." *Screening the Past* 5 (1998). www.latrobe.edu.au/screening the past/ (access date: 1999).

———. "Rivette and the End of Cinema." *Sight and Sound,* April 1992, 20–23.

———. "Two Decades in Another Country." In *Superculture: American Popular Culture and Europe,* ed. C. W. E. Bigsby. Bowling Green, Ohio: Bowling Green University Press, 1975.

Elsner, John, and Roger Cardinal, eds. *Cultures of Collecting*. Cambridge: Harvard University Press, 1994.

Farber, Manny. *Negative Space*. New York: DaCapo Press, 1998.

Foucault, Michel. *Michel Foucault: Power, Truth, Strategy*. Ed. Meaghan Morris and Paul Patton. Sydney: Feral Publications, 1979.

Freedberg, S. J. "Berenson, Connoisseurship, and the History of Art." *New Criterion* 7, no. 6 (February 1989): 7–16.

Freud, Sigmund. *Therapy and Technique*. New York: W. W. Norton, 1963.

Galassi, Peter. *Before Photography*. New York: Museum of Modern Art, 1981.

Gallagher, Catherine, and Stephen Greenblatt. *Practicing New Historicism*. Chicago: University of Chicago Press, 2000.

Godard, Jean-Luc. *Godard on Godard*. Ed. and trans. Tom Milne. New York: DaCapo, 1972.

Gombrich, E. H. *Art and Illusion: A Study in the Psychology of Pictorial Representation*. Princeton, N.J.: Princeton University Press, 1969.

Graham, Peter, ed. *The New Wave*. New York: Doubleday, 1968.

Gunning, Tom. "The Cinema of Attractions: Early Cinema, Its Spectator and the Avant-Garde." *Wide Angle* 8, nos. 3 and 4 (1986): 63–70.

———. "From the Kaleidoscope to the X-Ray: Urban Spectatorship, Poe, Benjamin, and *Traffic in Souls* (1913)." *Wide Angle* 19, no. 4 (October 1977): 25–61.

Hammond, Paul, ed. *The Shadow and Its Shadow: Surrealist Writings on the Cinema*. London: Polygon, 1991.

Hansen, Miriam. "Benjamin, Cinema, and Experience: 'The Blue Flower in the Land of Technology.'" *New German Critique* 40 (Winter 1987): 179–224.

———. "'With Skin and Hair': Kracauer's Theory of Film, Marseille 1940." *Critical Inquiry* 19, no. 3 (Spring 1993): 437–469.

Harvey, Sylvia. "What Is Cinema? The Sensuous, the Political, and the Abstract." In *Cinema: The Beginnings and the Future*, ed. Christopher Williams. London: University of Westminster Press, 1996.

Heidegger, Martin. *The Question Concerning Technology*. Trans. William Lovitt. New York: Garland, 1977.

Hess, John. "*La Politique des auteurs*: Part One: World View as Aesthetic." *Jump Cut*, no. 1 (May–June 1974): 19–22.

Hillier, Jim, ed. *Cahiers du Cinéma, the 1950s: Neo-Realism, Hollywood, New Wave*. Cambridge: Harvard University Press, 1985.

———. *Cahiers du Cinéma, the 1960s: New Wave, New Cinema, Reevaluating Hollywood*. Cambridge: Harvard University Press, 1986.

Jameson, Fredric. *Signatures of the Visible*. New York: Routledge, 1990.

Jay, Martin. *Downcast Eyes: The Denigration of Vision in Twentieth Century French Thought*. Berkeley: University of California Press, 1994.

Jenkins, Keith. *Re-thinking History*. New York: Routledge, 1991.

Kauffmann, Stanley. "A Lost Love." *New Republic*, September 8 and 15, 1997, 28–29.

Koch, Gertrud. *Siegfried Kracauer: An Introduction*. Trans. Jeremy Gaines. Princeton, N.J.: Princeton University Press, 2000.

Kracauer, Siegfried. *The Mass Ornament*. Cambridge: Harvard University Press, 1995.

———. *Theory of Film*. Princeton, N.J.: Princeton University Press, 2000.

Kramer, Hilton. "Grappling with the Mysteries of Taste." *New York Times*, February 11, 1979, D29.

Krauss, Rosalind. "The Ministry of Fate." In *A New History of French Literature*, ed. Denis Hollier. Cambridge: Harvard University Press, 1989.

———. *The Originality of the Avant-garde and Other Modernist Myths*. Cambridge: MIT Press, 1986.

Leutrat, Jean-Louis. "Traces That Resemble Us: Godard's *Passion*." *Sub-Stance* 51 (1986): 36–51.

MacCabe, Colin. *The Eloquence of the Vulgar*. London: BFI, 1999.

———. *Godard: Portrait of the Artist at Seventy*. New York: Farrar, Straus and Giroux, 2003.

Malraux, André. "Sketch for a Psychology of the Moving Pictures." In *Reflections on Art*, ed. Susanne K. Langer. Baltimore: Johns Hopkins University Press, 1958.

———. *The Voices of Silence*. Trans. Stuart Gilbert. Princeton, N.J.: Princeton University Press, 1978.

Marks, Laura. *The Skin of the Film: Intercultural Cinema, Embodiment, and the Senses*. Durham, N.C.: Duke University Press, 2000.

Martin, Adrian. "The Artificial Night: Surrealism and Cinema." *Surrealism: Revolution by Night*. Melbourne: National Gallery of Australia, 1993.

——. "The Body Has No Head: Corporeal Figuration in Aldrich." *Screening the Past* 10 (2000). http://www.latrobe.edu.au/screeningthepast/ (access date: 2000).

——. "Ultimatum: An Introduction to the work of Nicole Brenez." *Screening the Past* 2 (1997). http://www.latrobe.edu.au/screeningthepast/ (access date: 1997).

Metz, Christian. *The Imaginary Signifier: Psychoanalysis and the Cinema.* Trans. Celia Britton, Annwyl Williams, Ben Brewster, and Alfred Guzzetti. Bloomington: Indiana University Press, 1977.

Moullet, Luc. "Confession impudique d'un vieux cinéphile." *Cahiers du Cinéma* 497 (December 1995): 66–67.

Mulvey, Laura. "The Index and the Uncanny." In *Time and the Image,* ed. Carolyn Bailey Gill. New York: Manchester University Press, 2000.

Nachmanovitch, Stephen. *Free Play: Improvisation in Art and Life.* New York: Tarcher/Putnam, 1990.

Naremore, James. *Acting in the Cinema.* Berkeley: University of California Press, 1988.

Nichols, Bill. *Representing Reality.* Bloomington: Indiana University Press, 1991.

Nowell-Smith, Geoffrey. "On History and the Cinema." *Screen* 31, no. 2 (Summer 1990): 160–171.

Païni, Dominique. "Le cinéphile, la mélancolie, et la Cinémathèque." *Vertigo* 10 (1993): 61–65.

——. "La cinéphilie au risque du patrimonie." *Cahiers du Cinéma* 498 (January 1996): 54–57.

Pater, Walter. *The Renaissance: Studies in Art and Poetry.* In *Selected Writings of Walter Pater,* ed. Harold Bloom. New York: Columbia University Press, 1974.

Paul, William. "Uncanny Theater: The Twin Inheritances of the Movies." *Paradoxa* 3, nos. 3–4 (1997): 321–347.

Pearce, Susan. *On Collecting: An Investigation into Collecting in the European Tradition.* London: Routledge, 1995.

Penrose, Roland. *Man Ray.* London: Thames and Hudson, 1975.

Perkins, V. F. *Film as Film.* Baltimore: Penguin Books, 1972.

Ray, Man. *Self Portrait.* Boston: Little, Brown and Co., 1963.

Ray, Robert B. *The Avant-Garde Finds Andy Hardy.* Cambridge: Harvard University Press, 1995.

——. *A Certain Tendency of the Hollywood Cinema 1930–1980.* Princeton: Princeton University Press, 1985.

——. "Film Studies/Crisis/Experimentation." *Film Criticism* 17, nos. 2–3 (Winter/Spring 1993): 56–78.

Renoir, Jean. *My Life and My Films.* Trans. Norman Denny. New York: Atheneum, 1974.

Rohmer, Eric. *The Taste for Beauty.* Ed. Jean Narboni. Trans. Carol Volk. New York: Cambridge University Press, 1989.

Rosen, Philip. *Change Mummified.* Minneapolis: University of Minnesota Press, 2001.

Rosenbaum, Jonathan, Lauren Sedofsky, and Gilbert Adair. "Phantom Interviewers over Rivette." *Film Comment* 10, no. 5 (September/October 1974): 18–23.

——. *Moving Places.* Berkeley: University of California Press, 1995.

Rosenbaum, Jonathan, and Adrian Martin, eds. *Movie Mutations: The Changing Face of World Cinephilia.* London: BFI, 2003.

Rosenstone, Robert A. *Visions of the Past.* Cambridge: Harvard University Press, 1995.

Roud, Richard, ed. *Cinema: A Critical Dictionary.* New York: Viking, 1980.

Routt, William. "For Criticism." *Screening the Past* 9 (2000). http://www.latrobe.edu.au/screeningthepast/ (access date: 2000).

———. "L'Evidence." *Continuum: The Australian Journal of Media and Culture* 5, no. 2 (1990). http://kali.murdoch.edu.au/~continuum.

Sarris, Andrew. *The American Cinema: Director and Directions 1929–1968.* Chicago: University of Chicago Press, 1968.

———. *Confessions of a Cultist.* New York: Simon and Schuster, 1970.

———. "Preminger's Two Periods: Studio and Solo." *Film Comment* 3, no. 3 (Summer 1965): 12–17.

———. *The Primal Screen.* New York: Simon and Schuster, 1973.

Schivelbusch, Wolfgang. *The Railway Journey.* Berkeley: University of California Press, 1986.

Schlüpmann, Heide. "Phenomenology of Film: On Siegfried Kracauer's Writings of the 1920s." *New German Critique* 40 (Winter 1987): 97–114.

Schwarz, Arturo. *Man Ray: The Rigour of Imagination.* New York: Rizzoli, 1977.

Sobchack, Vivian. "The Active Eye: A Phenomenology of Cinematic Vision." *Quarterly Review of Film and Video* 12, no. 3 (1990): 21–36.

———. *The Address of the Eye: A Phenomenology of Film Experience.* Princeton, N.J.: Princeton University Press, 1992.

Sontag, Susan. "The Decay of Cinema." *New York Times Magazine,* February 25, 1996, 60–61.

Steinberg, Michael P., ed. *Walter Benjamin and the Demands of History.* Ithaca, N.Y.: Cornell University Press, 1996.

Stern, Lesley. "I Think, Sebastian, Therefore, I . . . Somersault." *Paradoxa* 3, nos. 3–4 (1997): 348–366.

Taussig, Michael. *Mimesis and Alterity: A Particular History of the Senses.* New York: Routledge, 1993.

Taylor, Greg. *Artists in the Audience: Cults, Camp, and American Film Criticism.* Princeton, N.J.: Princeton University Press, 1999.

Thomson, David. *A Biographical Dictionary of Film.* 3rd ed. New York: Knopf, 1994.

Truffaut, François. "A Certain Tendency of the French Cinema." In *Movies and Methods,* ed. Bill Nichols. Berkeley: University of California Press, 1976.

———. *Correspondence 1945–1984.* Ed. Gilles Jacob and Claude de Givray. Trans. Gilbert Adair. New York: Noonday Press, 1990.

———. *The Early Film Criticism of François Truffaut.* Ed. Wheeler Winston Dixon. Bloomington: Indiana University Press, 1993.

———. *The Films in My Life.* Trans. Leonard Mayhew. New York: Simon and Schuster, 1975.

Turvey, Malcolm. "Jean Epstein's Cinema of Immanence: The Rehabilitation of the Corporeal Eye." *October* 83 (Winter 1998): 25–50.

Ulmer, Gregory. "Fetishism in Roland Barthes's Nietzschean Phase." *Papers on Language and Literature* 14, no. 3 (Summer 1978): 334–355.

———. *Heuretics: The Logic of Invention.* Baltimore: Johns Hopkins University Press, 1994.

———. *Teletheory: Grammatology in the Age of Video.* New York: Routledge, 1989.

Vaughan, Dai. *For Documentary.* Berkeley: University of California Press, 1999.

Veeser, H. Aram, ed. *The New Historicism.* New York: Routledge, 1989.

Vernet, Marc. "The Fetish in the Theory and History of the Cinema." In *Endless Night: Cinema and Psychoanalysis, Parallel Histories,* ed. Janet Bergstrom. Berkeley: University of California Press, 1999.

White, Hayden. *Tropics of Discourse: Essays in Cultural Criticism.* Baltimore: Johns Hopkins University Press, 1978.

Willemen, Paul. "The Desire for Cinema: An Edinburgh Retrospective." *Framework* 19 (1982): 48–50.

———. *Looks and Frictions.* Bloomington: Indiana University Press, 1994.

Wollen, Peter. *Paris Hollywood: Writings on Film.* London: Verso, 2002.

———. *Readings and Writings: Semiotic Counter-Strategies.* London: Verso, 1982.

———. *Signs and Meaning in the Cinema.* Expanded ed. London: BFI, 1998.

INDEX

Christian Keathley is Assistant Professor in the
Film and Media Culture Program at Middlebury College, Vermont.

Milton Keynes UK
Ingram Content Group UK Ltd.
UKHW021821151223
434462UK00009B/699